Basic Education at a Distance

At the beginning of the twenty-first century, about one fifth of humanity is functionally illiterate. This means that they cannot participate fully in their societies or protect their basic rights. As most of these people live in the rural areas of the developing world, the task of helping them to gain access to basic education is formidable. Does open and distance learning have a role in reducing the growing numbers of undereducated people in the world?

Open and distance learning has been used in many ways in the recent past to provide both adult basic education and primary education. What lessons does this experience offer education policy makers?

Many existing policy documents link distance education with new information and communication technologies, portraying them as promising universal access and exponential growth of learning. Is this portrayal justified by experience?

Basic Education at a Distance answers these key questions, and in doing so, assesses the impact and effect of the experience of basic education at a distance all over the world and in a wide variety of forms. This is the first major overview of this topic for twenty years.

Chris Yates is Education Co-ordinator and **Jo Bradley** is Publications Co-ordinator at the International Extension College, Cambridge.

World review of distance education and open learning

A Commonwealth of Learning series
Series editor: Hilary Perraton

Higher Education through Open and Distance Learning
World review of distance education and open learning: Volume I
Edited by Keith Harry

Basic Education at a Distance
World review of distance education and open learning: Volume 2
Edited by Chris Yates and Jo Bradley

Editorial advisory group:

Maureen O'Neil	President, International Development Research Centre, Canada (chair)
Professor Hugh Africa	Vice-Chancellor, Vista University, South Africa
Professor Denise Bradley	Vice-Chancellor, University of South Australia, Australia
Dato' Professor Gajaraj Dhanarajan	President, Commonwealth of Learning
Sir John Daniel	Vice-Chancellor, Open University, Britain
Professor (Miss) Armaity Desai	Former Chairperson, University Grants Commission, India
Dr Maris O'Rourke	Director, Education, Human Development Network, World Bank
Hans d'Orville	Director, Information Technology for Development Programme, Bureau for Policy and Programme Support, UNDP
Dr Hilary Perraton	Director, International Research Foundation for Open Learning, Britain (secretary)

The world review of distance education and open learning is published on behalf of the Commonwealth of Learning.

The Commonwealth of Learning is an international organisation established by Commonwealth governments in 1988. Its purpose is to create and widen opportunities for learning, through Commonwealth co-operation in distance education and open learning. It works closely with governments, colleges and universities with the overall aim of strengthening the capacities of Commonwealth member countries in developing the human resources required for their economic and social development.

Basic Education at a Distance

World review of distance education and
open learning: Volume 2

Edited by Chris Yates
and Jo Bradley

London and New York

THE COMMONWEALTH *of* LEARNING

First published 2000 by
RoutledgeFalmer
11 New Fetter Lane, London EC4P 4EE

Simultaneously published in the USA and Canada
by RoutledgeFalmer
29 West 35th Street, New York, NY 10001

RoutledgeFalmer is an imprint of the Taylor & Francis Group

Typeset in Goudy by
HWA Text and Data Management, Tunbridge Wells
Printed and bound in Great Britain by
St Edmundsbury Press, Bury St Edmunds, Suffolk

British Library Cataloguing in Publication Data
A catalogue record for this book is available from the British Library

Library of Congress Cataloging in Publication Data
Basic education at a distance / edited by Chris Yates and Jo Bradley.
     p. cm. – (World review of distance education and open learning; v. 2)
     Includes bibliographical references and index.
     1. Distance education. 2. Open learning. 3. Basic education.
     4 Literacy. I. Yates, Chris, 1953– II. Bradley, Jo, 1942– III. Series

LC5800.B38 2000

371.3´5–dc21   00–036782

ISBN 0–415–23773–4 (hbk)
ISBN 0–415–23774–2 (pbk)

Contents

List of tables   vii
List of contributors   viii
Foreword   x
Acknowledgements   xii
List of acronyms and abbreviations   xiii

PART I
Introduction   I

1   Basic education at a distance: an introduction   3
    CHRIS YATES AND THOMAS TILSON

2   The elusiveness of integration: policy discourses on open
    and distance learning in the 1990s   27
    ELAINE UNTERHALTER, CATHERINE ODORA HOPPERS AND WIM HOPPERS

PART 2
Themes   49

3   Audiences for basic education at a distance   51
    LYNETTE ANDERSON AND BARBARA SPRONK

4   Basic education curriculum: contexts and contests   65
    RICHARD SIACIWENA AND JENNIFER O'ROURKE

5   Organisational and delivery structures   87
    TONY DODDS AND PALITHA EDIRISINGHA

6   Evaluation and quality   110
    JUDITH CALDER AND SANTOSH PANDA

7   The use of technologies in basic education   122
    KEITH HARRY AND ABDUL KHAN

8   Finance, costs and economics   138
    FRANÇOIS ORIVEL

PART 3
Applications   **153**

9   Literacy and adult education through distance
    and open learning   155
    USHA REDDI AND ANITA DIGHE

10 Basic education for refugees and nomads   173
    JASON PENNELLS AND CHIMAH EZEOMAH

11 The power of open and distance learning in basic education
    for health and the environment   192
    PAT PRIDMORE AND STEPHANIE NDUBA

12 Open schooling at basic level   205
    JANET JENKINS AND ARIEF S. SADIMAN

PART 4
Conclusion   **227**

13 Outcomes: what have we learned?   229
    CHRIS YATES

    Index   248

Tables

1.1   Models of basic education: a typology of practice and
provision   11

5.1   The main features of out-of-school programmes in
developing countries   92

8.1   Average GNP per capita in developed and least developed
countries   141

8.2   Expected number of years of education at age five   142

8.3   Public expenditure on education as a percentage of GNP   143

8.4   Unit cost as a percentage of the GNP per capita   145

8.5   Dependency ratios (% of 6–15 year-olds/16–65 year-olds)   146

10.1   Comparisons between situations of nomads and of refugees   175

13.1   Enrolment in key ODE institutions operating at the basic
level   231

13.2   Costs of basic education at a distance   233

Contributors

Lynette Anderson is Deputy Director, Institute of Distance and Continuing Education, University of Guyana.

Jo Bradley is Publications Co-ordinator, International Extension College, UK.

Judith Calder is Head of the Open and Distance Education for Lifelong Learning Research Group in the Institute of Educational Technology, Open University, UK.

Anita Dighe is Director, Centre for Extension Education, Indira Gandhi National Open University, India.

Tony Dodds is Professor and Director of the Centre for External Studies at the University of Namibia and a long-time former Director of the International Extension College, UK.

Palitha Edirisingha is Research Fellow, International Research Foundation for Open Learning, UK.

Chimah Ezeomah is Professor and Dean, Faculty of Education, University of Jos, Nigeria.

Keith Harry is a distance education information consultant and the former Director of the International Centre for Distance Learning, UK.

Catherine Odora Hoppers is Chief Research Specialist in the Human Sciences Research Council, Pretoria, South Africa, and former member of the International Consultative Forum Steering Committee for Education for All, Paris.

Wim Hoppers is Regional Education Adviser for the Netherlands Government Development Assistance, based in Pretoria, South Africa.

Janet Jenkins is an independent international consultant in open and distance education, UK and formerly a Director of the International Extension College and Programme Officer at the Commonwealth of Learning.

Abdul Khan is Vice Chancellor of the Indira Gandhi National Open University, India.

Stephanie Nduba is Head of Distance and Continuing Education, African Medical and Research Foundation, Kenya.

Jennifer O'Rourke is a consultant in adult and distance education based in Gabriola Island, British Columbia, Canada.

François Orivel is Professor, Institut de Recherche sur l'Economie de l'Education, Université de Bourgogne, France.

Santosh Panda is Professor of Distance Education and Director, Staff Training and Research at the Institute of Distance Education, Indira Gandhi National Open University, India.

Jason Pennells is Training Co-ordinator, International Extension College, UK.

Pat Pridmore is Senior Lecturer in international education and health promotion at the Institute of Education, University of London, UK.

Usha Reddi is Director, Commonwealth Educational Media Centre for Asia, India.

Arief S. Sadiman is Director, Centre for Communication Technology for Education and Culture and responsible for co-ordinating the Indonesian Distance Learning Network.

Richard Siaciwena is Professor and Director of Distance Education, University of Zambia.

Barbara Spronk is Executive Director, International Extension College, UK.

Thomas Tilson is Chief of Party, BESO Project, USAID/Ministry of Education, Ethiopia. He works for the Academy for Educational Development.

Elaine Unterhalter is Senior Lecturer in education and international development, Institute of Education, University of London, UK. She is a South African who researches and writes on educational policy and gender issues.

Chris Yates is Education Co-ordinator, International Extension College, UK.

Foreword

Just over ten years ago planners, policy makers and practitioners of education met in Jomtien, Thailand, to take stock of, reflect on, discuss and debate the state of the planet's provision for and performance in delivering basic education. Those who met at that First World Conference on Education for All were not at all happy with what they heard and discovered at that meeting.

Concerned about the educational deprivation of both children and adults, particularly women, and the parlous state of provision, especially among the developing nations of the globe, the Conference, through the nine articles of its declaration, urged nations, intergovernmental and international agencies, development and community organisations, educators and policy makers to mobilise the human, financial, physical and technological resources of the world to eradicate the unacceptable level of illiteracy and undereducation to which more than half the world's population was subjected at that time.

While much progress has been achieved since Jomtien, stocktaking in the last year, of national, regional and global performance, seems to indicate that there is still an unacceptably high level of deprivation especially among girl children and women. The sad fact is that, despite the global effort, in sheer numbers illiteracy and undereducation is expected to increase rather than decrease, at least during the first decade of this new century. Therefore calls for more and imaginative efforts to tackle the scourge of illiteracy can be expected to come from all those engaged in human development. A response to these calls will be required from others with an interest in such challenges. These others will include planners of education, teachers, scholars, government officials, non-government activists, political and community leaders and workers, as well as managers of international aid, lending and development agencies. These people need to know, understand and identify factors which help and those others which impede progress, in order to bring new ideas and design new strategies to tackle the problem. They will have to consider the accomplishments and failures of global efforts in reducing educational deprivation over the last decade and before. It is in this context, notwithstanding a number of recent reviews, that the publishers and editors of the *World review of distance education and open learning* series have developed this second volume.

As its companion first volume did for higher education, this book attempts to bring together global experience in the use of distance and open learning to meet the needs for basic education in a variety of situations. Given the magnitude of the global challenge to provide basic education to millions of children and adults, and the limitation of resources to do the same, it is surprising to note how little use has been made of mass education techniques for this purpose. One reason for this limited use may be a lack of knowledge and information on how distance education and open learning can be applied effectively in such situations. It is not only necessary to have knowledge of this application – knowledge of the limitations of such application is also useful. The case studies, analysis and critical assessment contained in this volume will help contribute to a better understanding of these and other related and relevant issues.

The Commonwealth of Learning, with its mission to enhance the world's knowledge of distance and open learning, is privileged to work with the community of distance educators to develop this World Review series. We are particularly pleased to have this volume published on the tenth anniversary of the Jomtien Conference. It is our hope that the knowledge and scholarship contained in the pages of this volume can make a useful contribution to the discussion of basic education. At the same time we also hope the experience gained and described in this volume can contribute to the eradication of an awful human situation, unnecessarily suffered by so many, for so little reason.

This volume could not have materialised but for the interest and commitment of so many people from across the Commonwealth. I am grateful to all of them, but especially to the authors, the editors of the volume Chris Yates and Jo Bradley, the managing editor of the series, Hilary Perraton, and the editorial advisory group of the series, for the time and effort which they so generously contributed to this effort.

Gajaraj Dhanarajan
President, Commonwealth of Learning

Acknowledgements

The editors wish to acknowledge the assistance received from the Commonwealth of Learning and the Editorial Advisory Group in the development of the plan for this book. We also received regular and close guidance from the series editor, Hilary Perraton.

Our colleagues in the Education and International Development Group of the University of London Institute of Education helped us to turn our initial ideas into a more coherent reality. We are also grateful to Roy Williams at Education for Development, Reading, for advice on a number of areas covered in the book.

We want to thank Keith Harry for compiling the index.

We owe a particular debt to the staff of the International Extension College (IEC), who sustained and encouraged us in the venture from start to finish.

Chris Yates would like to thank Libby Yates for her support throughout the long and arduous process.

Acronyms and abbreviations

ABET	Adult Basic Education and Training
ACPH	Acción Cultural Popular Hondureña
ACPO	Acción Cultural Popular (Colombia)
AID	Agency for International Development (USA)
AIDS	acquired immune deficiency syndrome
AIOU	Allama Iqbal Open University
AMREF	African Medical Research and Education Foundation
BBC	British Broadcasting Corporation
BESO	Basic Education Systems Overhaul (Ethiopia)
BEST	Basic Education Support Television
BFEP	Basic Functional Education Programme
BOCODOL	Botswana College of Distance and Open Learning
BOU	Bangladesh Open University
BOUOS	BOU Open School
CfBT	Centre for British Teachers
CIET	Central Institute for Educational Technology
CIPP	Context-Input-Process-Product
CLASS	Computer Literacy and Studies in Schools
CNED	Centre National d'Enseignement à Distance
COL	Commonwealth of Learning
CONFINTEA	International Conference on Adult Education
DAC	Development Assistance Committee (of OECD)
DE	distance education
DFID	Department for International Development (UK)
DL	distance learning
DNFE	Department of Non-Formal Education (Thailand)
ECCA	Emisoria Cultural de Canarias (Spain)
EDC	Education Development Center
EDEN	European Distance Education Network
EFA	Education for All
EFD	Education for Development
ERIC	Educational Resources Information Centre

ET	educational technology
ETV	educational television
EU	European Union
EWLP	Experimental World Literacy Programme
FEPRA	Functional Education Project for Rural Areas
FSU	former Soviet Union
G7	group of seven
GDP	gross domestic product
GTZ	Gesellschaft für Technische Zusammenarbeit (German Technical Co-operation)
HDI	Human Development Index
HIV	human immunodeficiency virus
ICDE	International Council for Distance Education
ICDL	International Centre for Distance Learning
ICT	information and communication technology
IDCE	Institute of Distance and Continuing Education
IDRC	International Development Research Council
IEC	International Extension College
IET	Institute for Educational Technology (UKOU)
IGNOU	Indira Gandhi National Open University
IIEP	International Institute for Educational Planning
IITT	Institute of In-service Teacher Training
ILT	initial literacy training
INADES	Institut Africain pour le Développement Economique et Social
INSAT	Indian National Satellite
IRI	Interactive Radio Instruction
ISCED	international standard classification of education
ISDN	integrated services digital network
JAMAL	Jamaican Movement for the Advancement of Literacy
MCDE	Malawi College of Distance Education
MOE	Ministry of Education
MOH	Ministry of Health
NAMCOL	Namibian College of Open Learning
NCERT	National Centre for Educational Research and Training
NCNE	National Commission for Nomadic Education
n.d.	no date
NFE	non-formal education
NFED	Non-Formal Education Division
NGO	non-government organisation
NICT	new information and communication technologies
NOS	National Open School
ODE	open and distance education
ODL	open and distance learning

OECD	Organisation for Economic Co-operation and Development
OJSS	Open Junior Secondary School
OLSET	Open Learning Systems Educational Trust
Oxfam	Oxford Committee for Famine Relief
PARI	Preventive Health programme
PHC	primary health care
PL	post literacy
PTAs	Parent Teacher Associations
RADECO	Radio-Assisted Community Basic Education
RAE	Refugee Adult Education
RP	rupee
SAEU	South African Extension Unit
SAIDE	South African Institute for Distance Education
SIDA	Swedish International Development Authority
SIDE	Schools of Isolated and Distance Education
SITE	Satellite Instructional Television
SOLO	Sudan Open Learning Organisation
SOLU	Sudan Open Learning Unit
SSC	Secondary School Certificate
TAD	Telematics for African Development Consortium
UFH-ABEP	University of Fort Hare Adult Basic Education Project
UIE	UNESCO Institute of Education
UK	United Kingdom
UKFIET	UK Forum for International Education and Training
UKOU	UK Open University
UNDP	United Nations Development Programme
UNESCO	United Nations Educational, Scientific and Cultural Organisation
UNHCR	United Nations High Commissioner for Refugees
UNICEF	United Nations Children's Fund
UNISA	University of South Africa
US	United States
USA	United States of America
USAID	United States Agency for International Development
VCR	video cassette recorder
WCEFA	World Conference on Education for All
WHO	World Health Organisation
YCMOU	Yashwantrao Chavan Maharashtra Open University

Part I

Introduction

Chapter 1

Basic education at a distance

An introduction

Chris Yates and Thomas Tilson

Everyone has the right to education. Education shall be free, at least in the elementary and fundamental stages. Elementary education shall be compulsory.
(Article 26, para. 1, Universal Declaration of Human Rights, 1948)

When ministers of education gather at UNESCO conferences, the old rhetorical drums continue to beat out the familiar call for the total eradication of illiteracy from the face of the earth (these days by the year 2000) with no reference to how it can be done ... One wonders what good purpose can possibly be served by such admittedly unattainable targets.
(Coombs 1985: 278–9)

Introduction: what's all the fuss about?

In March 1990, 155 governments and most of the world's major bilateral and multilateral donor agencies met in Jomtien, Thailand. They met to discuss and endorse a plan to achieve basic education for all, and to eradicate illiteracy globally by the year 2000. There were three main aspects to the issue:

- how to get all children enrolled in schools for at least four years and deliver a quality education to help them become literate
- how to recover literacy among the large numbers of 'over-age' children who have dropped out of school before achieving sustainable literacy
- how to bring basic education to more than 960 million adults who at that time were living in a state of illiteracy

The goal was to have basic education for all and universal literacy by 2000; an ambitious target indeed.

Ten years on, progress has been much slower than was hoped for. Despite enrolling an additional 50 million children in primary schools, today it is estimated that more than 130 million children still do not have access to primary education (DFID 1999: 11). And a further 150 million children start primary school but drop out before they have completed four years of education. Thus, over 40 per cent of primary-school-age children either never start school or drop out before they have acquired basic literacy skills. Two out of every three children not in school are girls.

Concerning adult education, current estimates suggest that globally about 900 million people over the age of 15 years remain illiterate (Watkins 1999: 1, DFID 1999: 13). If we accept these figures, then about 1.2 billion people alive today are living with the consequences of illiteracy: about a fifth of humanity. However, aggregate figures such as these mask important geographical, gender and ethnic disparities. Illiteracy affects some areas of the world and some groups of people far more than others. For example, most of the children not in school reside in South Asian and sub-Saharan African countries: 56 and 45 million respectively (Watkins 1999: 53). By 2015 it is predicted that the majority of the world's illiterate children will be concentrated in twenty or so sub-Saharan African states, often those which have suffered recent civil or border war, internal destabilisation and low rates of economic growth.

> Of the world's children aged between 6–11, about 12 per cent live in Africa. These children account for just over one third of all children out of school. By 2005, their share in the total number out of school will rise to just under one half and by 2015, three out of every four children of primary school age not in school will live in Africa ... The face of a child not attending school over the next decade is increasingly likely to be an African child.
>
> (Watkins 1999: 56)

We should remind ourselves, however, that international awareness of and commitment to the importance of providing basic education for all is relatively new. The world community has only publicly recognised and taken responsibility for this situation for a little over fifty years. It is only since the United Nations Declaration of Human Rights in 1948 that there has been concern with basic education for all. There followed the Experimental World Literacy Programme conducted by UNESCO between 1967 and 1973 and the numerous national literacy campaigns of the 1970s and 1980s (see Coombs 1985: 265–84, Arnove and Graff 1987 and chapter 9 in this volume for further details). Other important events include the Monrovia declaration of 1979, when members of the Organisation of African Unity adopted an action plan for the eradication of illiteracy in Africa, and the Udaipur conference on literacy in 1983 and its subsequent charter, which set similar goals for Asia. UNESCO called for 'Education for All' in its 1984–9 medium-term plan; the International Literacy year of 1990 and the 1997 conference on Adult Education in Hamburg all made significant statements. These initiatives bear testimony to the importance the world community has been claiming to attach to the issue of illiteracy.

Nevertheless, the problem of inequity and lack of education for all is serious. Regional disparities in investment have been growing significantly. In 1990 Lockheed and Verspoor showed that during the period 1965–85 annual pupil expenditure on primary education in low-income countries fell from US $41 to $31. In 1999, Watkins reported:

> Britain spends $3,553 per student at the primary level compared with $27 in Zambia. The US spends $5,000 per student ... compared with $12 in countries such as India and Nepal ... On average an OECD country spends $4,636 per student on primary and secondary education compared with $165 in the developing world.
>
> (Watkins 1999: 12)

However, such figures should be read in context. Education costs are largely a function of local (teacher) wage rates. As such, realistic comparisons are better made in terms of comparative GNP and comparisons between teachers' and average wage rates in the country under consideration (see chapter 8 in this volume for further discussion on these issues in relation to basic education provision).

To the quantitative dimension of the problem one must add a qualitative one. Much of what passes for primary education in tens of thousands of classrooms in the developing world might be described as little more than 'child-minding'. Often teachers who are poorly educated, trained, paid and professionally supported, stand in front of increasingly larger classes, with abysmally few teaching resources. The school buildings are frequently badly constructed or falling into disrepair. Furniture is scarce, dysfunctional or totally absent. Often there is no running water available and few or no toilet facilities. Coupled with this, structural adjustment programmes have resulted in policies of increasing cost sharing and recovery for schooling, through various kinds of local community levies. In such circumstances it is little wonder that in some contexts, for example in Kenya, enrolment rates are falling, as parents decide that the costs of schooling now outweigh its benefits.

The response to the Jomtien failure

The response to this abject failure, at the global level, has been to shift back the time frame another fifteen years to 2015 (OECD 1996). The goal of basic 'Education for All' remains a distant one for many, partly because of additional population growth, but also because of the inability of the present structures to cope with the scale and complexity of the challenge. And, it must also be said, the commitment of some governments and international agencies to achieving the original Jomtien targets appears questionable.

Research shows that, in real terms, total aid to the education sector was even lower in the mid-1990s than before the Jomtien conference. While some donors have re-allocated aid budgets in favour of basic education, many have not (Bennell with Furlong 1998, Mueller 1996, McGee et al. 1998). The peace dividend has not materialised. Debt levels have risen everywhere, and structural adjustment, the policy meant to bring relief through improved economic growth, has often further impoverished millions more of the poorest of the poor. Even more disconcertingly, we are already receiving warnings from academics and commentators that the 2015 targets in turn look unlikely to be realised (Bennell 1999, Colclough 1999, Watkins 1999). Oxfam have made one set of projections using current data and conclude:

> The number of children out of school will continue to decline, but far too slowly. About 96m children will be out of school in 2005. In 2015, a quarter of a century after the Jomtien conference, 75m will still be out of school.
>
> (Watkins 1999: 54)

The words of Coombs (1985), quoted at the beginning of this chapter, lamenting in the mid-1980s the unattainable folly of aiming at education for all by 2000, may ring just as true today for the new goal of basic education for all by 2015. We are now more aware than ever of the nature, extent, pattern and complexity of the challenge of basic education for all. The implications of putting back the deadline for its achievement are serious and involve growing inter- and intra-state disparities and inequalities in education, economy and social stability, as well as rising ethnic tensions, potential civil strife and resultant large-scale population movements.

In this new twenty-first century it seems a truism to many of the authors of this volume that more of the same will not do. Existing education institutions need to respond to the demands of a fast-changing world. It would appear that education structures, like so many of our other social institutions (e.g. the family or systems of governance) are becoming, as Giddens (1999) has put it, 'shell institutions'. Shell institutions may continue to look the same on the outside, but on the inside they are either changing in response to the growing forces of globalisation or becoming anachronistic. In the light of the scale of the Education for All (EFA) failure, existing forms of basic education provision simply do not seem to be up to the job. Even if the current education structures could change sufficiently from within, it is doubtful whether they could do so quickly enough to meet the new targets of gender equity by 2005, and basic education for all by 2015. Conventional education organisations are not noted for the speed of their internal change dynamic.

The questions for education policy makers concerned with providing basic education for all are thus: Are there any alternatives to conventional patterns of schooling and basic education provision? What can open and distance learning (ODL) approaches contribute to the Jomtien challenge? And how, and in what ways, might existing education institutions and systems develop and change from within? The first two questions are the subject of this book. The third is one which follows on from the answers to the first two. The formulation and implemention of basic education policy in relation to ODE is analysed in chapter 2. Other chapters review the experience of providing basic education for different audiences, through a range of open and distance education programmes and structures. Sometimes the provision is either complementary or supplementary to more conventional forms. In other situations, the chapters provide examples of how schools and colleges, and in some cases even universities, are changing from within and responding to the basic education challenge. Before we introduce such structures, however, it is important to define a few terms.

Defining our terms: basic, distance and open education

Basic education is a difficult term to define, because it can apply equally to young children, inside or outside schools, and to adults, inside or outside formal education structures or the labour market. It can relate to general life skills or to vocational capabilities. It is a term which must cross all cultural boundaries and yet retain some semblance of shared meaning. One solution would be to say that basic education is what normally occurs during the first nine years of schooling. But that would perhaps be overly simplistic. The Jomtien forum defined basic learning needs as comprising:

> both essential learning tools (such as literacy, oral expression, numeracy, and problem solving) and the basic learning content (such as knowledge, skills, values and attitudes) required by human beings to be able to survive, to develop their full capacities, to live and work in dignity, to participate fully in development, to improve the quality of their lives, to make informed decisions and to continue learning. The scope of basic learning needs and how they should be met varies with individual countries and cultures, and inevitably changes with the passage of time.
>
> (WCEFA 1990, Article 1)

Basic education thus refers to education addressed to both adults and children. It includes primary education programmes and programmes equivalent to primary and, in many countries, junior secondary education. It also includes those programmes with alternative curricula, including such areas as basic health, nutrition, family planning, literacy, agriculture and other life-related and vocational skills.

Distance education is an educational process in which for the majority of the time the learning occurs when the teacher and learner are removed in space and/or time from each other.

Open learning refers to 'an organisational activity, based on the use of teaching materials, in which the constraints on study are minimised either in terms of access, or of time and place, pace, methods of study or any combination of these' (Perraton 2000: 13).

Distance education at the basic level: a review of experience

Basic education provided at a distance has taken a wide variety of forms. Recently we have seen an increasing diversification of organisational form, as chapter 5 in this volume points out. The range of provision can however be considered under two main headings:

- in-school programmes: aimed mainly at children
- out-of-school programmes: aimed mainly at adults and school push-outs/drop-outs

In-school programmes

In-school programmes most often involve the delivery of approved state curricula to audiences located in conventional schools. They can be divided into those devised primarily for young children and those designed for older 'adolescent' children (often primary school drop-outs or push-outs) and adults. In-school programmes for children include quality enhancement programmes like the Interactive Radio Instruction (IRI) programmes (see Moulton 1994; Dock and Helwig 1999), along with the large-scale mass-media projects involving schools radio (see Jamison and McAnany 1978), and the educational television (ETV) experiments of the 1960s and 1970s in American Samoa, El Salvador, Colombia, Niger, and the Côte d'Ivoire (Schramm 1967, 1973, Arnove 1976).

More recently, satellite-based, multiple media schemes have emerged, going under the name of multichannel learning (Anzalone 1995a). The aims of such projects are basically to extend curricular reach, breadth and/or quality, compensate for education system shortcomings, or even in some cases substitute for, or replace, teachers.

In-school programmes for adults, delivering primary school curricula, adult literacy or various forms of vocational or community enhancement programmes, involve a wide range of models. These include open schools (see chapter 12 in this volume), and various kinds of study group fora or campaigns based on the use of existing government or private facilities.

Out-of-school programmes

Out-of-school primary education programmes have existed since at least 1914 (Lugg 1994: 17). They include the Australian and Canadian home studies programmes or schools of the air, often run by the external divisions of state or federal ministries of education. These are primarily correspondence programmes, supplemented by frequent radio contacts, which deliver the regular school curriculum to children living in isolated families or communities (Mukhopadhyay and Phillips 1994). In addition, various other approaches have been designed to serve smaller more focused populations, like nomadic or itinerant groups. For example in Lesotho, the herd boys' basic education programme was a literacy and numeracy project based on the study-group model. This project is particularly interesting, because it represents in some respects an early example of a multiple or 'new literacy' approach (as discussed by Street 1993 and Rogers *et al.* 1998), as it began by researching literacies as they were needed and used in the boys' personal life contexts. Basic education for nomadic and itinerant groups is discussed further in chapter 10. Recently we have also seen the emergence of basic education programmes for children (and adults) receiving long-term care in hospitals.

There is also one special application of IRI in the Dominican Republic which provided the first four years of primary school outside of formal schools. The subjects included mathematics, language and social science. Children would meet in groups every day under the supervision of a facilitator selected by the community. The one-hour lesson was delivered by radio using the usual IRI format which ensured active participation of the children. The ministry of education trained the facilitator, and provided ongoing support, developed the radio programmes and teachers' guides and managed the programme. Evaluations showed that children learned more mathematics and learned as much language as children attending traditional schools (Dock and Helwig 1999).

Out-of-school programmes for adults involve the provision of basic education though a wide range of different models of distance and open learning. These have included the *radiophonic and television schools* common in Latin America (e.g. Mexico's Radioprimaria and Brazil's Telecurso 2000 projects); more recently what have become known as *multichannel learning systems* (Anzalone 1995a); the many and various forms of *study group* system, including mass media campaigns, which were most common in the newly independent African states, e.g. Ghana, Zambia, and Tanzania; some new forms of *open schooling* found on a relatively small scale (a few thousand students) in southern Africa (e.g. Namibia, Botswana, South Africa); and mass provision involving tens or even hundreds of thousands in south and south-east Asia (e.g. in India, Indonesia and Bangladesh).

The in-school/out-of-school distinction is not always clear cut. Some models, like the African study centres of Zambia and Malawi, serve out-of-school audiences, but use school premises for face-to-face meetings. Similarly, the Bangladesh Open University Open School serves adults out of school, but through the school system (see below). Hence the classification of some models remains a matter of personal emphasis.

Models and approaches: progress and assessment

Using the in-school/out-of-school categorisation, we can identify and discuss seven main approaches or models of basic education provision, which have used distance education methods. Most of these have enjoyed varying levels of attention and use over the last thirty years. The models are:

- educational television
- schools broadcasting, including Interactive Radio Instruction
- radio learning groups, including radio forums, clubs and campaigns
- radiophonic schools
- open schools

- multichannel learning
- basic education training schemes.

Table 1.1 gives an indication of the range and scope of the models of provision.

Television

Educational television (ETV) systems

In-school ETV systems were mostly high-profile, large-scale and relatively expensive system-wide interventions, concerned mainly with improving the quality and reducing the unit cost of primary education provision. Experiments ran throughout the 1960s, 1970s and 1980s in several developing countries, including American Samoa, El Salvador, Colombia, Niger and Côte d'Ivoire (see Schramm 1967, Arnove 1976). Some projects addressed important equity issues. For example, 'the El Salvador instructional television system was the first school resource ever to be distributed equally across the seventh- through ninth-grade population' (Hornik 1988: 8). However, they were invariably school-focused initiatives, aimed primarily at children. The Côte d'Ivoire project did have a significant adult education component, but this was an exception. In some cases, e.g. in El Salvador (Schramm 1967) and the Ivory Coast (Ba and Potashnik, in press), they demonstrated a potential to improve the quality of educational process and outcome, while also raising internal rates of efficiency, by reducing student drop-out and repetition. However, generally they proved too costly for most developing countries to sustain or scale up. In most cases they were also beyond the technical capacity of the host countries to operate or maintain. As a result, by the mid-1980s all the ETV projects running in developing countries which had begun with external funding had been wound up, unable to continue without the very significant external aid. Evaluation reports generally yield a picture of disillusionment. ETV was in the main just too expensive or ineffective or both (Mayo 1990, Klees 1995: 399–400). Anzalone captures the mood well:

> The overall impression is that the use of television can be expensive and that it contributes little (and in some cases nothing) to student achievement. Television often arouses strong opposition on the part of teachers and sometimes resistance on the part of students. There is a striking lack of success in upgrading television use from an experimental phase to a permanent feature of national education.
>
> (Anzalone 1987: 39, cited in Mayo 1990: 288)

Not surprisingly, very few developing countries today use ETV for basic education. However, there are exceptions which have both survived and thrived: Brazil's Telecurso 2000, a project run by the Roberto Marinho Foundation, Mexico's Telesecundaria, and Portugal's Telescola are three longstanding projects which

Table 1.1 Models of basic education: a typology of practice and provision

Model	In-school programme examples	Out-of-school programme examples
Educational television	ETV projects in Côte d'Ivoire, El Salvador, American Samoa, Colombia and Niger. Others include Mexico's Telesecundaria and Portugal's Telescola.	Brazilian projects include the Secundo Grau, Minerva, Telecurso 2000 and Project Alphabetizar Constructir.
Radio learning groups, forums and campaigns		Farm forums in Canada, India, Ghana, Zambia, Benin and Senegal, Literacy, health and community development campaigns (many) e.g. On the Move (a UK BBC literacy campaign), Man is Health campaign in Tanzania.
Schools broadcasting	Australian 'Schools of the Air'. IRI projects in over 20 countries including Nicaragua, Kenya, Lesotho, South Africa and Nepal.	UK community education, IRI projects in Bolivia, Honduras, Nepal, Dominican Republic.
Radiophonic schools	Mexican Radioprimaria.	ACPO Colombia, ACPH Honduras, Radio ECCA Canary Islands, Radio Santa Maria Dominican Republic, and an IRI primary education programme in the Dominican Republic.
Open schools		National Open School India, Open Junior Secondary School Indonesia, Bangladesh Open University Open School.
Multichannel systems	Project No Drops, Philippines, multigrade schools in Costa Rica.	South Africa Radio Learning Project, Laiwo Karen Multichannel Learning Project in western Thailand, FEPRA AIOU Pakistan.
Basic education training schemes		Basic education through primary teacher education (many), e.g. in Tanzania, Pakistan, Indonesia. Adult literacy leader training at UNISA, South Africa. PETROBRAS worker training Brazil. INADES-formation basic education and farmer training programmes spread across ten countries in west, central and east Africa. AMREF health worker distance education training programme in Kenya and Uganda.

have basic education components and have reached large numbers of adults. Nonetheless, in the main, countries without oil wealth or significant mineral resources have understandably been wary of ETV.

However, the main conclusion of the late 1980s should perhaps now be challenged. Where developing countries have the technical infrastructure and indigenous public or private resources needed to fund such programmes, ETV can certainly attract sustained and sizeable audiences, and provide cost-efficient access for hundreds of thousands and in some cases millions of students (Oliveira and Jamison 1982, de Moura Castro 1999, Ortiz 1999). The schemes which have survived have usually been work oriented (e.g. the Brazilian Telecurso 2000). Whether such programmes are also cost-effective is, however, a question which remains to be tested.

Radio

Radio across the world is the great educational success story. No other medium has sustained its impact in the same way. Since 1924, when the BBC first introduced its schools broadcasting service, there have been numerous radio-led, basic education projects all over the world (Jamison and McAnany 1978, Young *et al.* 1991, Kaye and Harry 1982, Mayo 1999). The 1960s and 1970s were the era when educational radio thrived. Since then radio has been somewhat eclipsed by more glamorous media, like television and, more recently, information technology and moves to privatise the airwaves. There have been three radio-based models: schools broadcasting – including Interactive Radio Instruction (IRI); radio forums and mass campaigns; and radio schools. The first model occurs in-school, the latter two outside school.

Schools radio broadcasting and IRI

Both schools broadcasting and Interactive Radio Instruction are basically concerned with improving learning and teaching quality within the classroom. Schools broadcasting services can be found throughout the Commonwealth and in many other countries. Often modelled on the BBC approach, such services are designed to supplement the main task of teaching within schools. The role is to complement the work of teachers, by extending, enriching and providing a wider range of learning experiences for children who will live most of their lives within narrow geographical ranges. Schools broadcasting can thus be particularly important in those areas where broadcast television and other electronic media are yet to become established (Mayo 1999).

IRI was first developed in Nicaragua in 1974 and has been used in over twenty countries since then. The US Agency for International Development (USAID) has been the primary backer with a mission to 're-invent educational radio to serve the poorest children in the poorest nations of the world' (Dock and Helwig 1999: 9). What makes IRI distinctive are the following:

- carefully designed curricula based on the best practices, including findings from research
- radio programmes which are designed to be more than just supplementary or enrichment; IRI programmes usually focus on the core instruction, and lessons for a given subject and grade may be broadcast on a daily basis
- carefully developed scripts which incorporate the best pedagogical approaches, especially active participation of the learners during the radio broadcasts
- extensive use of formative evaluation during lesson development
- summative evaluations which determine the learning achievement gains resulting from the IRI programmes

The most successful radio programmes have been those which have maintained close congruence with teachers, their schools and the operational contexts (Hurst 1974, 1983, Dock and Helwig 1999). Further, projects which have paid close attention to the principles of rational curriculum design throughout the planning, preparation and implementation phases have had a particularly positive effect on educational outcomes. Such designs, far from alienating or de-skilling teachers as did ETV schemes, have in some cases served as important mechanisms for school-based in-service teacher training and upgrading. The programmes have, for example, often helped to introduce new and improved forms of classroom management and subject pedagogy.

It is also important to note that teachers who work regularly and over prolonged periods with IRI programmes need refresher courses and to be updated, if they are not to become habituated and bored with their role and undermine the impact of the IRI schemes (Dock 1999: 54).

Over the last twenty years, radio-led education projects have increasingly learned to use applied education principles drawn from both the behavioural and the constructivist paradigms, and this has had demonstrably positive learning benefits (Hornik 1988, Bosch 1997). The South African IRI project 'English in Action' deserves special mention, because it was particularly influential in shifting the IRI model away from a behaviourist model to a more constructivist approach as a learning design (see chapter 2 in this volume, p. 90). The ability of the IRI model to adapt to diverse and changing contexts and circumstances has been one of its greatest strengths.

Further, the IRI model has recently yielded some promising gender results:

> Concerning gender disparities, recent evaluation data suggest that when girls participate in IRI programs learning gains are achieved and IRI may benefit girls more than boys ... the potential for using IRI to improve educational quality and access for girls is promising.
>
> (Hertenberger and Bosch 1996: 31)

However, IRI has had mixed results in terms of national implementation and long-term sustainability. A number of projects have not proved sustainable.

Nevertheless, it is estimated that about 1 million students across various countries have been using IRI annually over the past fifteen years. Interestingly, some of the most successful projects did not result from close collaboration with a ministry of education or even extensive donor support. Examples of IRI projects which have had significant, sustained impact include mathematics in Bolivia and Venezuela, science in Papua New Guinea, English in South Africa and health in Bolivia.

One recent review suggests that the key factors determining the long-term sustainability of such projects include:

> ... vigorous local leadership, securing long-term financial commitment, marketing the project in the political and social arenas, building commitment and ownership among participants, working for integration into the education system, and regularly re-activating teachers and their supervisors.
>
> (Dock 1999: 58)

Radio forums, clubs and campaigns

The radio forum movement began in Canada in the early 1940s. In this model regular radio programmes, containing advice about modern farming and other community issues, were produced in collaboration with relevant professional agencies. The agricultural extension service, working in co-operation with the radio stations, broadcast innovative programmes to isolated farming communities living on the prairies. The 'Listen-Discuss-Act' pattern was encouraged and large audiences were reached. By 1949 the model had been exported and adapted in India where some of the regional stations of All India Radio began to use it. UNESCO support followed in 1956 and a better resourced programme began in Poona, which was later scaled up to other states with mixed results (Schramm 1967). More recently the model has been used to reach thousands of farmers with considerable success in All India Radio's 'Farm School Programme' (Dighe 1996).

The radio forum model was exported to a number of other countries, particularly in Africa, e.g. Ghana, Tanzania, Botswana (Young *et al.* 1991) and Senegal and Niger (Cassirer 1977, McAnany 1972). The francophone variant, known as the 'radio-club', is important in that the primary distinction between the forum and the club was an educational and political one. Unlike the forum, which was essentially a transmissionist, top-down deficit approach, the club model was more concerned with involving the listeners in the making of the programmes, in deciding the topics for investigation and discussion, in collecting the information needed, and in deriving solutions to locally defined 'problems'. As such, this club model represents an early example of the community-centred 'empowerment approach', now being called for by some recent postmodernist development thinking (e.g. Esteva and Prakash 1998, Carmen 1996, Craig and Mayo 1995).

Radio campaigns, like forums and clubs, often involve study groups, with print-based follow-up for clarification, contextualisation, decision making and subsequent action. But they differ in a number of important respects. First, they are planned to run for shorter periods and are often more tightly focused, sometimes on single issues. For example, the Man is Health campaign run in Tanzania in 1973 was primarily concerned with improving village health conditions (Hall and Dodds 1974, Young et al. 1991: 52–4). Secondly, because they are large scale, aiming to contact and influence the behaviour of tens or even hundreds of thousands of people, they often involve detailed co-ordination between several agencies, as it is unlikely that a single ministry or organisation would have the necessary resources, or skills, to run a campaign alone. This necessarily involves long lead times for planning and preparation, in many cases between six and eighteen months. Thirdly, it is important to have a co-ordinated delivery and support infrastructure in place on the ground. In the Tanzanian case, the existence of thousands of adult education officers to facilitate the implementation, along with broad-based grassroots political support, were important reasons for success. Fourthly, if the Listen-Discuss-Act approach is to work, the listeners actually have to discuss the ideas being conveyed by the radio. If the groups are too large, or the study group leaders poorly trained or supported, then stakeholder involvement and action can become more akin to compliance than ownership. Large-scale radio campaigns have been organised in a number of countries, including India, Tanzania, Botswana and Zambia.

But radio campaigns have not been confined only to the poorer regions. The UK and Canada have also both run extensive literacy campaigns involving radio. In the West, illiteracy is often something shameful. Illiteracy in these contexts is an embarrassment and as a result is hidden. In such circumstances, individual radio listening can reach people sensitively, thereby helping them to gain the confidence they need to go further and make use of more public group-based support facilities (Hargreaves 1980, Bates 1990).

Despite the scale of activity and its apparent initial success, the radio campaign approach, led, as it always was, by expatriates, collapsed more than a quarter of a century ago. It has not been revived since.

Radio schools

The radio schools model attempted to bring together the emergent multiple media approach to basic education provision: that of regular broadcasting, follow-up study group meetings, and simple print-based and other forms of media support. Interestingly the model has flourished most significantly in Latin America, where by the 1980s it had spread from its origins in Colombia in 1947 with the Catholic-church-based Accion Cultural Popular (ACPO), to some twenty-five countries in the region (Young et al. 1991: 55).

One of the most influential radio schools has been Radio ECCA in the Spanish Canary Islands (Cepeda 1982). Radio ECCA has been offering adult basic education programmes for more than thirty years. During its life, it is estimated that about 40 per cent of the adult population of the islands have been students with the school (Spronk 1997: 1). The Radio ECCA 'three pillars' approach (radio broadcasts, plus printed workbooks and weekly study groups) has been particularly successful and has served as a model for the establishment of a number of radiophonic schools in Latin America.

Often established primarily to serve adult audiences, the radio schools have generally provided a complementary and often vocationally or socially orientated curriculum, in contrast to that of the state-controlled curricula of the primary school. (Issues associated with basic education curriculum are discussed in chapter 4 of this volume.) However, where radio schools have attempted to supplement primary provision in-school, as in the various adaptations of the Australian 'schools of the air' model, Mayo reminds us that they have invariably experienced difficulties, including:

> (1) vague and unrealistic program objectives; (2) design flaws stemming from ignorance of the target audiences' (students and teachers) abilities and expectations; (3) reception difficulties due to faulty transmission and erratic power supplies; (4) scheduling conflicts; (5) receiver breakdowns and lack of repair facilities; (6) insufficient feedback; and perhaps most significantly, (7) lack of support structures within schools or other community institutions to reinforce the broadcast lessons.
>
> (Mayo 1999: 3)

The IRI non-formal primary education project in the Dominican Republic during the 1980s is, perhaps, a unique and successful example of using radio to provide primary education to young children outside formal school. The core subject areas were presented solely by radio through a one-hour daily broadcast. Children would meet in a group setting organised by a community facilitator. This programme was sustained for many years, and as indicated earlier, assessments of learning achievement were positive.

Radio, as a 'little medium', is important in an era of relentless globalisation (Giddens 1999), particularly when radio stations are locally owned and people have easy access to receivers. Radio can, given appropriate circumstances, impact positively on basic education provision and literacy levels. Broadcasting in local languages, stations remain connected to, and able to reflect the priorities of, the grass-roots communities. The delivery of basic education through radio networks, supported by active mobilisation structures on the ground, is important for the health of democracy. In an age of increasing globalisation, with the potential for extremes of emancipation and exploitation, the 'little media' can do much to counter the worst effects of 'big government'. If the big centralised media push down from above, then the local community radio stations can help to push up locally generated ideas and reactions from the grass roots. Without these local media pushing up vigorously from below, positive globalisation processes are unlikely to work. Public service and basic education radio projects can do much to improve the transparency of government, extend literacy and deepen civic participation.

Although large and internationally sponsored radio networks have existed for decades, radio remains a locally owned and operated institution in many societies. For this reason community broadcasters are able to provide information and entertainment programmes in listeners' mother tongues and in ways that meet the needs of illiterate individuals as well as those with little or no formal education. By the same token, radio is still an essential tool for promoting literacy and basic education at the grass-roots level.

(Mayo 1999: 1)

Issues associated with audience participation are discussed in chapter 3 of this volume.

Open schools

Open schools are important as an alternative route to basic and secondary school education. They currently represent the foremost evolutionary organisational form in terms of the numbers served and the sophistication of their institutional arrangements. Generally, they have been set up as dedicated structures by their national governments, to serve both children and adults. They are found in a wide range of locations including India, Indonesia, Brazil, Korea, the UK and Malawi. They are of particular interest to the high-population countries which are having difficulty expanding their school systems. Open schools use varying combinations of print, broadcast, face-to-face and, to a lesser extent, other media to deliver their programmes. Where they serve children, their curricula invariably mirror that offered in the state schools; equivalency of quality and the identity of the qualification being offered are of central importance to legitimacy. Where they serve adults, a broader variety of vocationally oriented courses may also be on offer. Under the prevailing ideology of the market, some schools (e.g. the National Open School in India) are required to recover an increasing proportion of their costs from student fees and other sources. This is a trend we can expect to continue in the future.

Bangladesh offers an interesting example because, unlike most other open schools, the Bangladesh Open School is an integral part of the national Bangladesh Open University (BOU). The BOU was established in 1992 with the BOU Open School (BOUOS) as one of its six founding schools. BOUOS offers school equivalency courses, including a two-year Secondary School Certificate (SSC) launched in 1995. The SSC programme includes courses in Bengali, English, mathematics, science, social science, agriculture, home economics and religion. By 1998 about 45,000 students had enrolled on the SSC programme. As such, the SSC is one of the BOU's largest programmes. In addition to school equivalency courses, the BOUOS also offers basic science and mathematics as part of the university's extensive non-formal education programme (Ali, Enamul Haque and Rumble 1997, Ministry of Planning 1996).

The quality and effectiveness of the regional outreach and support services are particularly important for school-level courses. As in the case of most other open schools, Bangladeshi audiences working at this level often lack the independent learning skills necessary to sustain motivation and develop understanding through distance learning. Without well-structured programmes and a supportive learning culture, it is easy for such models to become doors to failure. Hence it is important for institutions offering basic education programmes through an essentially independent learning approach to design effective, group-based support systems to complement the media-based, individualised elements. This group-based support can, however, be very expensive, being less amenable to economies of scale. How to maximise access, equity and quality, while at the same time controlling cost, is one of the central policy dilemmas facing educational planners working at this level. The open school structure, as potentially a very large-scale mass model, offers an interesting field for future research into these issues. A more detailed account of the evolution and development of the open schools model is given in chapter 12 of this volume.

Multichannel systems

Multichannel learning systems are less a kind of organisational structure, and more a mode of thinking which seeks to identify a set of key principles to guide the development of more effective and equitable education strategies. Multichannel learning is essentially a design and implementation strategy, which aims to find ways of integrating and reinforcing the learning which takes place both within and beyond conventional education structures. Multichannel learning attempts to combine a wider range of media than is conventionally used in current programmes. It recognises and attempts to harness formal, non-formal and informal learning, seeing all three as mutually reinforcing and complementary modalities of learning. In other words, multichannel learning recognises and uses 'multiple pathways to learning'.

Some countries are able to expose their citizens to rich learning environments with multiple pathways to learning both inside and outside the formal structures. Such situations provide greater opportunities for continuous skill development and learning reinforcement. In poorer countries there are fewer pathways to learning, and the interconnections between the formal learning experienced in structured situations and learning gained outside, in social contexts beyond the school, are fewer (Anzalone 1995b: 6). Multichannel learning attempts to build on, and build out from, the educational practices currently available.

The key assumptions are:

- multiple learning channels are better than single learning channels
- where possible, interconnections between channels should be fostered and used to reinforce and extend learning opportunities
- learners are perceived as 'sense-makers' and knowledge creators, rather than as recipients and users of communicated information

These principles necessarily place great emphasis on achieving a better understanding of learners' study motivations and life contexts, before designing messages and selecting the learning channels to convey them. Multichannel learning programmes are found both within and outside formal schooling structures and include initiatives like multigrade schooling, and UNESCO's Project No Drops in the Philippines (Sutaria 1995), along with community-based projects like the Laiwo Karen multichannel learning scheme in western Thailand (Laflin and Olssen 1995) and the Functional Education Project for Rural Areas (FEPRA) adult basic education project at the Allama Iqbal Open University (Warr 1992). Essentially, the concept attempts to draw together a great deal of the thinking and experience gained over the last forty years in areas like participatory learning, development communication and social mobilisation (Chieuw and Mayo 1995). In this sense multichannel learning is a concept which tries to take distance educators and educational technologists beyond sterile debates about separate provision, on to more holistic debates which explore productive interconnections among motivation, context, structural integration, methodology and outcome.

Basic education training schemes

Finally, there are numerous basic-level education and training programmes run in a wide range of contexts, both by dedicated distance education structures like open universities and by non-specialised structures in state ministries or commercial companies. This category includes a wide range of vocational and professional development programmes, both for the personnel who are involved directly in the development of basic education systems, like those training to be adult basic education trainers, and people working in commercial or government environments who undertake basic education courses as part of their own work or personal development. Three examples illustrate this last category.

The University of South Africa Adult Basic Education Scheme for basic education trainers   In the early 1990s, soon after the demise of the apartheid regime, an important aim in South Africa was to train approximately 150,000 adult educators over a ten-year period. A number of projects are concerned with meeting this target. The largest was the Adult Basic Education and Training (ABET) Project based at the University of South Africa (UNISA). The programme was piloted in 1995 with 2,200 students, supported by over fifty part-time tutors. The tutors received training and support from the central unit in Pretoria (the planned student tutor ratio is 1:40). In 1995, 78 per cent of students in the first cohort passed their exams.

Project ACESSO   Although they are comparatively rare, one can find vocationally orientated projects which include basic education components taught at a distance. One such project is ACESSO. ACESSO is a worker basic education training project of PETROBRAS, the Brazilian state-owned oil company and one of the biggest corporations in the world. Company site locations are frequently very isolated. The company relies on locally recruited labour, many of whom have received poor-quality formal education. In the late 1970s, in order to improve worker effectiveness, the company instigated print-led distance education vocational training programmes which included courses in basic education at primary and secondary levels. Although the numbers taking the courses were relatively low – in the hundreds (at the primary level 493 had enrolled, 128 had graduated and 303 were ongoing at the time of the first evaluation) – cost-effectiveness was demonstrated, as was the efficacy of using simple print-based correspondence materials (Oliveira 1988).

Primary teacher education (in-school programmes)   A number of distance teacher education programmes have had as one of their goals raising the basic knowledge levels of their target audiences, so that they can teach better. The early Kenyan teacher education programme at the University of Nairobi (Hawkridge *et al*. 1982) and more recently the Logos II project in Brazil (Oliveira and Orivel 1993) and the Northern Integrated Teacher Education Project in Uganda (Wrightson 1998) are all examples. The curriculum of the Logos II teacher education project, for example, offered adult basic education to teachers through distance education, which corresponded with the last four years of the primary school plus three years of secondary school. Logos II had to develop basic schooling and specialised teacher training programmes. Compared with other Brazilian education projects, modes and levels of education, Logos II was, from an economic perspective, a highly cost-effective system of training Brazilian primary teachers (Oliveira and Orivel 1993).

A word on new information technologies

Before concluding this summary of distance and open learning to support basic education, it is important to mention two new technologies which may become very important, even in developing countries. The first is the Internet, which is beginning to have significant impact in many areas, including education. Although the Internet will not reach many primary schools in developing countries during the next few years, it may well reach a large number of teacher training institutions. In many developed countries the Internet is quickly becoming a key component of many distance education programmes. It allows for the easy delivery of a wide range of instructional material, not only text, but also audio and video using streaming technology. In addition to materials provided directly by the institution offering the distance education courses, the Internet offers a wealth of information which can supplement and greatly enrich virtually any course being offered. Perhaps most importantly, the Internet through e-mail and chat services makes possible a high level of interactivity between instructor and students and among students. For example, joint activities can be carried out by a group of individuals located in distant corners of the world.

As well as supporting distance education courses, the resources available through the Internet could be used to greatly enrich traditional classes. In a sense, the use of the Internet to enrich traditional classrooms is akin to using schools broadcasting to enrich regular classrooms, but with far more variety. The Internet, with its obvious association with distance learning, could become an important technology for helping to improve the training of teachers, and other professionals, within the next few years.

Digital radio is another new technology with potential for supporting distance education. The WorldSpace corporation launched in 1999 the first of three satellites. When all are launched, they will reach about 80 per cent of the world's population. The AfriSat satellite is sending three beams of signals, each with sixty high-quality audio channels covering all of Africa and most of the Middle East. In 2000–1 WorldSpace plans to launch two additional satellites which will cover Asia and Latin America. The corporation has set aside about 10 per cent of its broadcasting capacity to the WorldSpace Foundation to use for education, health, the environment, women's issues and humanitiarian purposes, which can include support for open and distance learning programmes. There are four potential major advantages of the WorldSpace digital radio system:

- there are many channels
- it has very wide coverage with a single channel, for example, covering about one-third of the African continent
- the quality of the sound is exceptionally clear, which is of particular importance for educational programmes
- in addition to broadcasting audio signals, the satellites can be used to send any type of digital materials to schools, resource centres, health clinics, etc., including not only audio material, but also video, graphics and text; to receive this multimedia information, the radio is tuned to the appropriate channel, and the information received by the radio receiver is transferred directly to an attached computer

Currently, the major disadvantage of the WorldSpace system is the lack of availability and high cost of the digital radio receivers. Several Japanese companies are now producing receivers, but they are not yet widely available, and the cost begins at about US $200. In time, though, receivers should become readily available and the price should decline significantly. The issue of who controls the programming, and how, is likely to be important, particularly as it relates to educational quality and relevance. Technology questions relating to the provision of basic education through ODE are discussed further in chapter 7 of this volume.

Conclusion

Open and distance learning models for basic education are found in many areas of the world, in rich and poor contexts, cutting across different cultural boundaries and political persuasions. Some approaches have had their theoretical origins in Marxist, neo-Marxist or Christian liberation theory of the dependency era (Freire 1972, Youngman 1986), others are children of neo-classical market economics and the new forms of Western liberal modernisation (Schramm 1967, Jayaweera and Amunugama 1987). It is perhaps surprising to note the great variety of experience and form which has endured through time, space and many different forms of political and professional affiliation. Practice spans the ideological development theory divide.

Some programmes have survived for decades and then died suddenly, like Accion Cultural Popular in Colombia (Fraser and Restrepo-Estrada 1998). Others, like the Bangladesh Open School, are quite new and as yet remain relatively untested. However, if basic education is ever to become a universal good, this diversity of form and practice needs far greater attention, research, nurturing, experimentation and sustained support – from politicians, scholars, educational practitioners and funding agencies alike (see chapter 6 in this volume). Only then will we have any real chance of making a significant impact on levels of illiteracy. More of the same in the twenty-first century will simply not be enough. For, as a director of UNESCO's basic education division has reminded us:

> In countries where the unreached are a majority, principally in sub-Saharan Africa and South Asia, conventional education systems are often not only unaffordable and irrelevant but also alienating to many of those they are intending to serve.
>
> (Ordonez 1995: 19)

As we indicated at the beginning of this chapter, in the twenty-first century out-of-school structures like the open schools, which are aimed primarily at adults, are likely to become more prevalent, particularly in south and south-east Asia. In contrast, the need in sub-Saharan Africa will be for better and more responsive schooling for children, aimed at helping them to get in, stay in or get back into school. Yet open universities are also being established in Africa, in Tanzania and Zimbabwe.

Perhaps the greatest need is for ways to encourage non-traditional thinking about expanding and improving the quality of basic education. This is discussed in relation to health education in chapter 11 of this volume. If more of the same is not good enough for the next decades, and if distance education and open learning offer promising alternatives (Perraton 2000), then it is important for policy makers, educational leaders and donors to begin thinking of new approaches and alternatives. This book seeks to encourage debate on this issue. Finally, a discussion of the outcomes of the activity reviewed in this book is undertaken in the last chapter, chapter 13.

References

Ali, M., Enamul Haque, A. and Rumble, G. (1997) 'The Bangladesh Open University: mission and promise', *Open Learning*, June 12–28.

Anzalone, S. (1987) *Using Instructional Hardware for Primary Education in Developing Countries: A Review of the Literature*, Project BRIDGES, Cambridge, Massachusetts: Harvard University.

Anzalone, S. (ed.) (1995a) *Multichannel Learning: Connecting All to Education*, Washington, DC: Education Development Center.

Anzalone, S. (1995b) 'The case for multichannel learning', in S. Anzalone (ed.) *Multichannel Learning: Connecting All to Education*, Washington, DC: Education Development Center.

Arnove, R. (ed.) (1976) *Educational Television: A Policy Critique and Guide for Developing Countries*, New York: Praeger.

Arnove, R. and Graff, H. (eds) (1987) *National Literacy Campaigns: Historical and Comparative Perspectives*, New York: Plenum Press.

Ba, H. and Potashnik, M. (in press) *The Côte d'Ivoire Educational Television Project: Revisited 20 Years Later*, draft report, World Bank.

Bates, T. (1990) *Literacy by Radio: Lessons from Around the World*, paper presented at the International Symposium of Popular Literacy by Radio, Santo Domingo, Dominican Republic, 1–3 July.

Bennell, P. (1999) *Education for All: How Attainable is the DAC Target in Sub-Saharan Africa?* paper presented at the Oxford International Conference on Education and Development, Oxford: UKFIET/CfBT.

Bennell, P. with Furlong, D. (1998) 'Has Jomtien made any difference? Trends in donor funding for education and basic education since the late 1980s', *World Development* 26,1.

Bosch, A. (1997) *Interactive Radio Instruction: Twenty-Three Years of Improving Educational Quality*, Educational Training Technology Notes Series, 2, Washington, DC: World Bank.

Carmen, R. (1996) *Autonomous Development: Humanising the Landscape, an Excursion into Radical Thinking and Practice*, London: Zed Books.

Cassirer, H. (1977) 'Radio in an African context: A description of Senegal's pilot project', in P. Spain *et al.* (eds) *Radio for Education and Development: Case Studies*, 2, Staff Working Paper 266, Washington, DC: World Bank.

Cepeda, L. (1982) 'Radio ECCA, Canary Islands', in A. Kaye and K. Harry (eds) *Using the Media for Adult Basic Education*, London: Croom Helm.

Chieuw, J. and Mayo, J.(1995) 'The conceptual foundations for multichannel learning', in S. Anzalone (ed.) *Multichannel Learning: Connecting All to Education*, Washington, DC: Education Development Center.

Colclough, C. (1999) *Achieving Schooling for All in Sub-Saharan Africa: Is Gender a Constraint or an Opportunity?* Oxford/London: Oxfam/ActionAid.

Coombs, P. (1985) *The World Crisis in Education: The View From the Eighties*, New York: Oxford University Press.

Craig, G. and Mayo, M. (eds) (1995) *Community Empowerment: A Reader in Participation and Development*, London: Zed Books.

de Moura Castro, C. (1999) 'Brazil's Telecurso 2000: The flexible solution for secondary school equivalency', *TechKnowLogia*, November/December, Knowledge Enterprise Inc. Available HTTP: *http://www.techKnowLogia.org*

DFID (1999) *Learning Opportunities for All: A Policy Framework for Education*, London: Department for International Development.

Dighe, A. (1996) 'Farm and home programmes of the All India Radio: A case study', in Course 7 *Non-Formal and Adult Basic Education at a Distance*. Reader, Cambridge: University of London/International Extension College MA in Distance Education.

Dock, A. (1999) 'Success and sustainability', in A. Dock and J. Helwig (eds) *Interactive*

Radio Instruction: Impact, Sustainability, and Future Directions, Education and Technology Notes Series, 4, 1, Washington, DC: USAID/World Bank.

Dock, A. and Helwig, J. (eds) (1999) *Interactive Radio Instruction: Impact, Sustainability, and Future Directions*, Education and Technology Notes Series, 4, 1, Washington, DC: USAID/World Bank.

Esteva, G. and Prakash, M. (1998) *Grassroots Post-Modernism: Remaking the Soil of Cultures*, London: Zed Books.

Fraser, C. and Restrepo-Estrada, S. (1998) *Communicating for Development: Human Change for Survival*, London: I. B. Tauris.

Freire, P. (1972) *Cultural Action for Freedom*, Harmondsworth, Penguin.

Giddens, A. (1999) *The Reith Lectures: Runaway World*, London: BBC.

Hall, B. and Dodds, T. (1974) *Voices for Development: The Tanzanian National Radio Study Campaigns*, Cambridge: International Extension College.

Hargreaves, D. (1980) *Adult Literacy and Broadcasting: The BBC Experience*, London: Francis Pinter.

Hawkridge, D. *et al.* (1982) 'In-service teacher education in Kenya', in H. Perraton (ed.) *Alternative Routes to Formal Education*, Baltimore/London: Johns Hopkins University Press for the World Bank.

Hertenberger, L. and Bosch, A. (1996) *Making Interactive Instruction Even Better for Girls: The Data, the Scripts and the Potential*, Washington, DC: Education Development Center.

Hornik, R. (1988) *Development Communication*, New York/Maryland: Longman/University Press of America.

Hurst, P. (1974) 'Educational technology transfer: Tactics on innovation', *British Journal of Educational Technology*, 5,1.

Hurst, P. (1983) *Implementing Educational Change: A Critical Review of the Literature*, EDC Occasional Papers No. 5, London: Department of Education in Developing Countries, University of London Institute of Education.

Jamison, D. and McAnany, E. (1978) *Radio for Education and Development*, London: Sage.

Jayaweera, N. and Amunugama, S. (1987) *Re-thinking Development Communication*, Singapore: AMIC.

Kaye, A. and Harry, K. (eds) (1982) *Using the Media for Adult Basic Education*, London: Croom Helm.

Klees, S. (1995) 'The economics of educational technology', in M. Carnoy (ed.) *International Encyclopedia of Economics of Education*, Oxford: Pergamon, second edition.

Laflin, M. and Olssen, M. (1995) 'Multichannel learning at the community level', in S. Anzalone (ed.) (1995) *Multichannel Learning: Connecting All to Education*, Washington, DC: Education Development Center.

Lockheed, M. and Verspoor, A. (1990) *Improving Primary Education in Developing Countries: A Review of Policy Options*, Washington, DC: World Bank.

Lugg, D. (1994) 'Primary and secondary distance education in Victoria, Australia', in M. Mukhopadhyay and S. Phillips (eds) *Open Schooling: Selected Experiences*, Vancouver: Commonwealth of Learning.

McAnany, E. (1972) *Radio Clubs of Niger*, Stanford: University of Stanford, Institute of Communications Research, reprint.

McGee, R., Robinson, C. and van Diesen, A. (1998) *Distance Targets? Making the 21st Century Development Strategy Work*, London: Christian Aid.

Mayo, J. (1990) 'Unmet challenges: Educational broadcasting in the third world', in D.

Chapman and C. Carrier (eds) *Improving Educational Quality*, New York: Greenwood Press.

Mayo, J. (1999) 'Radio's role in education and development: Introduction and overview', in A. Dock and J. Helwig (eds) *Interactive Radio Instruction: Impact, Sustainability, and Future Directions*, Education and Technology Notes Series, 4, 1, Washington, DC: USAID/World Bank.

Ministry of Planning (1996) *Bangladesh Open University Project Proforma: Revised Scheme for the Establishment of the Bangladesh Open University* (1991–1999) Dhaka: Government of Bangladesh.

Moulton, J. (1994) *Interactive Radio Instruction: Broadening the Definition*, LearnTech Case Study Series, 1, January, Washington, DC: Education Development Center.

Mueller, J. (1996) *Literacy and Non Formal (Basic) Education: Still a Donor Priority?* Occasional Papers Series 1, 3, Reading: Education for Development.

Mukhopadhyay, M. and Phillips, S. (eds) (1994) *Open Schooling: Selected Experiences*, Vancouver: Commonwealth of Learning.

OECD (1996) *Shaping the 21st Century: The Contribution of Development Co-operation*, Development Assistance Committee, Paris: Organisation for Economic Co-operation and Development.

Oliveira, J. (1988) *Project ACESSO: An Application of Distance Learning for Professional Training*, Washington, DC: Economic Development Institute of the World Bank.

Oliveira, J. and Jamison, D. (1982) 'Evaluation of the Brazilian Telecurso Secundo Grau: Summary and policy implications', in H. Perraton (ed.) *Alternative Routes to Formal Education: Distance Teaching for School Equivalency*, Baltimore/London: Johns Hopkins University Press for the World Bank.

Oliveira, J. and Orivel, F. (1993) 'Logos II in Brazil', in H. Perraton (ed.) *Distance Education for Teacher Training*, London: Routledge.

Ordonez, V. (1995) 'More of the same will not be enough', Education Commentary in *The Progress of Nations*, New York: United Nations Children's Fund.

Ortiz, V. (1999) 'Open and distance education programmes in Latin America', in G. Farrell (ed.) *The Development of Virtual Education: A Global Perspective*, Vancouver: Commonwealth of Learning.

Perraton, H. (2000) *Open and Distance Learning in the Developing World*, London: Routledge.

Rogers, A., Holland, D., Maddox, B., Millican, J., Newell-Jones, K., Papen, U., Robinson-Pant, A. and Street, B. (1998) *Changing Post Literacy in a Developing World*, London: Department for International Development.

Schramm, W. (1967) 'Ten years of the Rural Radio Forum in India', in W. Schramm (ed.) *New Educational Media in Action: Case Studies for Planners* 1, Paris: UNESCO International Institute for Educational Planning.

Schramm, W. (1973) *Big Media Little Media*, London: Sage.

Spronk, B. (1997) *Report on Radio Schools in Latin America*, Cambridge: International Extension College, mimeo.

Street, B. (1993) 'Introduction: The new literacy studies', in B. Street (ed.) *Cross-Cultural Approaches to Literacy*, Cambridge: Cambridge University Press.

Sutaria, M. (1995) 'Multichannel learning: The Philippines experience', in S. Anzalone (ed.) *Multichannel Learning: Connecting All to Education*, Washington, DC: Education Development Center.

Warr, D. (1992) *Distance Teaching in the Village*, Cambridge: International Extension College.

Watkins, K. (1999) *Education Now: Break the Cycle of Poverty*, Oxford: Oxfam International.

WCEFA (1990) (World Conference on Education for All) *The World Declaration on Education for All: Meeting Basic Learning Needs*, New York, Inter-Agency Commission.

Wrightson, T. (1998) *Distance Education in Action: The Northern Integrated Teacher Education Project*, Cambridge: International Extension College.

Young, M., Perraton, H., Jenkins, J. and Dodds, T. (1991) *Distance Teaching for the Third World: The Lion and the Clockwork Mouse*, Cambridge: International Extension College, second edition.

Youngman, F. (1986) *Adult Education and Socialist Pedagogy*, London: Croom Helm.

Chapter 2

The elusiveness of integration

Policy discourses on open and distance learning in the 1990s

Elaine Unterhalter, Catherine Odora Hoppers and Wim Hoppers

At Jomtien in 1990, the governments, international organisations and non-governmental organisations (NGOs) gathered for the World Conference on Education for All (WCEFA) jointly acknowledged that the aspiration for universal basic education had not been met. This failure was most evident with regard to people who were discriminated against, politically, socially, economically and culturally. Although the conference referred to this category as 'marginal' groups, their numbers were estimated in 1990 at well over a billion adults and children, amounting to at least one fifth of the world's population (WCEFA 1990). They were thus not numerically 'marginal', but rather politically and culturally located outside the mainstream of what was seen to be the promise of the new decade and the century to come.

The Education for All (EFA) initiative, supported by governments, international organisations and large NGOs, had two aims. Firstly to provide universal access to and completion of primary education by all the world's children by the year 2000; secondly to halve the 1990 level of adult illiteracy by the end of the decade (Hallak 1990). An International Consultative Forum on Education for All was set up to monitor progress and follow up regional meetings, and a mid-decade review took place at Amman in 1995. The EFA decade was reviewed in a meeting convened by UNESCO in Dakar, Senegal, in April 2000 (UNESCO 2000).

The gathering at Jomtien highlighted the very large numbers of children out of school and illiterate adults worldwide. These figures destabilised some of the confident assertions or aspirations for a new global order which were formulated in the wake of the end of the cold war, the demise of apartheid, and the commitments to try to find peaceful solutions to long-running conflicts. The notion of a significant proportion of the world's population who were uneducated sat uncomfortably with what was seen in 1990 as a new age of great promise, and Jomtien was partly an attempt to include education in the expansive dreams for peace for the new decade and the new century. Indeed a stress on the powers of education to contribute to the conditions for economic growth, political stability, social integration and environmental sustainability was a *leitmotiv* of all the major international conferences of the decade (Unterhalter 2000).

Open and distance learning (ODL) featured in a number of different guises over the decade in global strategies to integrate so-called marginal populations with the mainstream. In many policy documents addressing education for all in the 1990s, new information and communication technologies (NICT), with ODL in their wake, became freighted with particular significance. The links between ODL and global communication technologies were often portrayed as promising universal access and exponential growth of learning. In the Jomtien Declaration this linkage seemed to be seen as a new 'synergistic effect' which would bring continued educational progress (WCEFA 1990). ODL was believed to offer a connection between new technologies and aspirations for equality and democracy. In the policy documents developed during the 1990s, by both multilateral and a number of bilateral agencies, NICT, attached to ODL, are often described as more than just one of a range of strategies available to governments, NGOs or community-based organisations to tackle the lack of quality formal education available. As the decade progressed, they were increasingly promoted (despite little research and investment) as a key strategy, which, by the 'synergistic effect' of correct policy, cheaply available technology and the growth of 'knowledge', would open educational doors to the excluded. ODL therefore came to be seen to have a very particular role to play in helping to usher in what was confidently believed could be a golden age for economic, political and social policy.

Educational technologies then, particularly those associated with ODL, have often during the 1990s been linked with both effective learning and equality of learning opportunity. Although the alleged synergy of technology and improved communication through ODL was generally, as the decade progressed, only weakly evident in addressing the needs of the poorest (Perraton 2000, Yates 1998, Mueller 1996, UNDP 1998), their potential continued to be advocated. How the argument for their use continued to be made, despite scant evidence of their efficacy, is explored in this chapter. The chapter focuses on education policy documents, because these represent a powerful framework through which governments or NGOs appealed both to the constituencies they represented and the donors from whom they sought development assistance.

The next part of the chapter provides an overview of the challenges and aspirations of the decade and some of the major multilateral and bilateral policy initiatives of the period which addressed adult and basic education, linking this with ODL. There follows a critical examination of a number of themes which emerge from the policy documents, relating to the links made in these between ODL and the role of technologies. The final sections of the chapter consider the implications of the policy formulated, looking at reasons for the differences between the aspiration and the implementation at the international, regional and national levels.

The challenges and aspirations of the decade

Despite the high expectations of the peace dividend to arise from the end of the Cold War, the 1990s were far from peaceful. The scale of death and devastation in local wars, such as in Rwanda, Somalia, former Yugoslavia, and East Timor, was enormous. In many parts of the world large populations suffered homelessness, hunger and the destruction of social institutions. At the global level, the gap between the richest countries and the poorest grew to unprecedented levels, and within individual countries there were huge differences between the access to national income of the richest and poorest segments.

Complex measurements, such as the human development index and the human poverty index formulated by the United Nations Development Programme (UNDP), and used to map the distribution of social development, not just per capita income, showed that, even in countries with some of the highest levels of human development, Canada and France, there were significant problems with poverty and large illiterate populations (UNDP 1998: 28). Human development was not well distributed. In 1998 the USA had the highest per capita income in terms of purchasing power, and was home to 143 out of the 225 richest people in the world (a group whose wealth exceeded that of the GDP of whole continents). However in 1998, the USA also had the highest levels of poverty of seventeen industrialised countries surveyed by UNDP (UNDP 1998: 29–30).

The persistence of war and poverty went side by side with three other features of the decade remarked on by a number of commentators. These comprised, firstly, increasing democratisation and the extensive growth of civil society organisations, which expanded and deepened notions of the political terrain and challenged existing understandings of markets (DAWN 1995, Held 1995, Sen 1999). A second feature involved environmental change, whose social, political and economic consequences were felt in large-scale floods and fires. Some of these disasters were crippling for efforts to achieve social development in many poor countries. A third feature concerned globalisation, which has entailed the use of NICT to achieve a qualitatively different level of economic, political and cultural interconnection (accompanied paradoxically by high levels of divergence) from that known in previous epochs (Castells 1996, Giddens 1999).

Thus, while the decade opened with the fall of the Berlin wall in November 1989 and the release of Nelson Mandela in February 1990, both appearing to signal previously undreamed of hopes for a better future, it ended with fresh pains of ethnic hatreds in parts of Europe, Africa and south-east Asia. The immensity of the north-south divide was also accentuated by the general intransigence of the group of seven (G7) countries with regard to Third-World debt and development assistance, although Britain did undertake some bold steps regarding debt relief in the last weeks of the century. All these events highlighted barriers to democratisation and many of the failures of redistribution, despite heightened concern with these aspirations. The decade had witnessed a process of moderating high hopes.

Within the broad challenges outlined above, the issue of the right to education, already anchored and enshrined in the 1948 Universal Declaration of Human Rights, was to assume a central place in international conferences and subsequent declarations. It was accompanied by a critical scrutiny of many features of education, particularly those associated with quality and relevance, assessment, governance and financing (Buchert 1998, Colclough *et al*. 1997, Leach and Little 1999, Jansen and Christie 1999). The challenge, not always clearly confronted, was how not to lose the aspiration for justice in a context of increasing pressures of a market ideology.

During the decade, pressure toward increasing access in education was signalled with the declaration of 1990 as UN International Literacy Year. This drew attention to the demands for literacy by youth and adults; women's demands were given a special prominence. In the same year the World Conference on Education For All, held in Jomtien, Thailand, issued the Jomtien Declaration on Education for All and its Framework for Action. The momentum for Education for All expressed at Jomtien was encapsulated in the first two Articles of the Conference Declaration. Article 1 stated that every child, youth and adult shall be able to benefit from educational opportunities *designed* to meet their basic learning needs. Article 2 was explicit that to serve the basic learning needs of all required more than just a recommitment to basic education as it now existed. What was needed was an 'expanded vision' which surpassed present resource levels, institutional structures, curricula, and *conventional delivery systems*, while building on the best in current practices (WCEFA 1990). The implications of these two articles were that every child, youth and adult should benefit from educational opportunities, and that education would be diversified, made content relevant, and designed to meet what was defined at Jomtien as their 'basic learning needs'.

Soon after Jomtien came the children's summit convened in New York, in which the rights of the child to education were strongly underlined. In 1992 at the Rio conference on the environment and development, renewed emphasis was placed on the fact that the education of adults was crucial in the protection of the environment and ensuring sustainable livelihoods.

The right of women to education was woven in with the population issues of the Cairo conference on population and development in 1994. This was a prominent feature of the poverty eradication focus of the 1995 Copenhagen social summit, and the Beijing women's conference later the same year. The year 1996 saw the global mid-decade review of Education for All, which ended with the Amman affirmation of the commitments made at Jomtien. In the following year (1997) the Fifth International Conference on Adult Education (CONFINTEA V) re-established the importance of adult education as an essential part of any education system. This gathering underscored the fact that the new vision of adult learning was not only multisectoral and diverse, but that it was located squarely within the framework of sustainable human development (Odora Hoppers 1997).

With the Fifth World Conference on Adult Education (CONFINTEA V) came an emphasis on the need to reinforce democracy by strengthening the learning environments and ensuring the participation of citizens. CONFINTEA V also stressed the need to counter the polarity between those who have access to information and those who do not, by promoting the right to work, improving conditions and quality of adult learning, and creating learning environments which are conducive to life-long learning. These learning strategies include promoting workplace learning, and community extension programmes for rural and isolated areas, as well as ensuring the universal right to literacy (UNESCO 1997a).

The 1990s was thus a decade of unprecedented international concern with expanding access to education and using new approaches for the design and delivery of education. Growing concerns with deepening democracy and including the marginal were key aspirations of the decade. How was ODL presented in the policy discourses of these international gatherings?

Open and distance learning in international policy discourses

Jomtien's emphasis on Education for All, its call for educational opportunities designed to meet basic learning needs, and the recognition that the expanded vision needed to reach beyond conventional delivery systems, should have given a major boost to the consideration of ODL as a philosophy and a strategy for realising rapid exponential growth of participation in education. Indeed strong international attention emerged around the time of the Jomtien conference on the potential of global communication technologies for improved access to information and enhanced communication, as expressed in the Preamble of the World Declaration on Education for All (WCEFA 1990: 2). In subsequent world conferences on education the significance of such new information and communication technologies (NICT) was also noted in relation to opening up access to learning and thus promoting equal opportunity and democracy. At the same time, however, it was striking that in none of these conferences was this general attention to NICT reflected in the endorsement of a future central role of distance learning as a delivery mode for education (Hoppers 2000). As we shall see, it was only towards the end of the decade, and even then in the more restricted context of agency policy papers, that the connection between NICT and the broader notion of ODL became an explicit policy issue.

It is worth examining factors which could have contributed to this hesitancy displayed towards ODL in momentous conferences devoted to Education For All. The first of these is the knowledge available on ODL experiences related to basic education. Here it should be pointed out that during the 1980s ODL (especially distance learning) had gained in importance as a cost-effective means to improve access and quality in education at all levels. It had achieved some recognition throughout the developing world as a legitimate policy option for formal school systems (Nettleton 1991:102). In Africa, particularly, it had become acceptable as an alternative to regular education delivery at secondary and higher levels of education, when the need for rapid expansion began to outstrip the resources available. This led to experiments with 'open secondary schools', correspondence programmes and the like (Dodds 1994).

It was recognised, however, that ODL had been least often attempted at primary level. This had been attributed to the importance of the socialisation role of education at this level, the need for greater supervision, and the complexity of designing appropriate materials for children (Nettleton 1991: 103). Nevertheless, during the 1980s two types of programmes emerged which were carried out with some degree of success: these were in-school programmes of 'Interactive Radio Instruction' (IRI) and programmes of educational radio as an outreach facility for out-of-school youth. The first type usually involved short radio lessons, which were highly interactive, in that learners were continuously prompted to respond in various ways. The second involved one or more hours of listening followed by group work led by para-professionals (Nielsen 1991: 125–6).

A good part of the distance learning (DL) experience had been summarised by Nielsen in a paper for the International Development Research Council (IDRC) as an input to the Jomtien Conference (Nielsen 1991). It is here that we come to the second factor which may have contributed to a fair degree of caution towards ODL: the apparent *problematic nature of DL in the context of basic education*. Nielsen's analysis raised the following critical points in a provisional assessment of DL in relation to mainstream education:

- The emphasis of 'classical' DL on mass production of learning and on delivery of a curriculum in digestible chunks of information for learner consumption led to insufficient attention to the human interaction dimension of learning and the social construction of knowledge.
- There is little space for relating learning to the local context and orientating activities towards cultivating a disposition and competencies for social change.
- DL is based on a value system which is individualistic and attaches great importance to the written word; thus it is often culturally alien to local traditions of communality and oral interaction; this effect is only strengthened by the use of a foreign language of communication.
- DL programmes do not have the same status as conventional ones, as they deviate from prevailing conceptions as to what education is all about.
- Teachers often fear being displaced by externally produced media, leaving them in a very subservient position, resulting in progressive 'de-professionalisation'.
- DL programmes tend to be developed outside the mainstream education management network, and thus have problems when it comes to their institutionalisation and the soliciting of routine financial support (Nielsen 1991: 136–9).

Some of the above points were more applicable to separate DL programmes for out-of-school youth than for in-school education. Yet both types have suffered from being regarded as stop-gap measures, the need for which would disappear once teachers were sufficiently qualified to handle learner-centred methodologies, or once sufficient numbers of conventional school places were created. Thus DL programmes for this critical group generally did not have a long life and rarely survived once the original goal for which they were established had been achieved. In fact a major problem for DL has been the apparent lack of strategic planning in its use for classroom instruction, based on a clear view of how it fits within an overall programme of educational change and development (Nielsen 1991: 144–6).

Our contention is that this second factor – i.e. the problematic nature of distance learning in basic education – has contributed significantly to the hesitancy of the major actors in education present at the world conferences (i.e. policy makers, agency personnel, professional educators) to fully endorse a widespread use of DL in promoting access and quality.

A third factor which is of some importance concerns the very nature of the conference declarations. Their emphasis tended to be on general advocacy for action, more than on the elaboration and promotion of specific strategies for reaching the goals. This meant that, in the midst of uncertainties surrounding the actual value of NICT in the context of basic education and the rather mixed notions concerning the state of practice regarding ODL, only vague generalisations found their way into conference documents or declarations.

A final factor underlying the cautious attitude to ODL may concern the assumed synergy between distance learning and open learning. While distance learning is a delivery strategy, open learning is regarded as a statement about a philosophy of education, in which particular value is given to certain underlying principles. Chief among these are those of 'learner centredness', 'flexibility in learning', the 'removal of unnecessary barriers to access' and the 'recognition of prior learning and experience'. While these principles can find expression in certain forms of distance learning, the two notions are not necessarily identical. Yet, particularly during the latter part of the 1990s, they have come to be connected in the wider notion of ODL.

While the Jomtien documents make no reference to DL as a particular mode of delivery for primary or adult education, the notion of open learning lies at the heart of the first two Articles of the Jomtien Declaration. These constitute a clear endorsement of the value of informal education to inform and educate people on social issues (WCEFA 1990: 46, 56). Yet, these statements are not followed either by further articulation of the philosophy of open learning or by discussions on modes of delivery with respect to distance learning. In fact, by 1996, it was openly stated that the expanded vision of basic education espoused in Jomtien had been reduced to a single emphasis upon putting more children into school (EFA 1996: 9).

Jomtien did recognise the need to keep a watchful eye on emerging technologies, as their suitability for the education process was deemed to change rapidly over time, but by the mid-1990s the interest was somewhat different, as was witnessed at the Amman mid-decade review. None of the four commissions of the conference, or for that matter the eight open dialogue sessions, focused any attention on the principles or potentialities of open or distance learning. Instead, the final report made the muted criticism that 'the use of media for educational purposes has lived up only modestly to the challenges set forth in the Jomtien declaration' and warned that 'in too many countries the potential of the media goes largely untapped' (EFA 1996: 27).

The final communiqué from Amman also regressed to the rather traditional position that 'while we must make better and wider use of technology and media, they can complement, but never replace the essential role of the teacher as the instructor, guide and example for the young' (EFA 1996: 17). Repeatedly, the document underscores the fact that the 'All' dimension of the Jomtien vision still needs more attention, and that a change is needed in the mind frame of planners and educators worldwide in recognising the bridge between formal and non-formal education. Yet, five years after Jomtien, even some developing countries still spoke of achieving EFA within a few years, apparently confusing EFA with universal primary education (EFA 1996: 37).

The Hamburg Declaration on Adult Learning and its Agenda for the Future took a broad view of learning and the range of opportunities available for promoting it. In fact, Hamburg, through its promotion of life-long learning, underscored the importance of open learning as a basis for improving access, flexibility, and learner-centredness. Both traditional and modern media need to become accessible to adult learners wherever they are and for any purpose. In the Agenda for the Future, one article, devoted to the media, information and communication technology, stated that better synergies were needed between media, information technologies and adult learning, by 'ensuring equal access and sustainability of ODL systems, the media, and the new information and communication technologies, and by using new technologies to explore alternative ways of learning' (UNESCO 1997a: 23–4). It urged that institutions of formal learning should open up their doors to learners of all categories, and adapt their programmes to meet learning needs; and that opportunities for adult learning should be created in flexible ways, taking into account the diverse nature of the clientele in new institutional formats (UNESCO 1997a: 13–14). But once again, the document fell one step short of articulating either a philosophy or a strategy for ODL.

This ambiguity at international levels was to encounter further vagueness at regional levels. In April 1998 the Seventh Conference of African Ministers of Education came out with its Durban Statement of Commitment, which confirmed the importance of access to all levels of formal and non-formal education as a prerequisite for the development of democracy. Yet, when distance learning was mentioned, it was slotted back into the realm of higher education as a means of increasing access to that level (UNESCO 1998: 22).

Open and distance learning in agency policies

The policy turn taken at Jomtien, with its stress on the need to prioritise basic education for children and adults, was rearticulated in a wide variety of agency documents. The World Bank added its own policy text for the decade, *Priorities and Strategies for Education*, published in 1995 (World Bank 1995). Large-scale education interventions, like the District Primary Education Programme in India or the Strengthening Primary Education Programme in Kenya, which brought together government and NGO mobilisation around education for all, were implemented in the wake of Jomtien. In parallel with large-scale national interventions like these, a very large number of other initiatives on a medium, small and micro level also worked towards the goals of EFA (Little, Hoppers and Gardner 1994, Colclough and Lewin 1993, Bennell and Furlong 1997, Buchert 1998, Perraton 2000). But despite such initiatives, and despite the periodic meetings and resolutions of the international community in terms of the Jomtien machinery, the very large numbers of adults and children without basic education did not decline dramatically as the decade progressed (UNESCO 1998, Bellamy 1999, Bennell 1999).

Towards the end of the decade, the chimeric quality of the Jomtien-inspired solutions to the problem of basic education for all led to new rounds of strategising among certain development assistance agencies. Some of these were bilateral agencies like DFID, the Swedish International Development Authority (SIDA) and Netherlands Development Assistance, acting in response to the realisation that the Jomtien goals were unreachable without a rethinking of development assistance in relation to national policies and strategies (DFID 1999, Gustafsson 1999, Netherlands 2000). A prominent role in stimulating fundamental discussions on promoting access was taken up by prestigious international NGOs like Oxfam, which wanted to build a new worldwide popular consciousness about demands for education (Watkins 1999). Within this climate there also arose an increased interest in exploring the systemic dimensions of basic education and in examining the relevance of alternative pathways and methodologies for learning linked to the mainstream. The concept of open learning has come to serve here as a central reference point for exploring a range of options with the potential to reach beyond the specific confines of conventional distance learning (World Bank 1999b, Commonwealth Secretariat 1999, Hoppers 2000).

In the late 1990s new thinking was also emerging from international bodies like UNESCO and the World Bank. In these bodies, side by side with some analysis of why the aspirations of Jomtien had not been met – analyses which tended to stress poor delivery and limited institutional capacities (Colclough *et al.* 1997, Buchert 1998) – new solutions were being proffered, which appeared to leapfrog the institutional problem. These solutions were linked to the promise of new information and communication technologies (NICT) to deliver where older programmes implemented through governments and NGOs had faltered or failed.

In 1997, UNESCO issued a policy paper, *Open and Distance Learning: Prospects and Policy Considerations* (UNESCO 1997b). This document was not so much a position paper as a strategic intervention into the policy debate which, in the words of the Director of the Higher Education Division, was intended as 'a contribution to the on-going discussion on the ever wider role that ODL is expected to assume in the educational landscape of tomorrow' (Dias 1997: 1). In the UNESCO document ODL became increasingly seen as an important and positive application of NICT. Optimistic readings of the potential of these technologies for widening access to education featured in a preliminary conference paper by the Chief of the World Bank Electronic Media Centre (Knight 1996).

Similar optimism is reflected in two World Bank papers published at the end of the decade. The *World Development Report* for 1998/9 had as its theme 'Knowledge for Development' (World Bank 1999a). Here World Bank writers constructed an argument that the new knowledge revolution would result in increased social benefits for all, and specific benefits to the poor (Wolfensohn 1999). This theme emerged again in the World Bank Education Sector paper circulated as a discussion document in 1999 (World Bank 1999b). Fortunately, this 1999 World Bank paper is much less directive and assertive about whose ideas are decisive in particular contexts than the World Bank 1995 paper (World Bank 1999b: 46). This is a notable shift: policy documents written at the end of the decade, like the UNESCO policy paper, the two 1999 World Bank papers and the DFID education policy paper, appear as less prescriptive texts than the Jomtien Declaration and the 1995 World Bank strategy paper. These papers were all presented as contributions to a debate and explicitly noted that they invited discussion of their arguments (Dias 1997, Wolfensohn 1999: iv, World Bank 1999b: 53–4, DFID 1999: 43).

The increased interest in debate among international education agencies is perhaps an indication, not only that there is grave concern about the realisation of the original goals of Jomtien, but that more specifically there is a significant lack of clarity about the possible contribution which can be made by ODL. There is no coherent international understanding as to how in different developmental contexts new technologies can best be used to enhance formal and lifelong learning. In addition, there is little clarity as to how the principles of ODL can be applied to improve access and quality, *irrespective of what technologies can suitably be invoked*. Thus, while it is a gain that ODL has now become a policy issue, it is effectively still an agenda which is waiting to be defined.

The above does not mean that no pointers exist which could help to formulate such an agenda. In many parts of the developing world in recent years initiatives have been taken by governments, NGOs, donor agencies and private sector companies, often in partnership with one another, to begin to explore the dimensions of such an agenda. These include the many efforts to introduce NICT in schools and in arrangements for teacher education and support, and further experimentation with the use of different electronic media to reach adult and out-of-school learners. A notable example in this respect has been the UNESCO programme 'Learning without Frontiers', which has become a vehicle to open up dialogue on the relevance of NICT and ODL in relation to the goals of Jomtien in a wide variety of countries. UNESCO has done further work on the introduction of ODL in nine 'high-population countries', also with a view to promoting access and quality. Other leading agencies have been the Commonwealth of Learning (COL), IDRC and the World Bank.

While many of these initiatives have focused explicitly on NICT issues within conventional education, others have intentionally explored a wider systemic agenda, in which a variety of modern and more traditional technologies (radio, print) can contribute to mixed-mode arrangements. Thus boundaries between contact and distance interaction, full-time and part-time, formal and nonformal provisions are beginning to be blurred. Although much of this work tends to be implemented in secondary and higher education, the possible lessons for basic education – both for youngsters and for adults – are beginning to be explored as well. The hope is that sooner or later the feedback from this work will begin to enter policy discussions and give new expression to the 'expanded vision' of Jomtien.

It can be seen that concern with the possibilities of ODL was a feature of many debates and discussions linked to the expansion and transformation of education in the 1990s. We now want to look in some more detail at certain features of the ways in which the discourse around the potential of ODL was constructed.

Metonymy, ambiguity and silence: constructing the discourse of the synergistic effect

In this section we shall attempt to analyse the discourse on ODL further. This is partly in order to promote understanding about the disappointing progress during the 1990s in explicating an agenda for ODL, and partly so as to help lay a basis for focused action in policy and practice in years to come. We shall look at how in the policy discourse a number of ideas were yoked together, so that ODL continued to be seen to promise a 'synergistic effect' in addressing the needs of the marginal. This effect concerns first of all the link between global communication technologies and ODL, and thus the primacy of modern technology, and secondly the link between the 'components' of ODL, i.e. open learning and distance learning.

The subtle notion of a synergistic effect, resulting from the links between NICT and policy oriented to the expansion of basic education, is present both at the beginning of the decade and at the end. Interestingly the idea does not change in the ten years between the Jomtien Declaration in 1990 and the World Bank Education Sector paper of 1999. The Preamble to the Jomtien Declaration of 1990 noted:

> Today, the sheer quantity of information available in the world – much of it relevant to survival and well-being – is exponentially greater than that available only a few years ago, and the rate of its growth is accelerating. This includes information about obtaining more life-enhancing knowledge – or learning how to learn. A *synergistic effect* occurs when important information is coupled with another modern advance – our new capacity to communicate. These new forces, when combined with the cumulative experience of reform, innovation, research and the remarkable educational progress of many countries, make the goal of basic education for all – *for the first time in history* – an attainable goal.
>
> (WCEFA 1990: 2, our emphasis)

In 1999, the World Bank's *World Development Report*, while noting how much still remained to be done in expanding basic education, remained confident in the powers of NICT to achieve this:

> Despite the expansion of enrolments in recent decades, success in extending quality education to all has been limited, and new challenges have emerged. In still too many settings, some groups – the poor, girls, adults who have long since left school without learning basic skills – have not shared in the gains. Many school systems in developing countries fail to meet even basic academic standards. Meanwhile demand for secondary and tertiary education is rising

faster than the public sector can provide it. *Solving information problems* in education systems *is the key* to addressing these challenges.

(World Bank 1999a: 55, our emphasis)

In both these extracts education is linked with increasing access to information. Both see progress as achieved by exogenous forces, which supplement the deficits of 'developing countries'. It is assumed that human agency and the appropriate supply of information technology will overcome complex structural problems in education systems. It is also implied that NICT are inclusive and have the capacity to overcome the educational exclusions of the past. What is not canvassed at all are notions of education and international development concerned with reflexive analysis or empowerment and the extent to which these can or cannot be fostered through the use of NICT.

A slightly more measured, but still optimistic, assessment of NICT appears in the 1999 World Bank Education Strategy paper. Here, in a section which deals with 'top-down or global priorities', three strategies are discussed as 'interventions [which] are likely to have a big impact on the quality of teaching and learning' to meet the needs of the poorest. These are, firstly, early education interventions with very young children and complementary programmes in school health and nutrition; and, secondly, systemic reform, which entails education sector reform happening in a holistic, rather than piecemeal, fashion. The third 'priority intervention' identified by the World Bank is what it terms 'innovative delivery', which is seen to entail the following elements only: 'distance education, open learning and using new technologies' (World Bank 1999b: 38). In this strategy paper, the Bank sees ODL, not so much as a 'key' reform or strategy, but as a very powerful opening. In the sub-section discussing innovative delivery, the text reviews what has been achieved worldwide through distance education in the use of radio for students and television for students and teachers. It goes on to conclude:

New technologies, especially the Internet, offer policymakers additional alternatives for delivering education and training to learners of all ages. These technological possibilities *can reduce costs, increase access, and expand the range and quality of education and training options.*

(World Bank 1999b: 42, our emphasis)

While this is not the hyperbolic language of the 'synergistic effect' at Jomtien in 1990, or the 1998/9 World Bank notion of NICT as 'a key' to solving the problems of lack of access to education, it is not so distant from the confidence of those two texts. Of all the innovations in education delivery, ODL is singled out in this 1999 text. What is stressed are its *possibilities* or implied potential to solve some of the apparently intractable problems of the cost of education, the lack of access or motivation for key groups, and the quality of learning.

The significance given to the possibilities offered by ODL is of interest, as this area, unlike early education interventions and systemic reform, is not supported by extensive research. The potential of distance learning in relation to basic education is generally not well documented, except perhaps in areas like Interactive Radio Instruction and teacher education. Moreover, work on distance learning does not have a widely used and well-known form of action, like reflective practice, which highlights the need for comprehensive institutional changes – joined-up government – to support reforms in the education system. In fact, it has been observed that the alleged synergy between NICT and ODL was only weakly evident in addressing the needs of the poorest (Perraton 2000, Yates 1998, Mueller 1996, UNDP 1998).

Indeed the way the argument is made in the World Bank paper is puzzling. It moves from the achievements of education programmes using radios, which can be generally low cost and responsive to local conditions, to the potential of 'new technologies' (presumably digital) and the Internet. These are very high-cost technologies. Research on who uses computer-mediated communication, and how it is used, brings out how few opportunities it offers to those who do not belong to dominant groups, and how much it in fact reproduces existing political, economic and cultural patterns of power (Adeya 1996, Drykton 1996, Lax 1998, Mason 1998). This raises the question of why these issues are not alluded to? What is being signalled by the way in which ODL is placed as central to the expansion of basic education? How do the policy texts construct the discourse of the unlimited potential of ODL?

In our view they do so, firstly, by evading questions about the nature and ownership of information communication technologies, and secondly, by equating open learning with distance learning. In the remainder of this section we focus on the issue of the ways in which the technologies of ODL are presented.

In many of the texts in which the relationship between NICT and ODL is featured it is implied that the technologies, because they are new, will reform and improve relations between administrators, teachers and learners. Sometimes it is implied that NICT will be able of themselves to do the work of education, without trained teachers, good learning materials, children or adults whose lives are peaceful and healthy. These assumptions are evident in the passages quoted above from the World Declaration, the UNESCO policy paper and the World Bank papers.

A further example of the inordinate power assigned to new technologies to expand education comes from an extract from the 1999 *World Development Report*:

> The need for developing countries to increase their capacity to use knowledge cannot be overstated. Some are catching on, developing national knowledge strategies, and catching up. But most need to do much more, much faster, to increase their knowledge base, to invest in educating their people and to take advantage of the new technologies for acquiring and disseminating knowledge. Countries that postpone these tasks will fall behind those that move faster, and the unhappy consequences for their development prospects will be hard to remedy.
>
> (World Bank 1999a: 16)

The implication is not only that technology can do the work of 'educating people', but that if poor countries fail to take advantage of these technologies they will become poorer.

Generally it is never considered who owns the technologies being advocated and what the implications of the patterns of ownership are. To the extent that these issues are raised at all, what is stressed is the expense of the new technologies. However, Glennie and Gultig of the South African Institute for Distance Education have posed this question very sharply and not only in terms of costs. They point out that the problems with the multinational ownership of many of the technologies entailed in distance education are partly the direct costs entailed. There are also heavy indirect costs, for example, the brakes which the buying-in of technology and packages puts on local innovation and knowledge production, and the problems of heavy and recurrent maintenance (Glennie and Gultig 1998). Orivel points out in chapter 8 of this volume how increasing use of ICT for basic education in schools increases costs and does not save money.

The obfuscation of the issues of ownership is only strengthened by the persistence of another assumption permeating the policy discourse, which is that the introduction of new technologies to assist basic education must, in and of itself, be beneficial. A teleology which assumes that technology will always improve conditions is built into many of the arguments. But benefits cannot be read off from the technology itself. The technology does not exist outside the agency of historically situated groups who use it for good or for ill. The technological determinism which suggests that all technology must improve conditions is clearly incorrect. Glennie and Gultig show how complex the questions and decisions are concerning new technologies for a government, like South Africa's, struggling to bring about social change, expand education and make use of the potential of distance learning (Glennie and Gultig 1998).

DFID's 1999 education policy paper, virtually alone among the texts analysed for this chapter, robustly raises critical questions about divisions within and between countries regarding access to NICT and works these critiques into the policies it develops (DFID 1999: 35). However this text too lists the potential of NICT to improve education in a number of specific areas. These are education sector management, increased access for teachers and for adult learners, and the enhancement of quality (DFID 1999: 36–7). The DFID text gives no indication that this potential is as yet largely unknown and untested among the marginalised and excluded.

The comforts of metonymy: is distance learning equivalent to open learning?

The discourse regarding the unbounded possibilities of distance learning for the expansion of basic education relies on open and distance learning being linked together as a single concept. This implies that all distance learning carries the relationships of equality and learner-centredness implied by the term 'open learning' (Kaye 1989, Harasim 1989, Lewis, Whitaker *et al.* 1995, Hoppers 2000). The framing of the single notion of *open and distance learning* relies on metonymy, which is where a part, or a single attribute, is taken to be the whole. In this case a part – the technological capacity and promises of NICT working over distances – is taken to stand for the whole equality agenda of open learning. Through the utilisation of metonymy it is implied in the language of the policy texts that all distance learning and all uses of NICT facilitate open learning, which is itself implied to be oriented to social justice; all technologies associated with distance learning assist in opening learning. Similarly, it is thereby implied that open learning can only be realised through distance learning.

Through what are seen as neutral technologies which breach geographic (often seen as equivalent to social) distances, difficulties of inequality will be overcome – that is, openness between learners of different backgrounds and between learners and teachers will be achieved. By a particular elision of assumptions, the humanistic aspiration for equality inherent in the framing of open learning becomes attached to, and valorises, uncritical understandings of distance learning.

Below are further examples of the ways in which distance and open learning are elided in the policy discourse. The Jomtien Declaration does not use the phrase 'open and distance learning', but in Article 2, referred to above, the notion that new technologies can service an expanded vision of widening access and equity through ODL is implied.

> New possibilities exist today which result from the convergence of the increase in information and the unprecedented capacity to communicate. We must seize them with creativity and a determination for increased effectiveness ... the expanded vision encompasses ... universalising access and promoting equity.
>
> (WCEFA 1990: 4)

Later in the Declaration, when for example in Article 5 which deals with 'Broadening the means and scope of basic education' reference is made to a variety of technologies, we read these assuming that they promote access and equity.

> All available instruments and channels of information, communication and social action could be used to help convey essential knowledge and inform and educate people on social issues. In addition to the traditional means, libraries, television, radio and other media can be mobilised to realise their potential towards meeting the basic education needs of all.
>
> (WCEFA 1990: 6)

Similar elisions are apparent in the 1995 World Bank paper, *Priorities and Strategies in Education*. This document identifies major challenges with regard to access, equity and quality in education for what it sees as 'overlapping disadvantaged groups', sometimes called 'underserved groups'. These are defined as 'the poor, linguistic and ethnic minorities, nomads, refugees, and street and working children' (World Bank 1995: 3). Chief among these are girls and women, whose education is seen as key to reducing fertility, improving the health of the whole population, and increasing GDP (World Bank 1995: 28–31, 113–14) . In this particular approach to equity and social inclusion, the use of distance education through NICT is confidently claimed to improve the quality of provision to 'the marginal'.

> New technologies stand to improve the efficiency of education through software tools that improve student performance and through new means of providing instruction and educational resources to underserved populations.
> (World Bank 1995: 84)

No research is referred to which supports this. Hoppers has discussed some of the research commissioned on distance education for basic learning by the World Bank and other agencies as inputs into the Jomtien process. These studies raised a variety of issues concerning effectiveness, relevance and cultural appropriateness of distance learning methods, and were rather circumspect in the recommendations they made about the utility of distance learning technologies for improving access and quality (Hoppers 2000: 10). These points, some of which were raised by Nielsen (1991), do not appear to have influenced the policy discourse. Instead later in the text of *Priorities and Strategies*, after a discussion of how a number of small projects indicate that computer-based instruction and the use of new communication technologies (satellites and fibre optics) aid pupil achievement, and that expansion of tertiary education depends on harnessing NICT, a warning is issued that 'failure fully to use this technology carries the risk of further increasing the gap between these [developing] countries and industrial ones' (World Bank 1995: 85).

These passages, like those in the Jomtien Declaration, signal that distance education technologies unproblematically open up education to 'underserved populations'. Acquiring education by this means, it is implied, will lessen the social distances which lead to dysfunctional social problems, like inappropriate fertility rates among the poor and unproductive use of their labour. Moreover, not only will distance learning open up the barriers within societies and nations, but failure to use these technologies will result in further barriers, a further distancing of the poor from the rich. The victims, in this case poor developing countries, or the underserved groups in those countries, are thus doubly blamed; firstly for being uneducated and thus not integrating sufficiently with the interests of the powerful, and secondly for not making use of NICT and therefore remaining poor. By this discursive framing, rich dominant countries, or powerful classes in poor countries, are absolved from all responsibility. They are merely the benevolent conduit of insight into this situation and the source of redemptive technologies to solve problems.

The UNESCO document of 1997 contains the most detailed treatment of all the texts under review with regard to open and distance learning. In this document the concept of ODL in a range of educational and regional settings is examined in some detail. From this discussion a number of policy and strategy considerations are developed. These note the need for policy to address the rationale for the use of ODL, the structures and institutions which may be involved in design and delivery, some implementation, funding and quality issues, evidence from a number of countries of barriers encountered when ODL is introduced, and some critical reflection on technology. The context for the paper is UNESCO's commitment to and popularisation of lifelong learning in the 1990s (Delors 1996). Lifelong learning carries many of the assumptions of flexibility and learner centredness of open learning. The UNESCO paper elides open and distance learning in the following way:

> Open and distance learning is often used when one wants to address a whole range of related forms of teaching and learning, without concentrating too much on exact delineation and definition. It stresses at the same time openness concerning access, organisation and methods, flexibility in delivery and communication patterns, and the use of various technologies in support of learning. Although most of this paper addresses distance education and distance learning in particular, the broader term is chosen in order to stress policy aspects rather than technicalities.
>
> (UNESCO 1997b: 10).

A discursive shift from Jomtien and the World Bank 1995 paper is evident here. While these two texts saw distance education as opening learning to 'communities' or underserved groups, this text pivots the open learning on the lifelong learning aspirations of individuals served by distance technologies. Thus, in the previous texts distance education technologies opened learning to the socially excluded, whereas in this text open learning strategies for all are serviced by distance education. Here the beneficiary of ODL is not 'the community' or 'the economy', but 'the learner'. It is the learner who is specifically addressed as the beneficiary of policy:

> To the learner open and distance learning means more open access and thereby a wider range of opportunities for learning and qualification. The barriers which may be overcome by distance learning include not only geographical distance, but also other confining circumstances such as personal constraints, cultural and social barriers and lack of educational infrastructure ... Open learning also means a more learner-centred approach, allowing greater flexibility and choice of content as well as organisation of the learning programme.
>
> (UNESCO 1997b: 8)

It can be seen here that ODL engages with questions of learner autonomy. It resonates with concerns with democracy and individual rights.

What is the research base for these assumptions concerning the equalising potential of ODL, the ways in which it creates openings for learners? The largest body of research in this area is on higher education or on the use of ODL by the highly educated. Here there are two sharply distinct views on the issue of equality. Some see distance education as enhancing learner participation, both in terms of increasing access, because of its flexibility, and in terms of its process, because of the flattening of hierarchies between learner and teacher, and the enhanced communication possibilities between learners (Graddol and Swann 1989, Harasim 1990). On the other hand, a number of researchers point out how distance education and the use of computer-mediated communication for educational programmes amplify existing divisions, either embedding the authority of the teacher, or privileging access by and the voices of students from dominant groups, or emphasising the power of a particular language, generally English (Evans 1995, Stokes and Stokes 1996, Earle 1999, Perraton 2000). There is thus no sustained body of opinion which confirms that distance education is an equaliser, an opener of opportunity.

The lack of research is most evident in relation to the use of ODL for basic education programmes. Assumptions about the value and contribution of NICT to the lives of marginal groups abound. As we have seen, actual experiences of initiatives have been limited and, even though more concerted effort is now made in order to understand the dynamics of ODL approaches in different developmental situations, it is still far too early to draw general conclusions. It has, however, become clear that experiences need to be seen as highly contextualised, depending not only on the particular blend of organisational and methodological arrangements, but also on the perceptions and commitment of local groups directly involved in such initiatives. These range from young and adult learners, through their local organisations, to service providers and various sectoral authorities. Systematic action-oriented research will have to demonstrate how such arrangements to support learning can work, under what conditions, at what costs, and to whose benefit. This needs to be accompanied by critical investigations of pedagogical practices under ODL and of processes of decision making. Many such initiatives will be required in order to move forward and 'expand our vision' as to what ODL can really contribute to the practice of basic learning for all.

Conclusion: grand aspirations and small implementation

In this chapter we have shown how throughout the 1990s claims were made that, as part of redressing the lack of provision in basic education worldwide, a synergistic effect would become apparent, resulting from the combination of new communication technologies, distance education and correct policy. Very little research substantiated this assertion. Moreover, it appeared to be highly problematic to explicate the use of NICT in the actual development of strategies for ODL in the context of the Jomtien and Hamburg agendas. The discourse of

ODL did not become an integrated part of the wider discourse on the policy implications of Education for All. Only small amounts of development assistance money or Third-World governments' education budgets were spent on ODL for basic education, yet confident assertions continued to be voiced in agencies regarding the equalising and inclusive capacity of ODL.

Why did the discourse become so detached from the reality? Detailed empirical research at national and local levels is needed to uncover some of the answers to this, but our discourse analysis itself suggests some answers. Firstly, the weight of history and the scale of the need worldwide for basic education, both stressed in the Jomtien documents, called for a particular national, regional and international mobilisation. In 1990 ideas about democracy and human rights did not have the same inclusive global power which they assumed as the decade proceeded. The promised 'synergistic effect' of new technologies for ODL might have been partly a metaphor for some force which could drive forward the vision of Education for All. The promise of new technologies, indeed their newness, might have been part of the culture which the international organisations framing the Jomtien Declaration wished to invoke, in their efforts to stimulate regional and national change in policy regarding basic education. In 1990, therefore, the discourse might have been detached from the reality, because that was part of creating a vision of a new reality, a different future, where all children would be in school and adult illiteracy would be halved.

Secondly, the detachment of the discourse from the reality in 1999 may be read in a less optimistic light. Throughout the 1990s NICT established themselves as a worldwide business, and side-by-side with this have emerged as powerful political and economic forces promoting the marketisation of education. The development of NICT has generally been led by private corporations, although there are many examples of state- and private-sector partnerships in this field. Education has become a huge new area of expansion for these technologies. It is important to the corporations which own them that governments and international organisations appreciate their potential and buy the corporations' products. Do the policy texts of the late 1990s perhaps indicate that some multilateral and bilateral donor agencies were too willingly attaching themselves to the aspirations for new technologies to drive forward education expansion?

It appears that the vision of education for all has now partly been harnessed to multinationals, who promise a 'synergistic effect'. They do this, not to mobilise new strategies in expanding and improving basic education, but to promote their products, their technologies, their dreams. It is possible that these may offer untold benefits, but the research base to substantiate this remains remarkably thin. Most significantly we know little to nothing of how learners, teachers and managers engaged in basic education programmes – as opposed to policy makers – view developments in ODL. Without some understanding of their experiences the promised synergy will continue to be elusive.

Thirdly, we have seen that it has been very difficult to operationalise the notion of ODL. This is only partly because of the continued subservience of ODL to the problematics of modern technologies in education. There remains the unresolved and largely problematical marriage between open learning and distance learning, and the conceptual and operational unclarity which permeated the discourse throughout the decade. This was to result in lost opportunities at crucial moments of policy formulation at the international level. The ODL movement has not succeeded in pushing through an image of a consolidated perspective or philosophy, which could respond to the policy initiatives being advocated at the international level. In particular, it could be argued that ODL has not been able to develop realistic strategies for reaching marginalised groups.

In our view, an ODL vision in the twenty-first century would need to go beyond the trappings of high technology, if it is to realise the value and relevance of open learning principles for meeting the learning needs of those truly 'unreached' groups. Although Jomtien may be criticised for its weak articulation of alternative delivery strategies, the onus remains on the advocates of ODL to develop coherent strategies and ensure their integration into policies.

References

Adeya, N. (1996) 'Beyond borders: The Internet for Africa', *Convergence: The Journal of Research into new Media Technologies*, 2, 2.

Bellamy, C. (1999) *The State of the World's Children 1999: Education*, New York: UNICEF.

Bennell, P. (1999) 'Education for All: How attainable is the DAC target in sub-Saharan Africa?', Plenary address to the Oxford International Conference on Education and Development convened by UKFIET.

Bennell, P. and Furlong, D. (1997) *Has Jomtien Made any Difference? Trends in Donor Funding for Education and Basic Education Since the Late 1980s*, Brighton: Institute of Development Studies, University of Sussex.

Buchert, L. (ed.) (1998) *Education Reform in the South in the 1990s*, Paris: UNESCO Publishing.

Castells, M. (1996) *The Information Age: Economy, Society and Culture*, Oxford: Blackwell.

Colclough, C. and Lewin, K. (1993) *Educating All the Children: Strategies for Primary Schooling in the South*, Oxford: Clarendon Press.

Colclough, C. et al. (eds) (1997) *Marketizing Education and Health in Developing Countries: Miracle or Mirage?* Oxford: Oxford University Press.

Commonwealth Secretariat (1999) *Diversifying Education Delivery Systems: Reviving the Discourse on the Formal/Nonformal Interface*, Report of a workshop on nonformal education, Gaborone, Botswana, 23–6 June.

DAWN (1995) 'Rethinking social development: DAWN's vision', *World Development*, 23, 11: 2001–4.

Delors, J. (1996) *Learning: The Treasure Within*, Report of the International Commission on Education for the Twenty-first Century, Paris: UNESCO.

DFID (1999) *Learning Opportunities for All: A Policy Framework for Education*, London: Department for International Development.

Dias, M. (1997) 'Foreword', in UNESCO, *Open and Distance Learning: Prospects and Policy Considerations*, Paris: UNESCO.

Dodds, T. (1994) 'Distance learning for pre-tertiary education in Africa', in M. Thorpe and D. Grugeon (eds) *Open Learning in the Mainstream* London: Longman.

Drykton, J. (1996) 'Cool running: The contradictions of cybereality in Jamaica', in R. Shields (ed.) *Cultures of Internet: Virtual Spaces, Real Histories, Living Bodies*, London: Sage.

Earle, A. (1999) 'CMC – an equalising force in higher education?', Unpublished paper prepared for Science and Technology Group, Institute of Education, University of London.

EFA (1996) *Education for All: Achieving the Goal*, Final report of the mid-decade meeting of the International Consultative Forum on Education for All, 16–19 June, Amman, Jordan, Paris: UNESCO.

Evans, T. (1995) 'Globalisation, post-Fordism and open and distance education', *Distance Education* 16, 2: 256–69.

Giddens, A. (1999) *Runaway World*, Cambridge: Polity.

Glennie, J. and Gultig, J. (1998) 'Educational technology and social issues: realising the promise, diminishing the threat', Address delivered to the parallel convention on 'Education and technology in the Commonwealth: Making the transition', Commonwealth Conference of Education Ministers, Gaborone, Botswana, 28–30 July.

Graddol, D. and Swan, J. (1989) *Gender Voices*, Oxford: Blackwell.

Gustafsson, I. (1999) 'Are genuine partnerships evolving? Some reflections from an agency perspective', Plenary address to the Oxford International Conference on Education and Development convened by UKFIET.

Hallak, J. (1990) *Investing in the Future: Setting Educational Priorities in the Developing World*, Paris: UNESCO.

Harasim, L. (1989) 'Online education: A new domain', in R. Mason and A. Kaye (eds) *Mindweave: Communications, Computers and Distance Education*, Oxford: Pergamon.

Harasim, L. (1990) *Online Education: Perspectives on a New Environment*, London: Praeger.

Held, D. (1995) *Democracy and the Global Order: From the Modern State to Cosmopolitan Governance*, Cambridge: Polity.

Hoppers, W. (2000) 'Nonformal education, distance education and the restructuring of schooling: Challenges for a new basic education policy', *International Review of Education*, 46, 1, March.

Jansen, J. and Christie, P. (eds) (1999) *Changing Curriculum: Studies on Outcomes-Based Education in South Africa*, Kenwyn: Juta and Co.

Kaye, A. (1989) 'Computer-mediated communication and distance education', in R. Mason and A. Kaye (eds) *Mindweave: Communications, Computers and Distance Education*, Oxford: Pergamon.

Knight, P. (1996) 'Destined to leapfrog: Why a revolution in learning will occur in Brazil, Russia and South Africa', Unpublished paper presented at the Second International Conference on Distance Education in Russia, Moscow.

Lax, S. (1998) 'Democracy and communication technologies: Superhighway or blind alley?', *Convergence*, 4, 3: 30–7.

Leach, F. and Little, A. (eds) (1999) *Education, Cultures and Economics: Dilemmas for Development*, London: Garland.

Lewis, J., Whitaker, L. et al. (1995) *Distance Education for the 21st Century: The Future of National and International Telecomputing Networks in Distance Education*, Creskill: Hampton Press.

Little, A., Hoppers, W. and Gardner, R. (eds) (1994) *Beyond Jomtien: Implementing Primary Education for All*, Basingstoke: Macmillan.

Mason, R. (1998) *Globalising Education: Trends and Applications*, London: Routledge.

Mueller, J. (1996) *Literacy and Non Formal (Basic) Education: Still a Donor Priority?* Occasional Paper Series 3, Education for Development, University of Reading.

Netherlands (2000) *Education: A Basic Human Right; Development Cooperation and Basic Education: Policy, Practice and Implementation*, The Hague: Ministry of Foreign Affairs, DCO/OO.

Nettleton, G. (1991) 'Uses and costs of educational technology for distance education in developing countries: A review of the recent literature', in M. Lockheed, J. Middleton and G. Nettleton (eds) *Educational Technology: Sustainable and Effective Use*, IBRD, PHREE background paper series, PHREE/91/32, Washington, DC: World Bank.

Nielsen, H. (1991) 'Using distance education to extend and improve teaching in developing countries', in IDRC (ed.) *Perspectives on Education for All*, Ottawa: IDRC Social Sciences Division.

Odora Hoppers, C. (1997) *Adult Education for Change and Sustainable Human Development: Mandate for Action from Five World Conferences*, paper prepared for the Expert Working Group for CONFINTEA V, Hamburg: UIE.

Perraton, H. (2000) *Open and Distance Learning in the Developing World*, London: Routledge.

Sen, A. (1999) *Development as Freedom*, Oxford: Oxford University Press.

Stokes, P. and Stokes, W. (1996) 'Pedagogy, power politics: Literate practice online', *Computers and Texts*, 13, 5.

UNDP (1998) *Human Development Report*, Oxford: Oxford University Press.

UNESCO (1997a) *Adult Education: The Hamburg Declaration: The Agenda for the Future*, Fifth International Conference on Adult Education 14–18 July, Hamburg: UIE.

UNESCO (1997b) *Open and Distance Learning: Prospects and Policy Considerations*, Paris: UNESCO Division of Higher Education.

UNESCO (1998) *The Durban Statement of Commitment*, Seventh Conference of Ministers of Education of African Member States (MINEDAF VII), Durban, South Africa, 20–4 April.

UNESCO (2000) Education for All Forum online. Available HTTP: *http://www.unesco.org/education/efa/index.html*

Unterhalter, E. (2000) 'Transnational visions of the 1990s: contrasting views of women, education and citizenship', in M. Arnot and J. Dillabough (eds) *Challenging Democracy: Feminist Perspectives on the Education of Citizens*, London: Routledge (forthcoming).

Watkins, K. (1999) *Education Now: Break the Cycle of Poverty*, Oxford: Oxfam.

WCEFA (1990) *World Declaration on Education for All and Framework for Action to Meet Basic Learning Needs*, World Conference on Education for All, 5–9 March, Jomtien, Thailand.

Wolfensohn, J. (1999) 'Foreword' in World Bank *Knowledge for Development: World Development Report 1998/9*, Oxford: Oxford University Press.

World Bank (1995) *Priorities and Strategies in Education: A World Bank Review*, Washington, DC: World Bank.

World Bank (1999a) *Knowledge for Development: World Development Report 1998/9*, Oxford: Oxford University Press.

World Bank (1999b) *Education Sector Strategy Draft Paper*, Washington, DC: World Bank.

Yates, C. (1998) *A Review of Open and Distance Learning Research in Primary and Adult Basic Education*, Cambridge: International Research Foundation for Open Learning.

Part 2

Themes

Chapter 3

Audiences for basic education at a distance

Lynette Anderson and Barbara Spronk

Who are the audiences for basic education at a distance? This is a central question, given the 'learner-centred' approach which educators in this field tend to claim. Yet the answer is far from straightforward, because the term 'audience' has several possible meanings. One possible meaning is 'potential audiences', that is, the entire range of people – or, more accurately, groups of people – who might be able to benefit from education at this level. Another possibility is 'actual audiences', referring to those people who actually take up the opportunities for basic education which are on offer.

These two audiences differ considerably in size. As one might expect, given the attention currently being devoted to ways of making 'education for all' a reality, the actual audiences for basic education are far less numerous than the potential audiences. As other chapters in this book make clear, we are a long way from making basic education available to all who might benefit from it. This is where the approaches of distance education become relevant.

The appeal of distance education approaches to this work lies in their potential, through the use of communication technologies, to bridge distances and extend the reach of the expertise and experience which educators have to offer. 'Reaching' audiences is not the same as 'teaching' them, of course. In order to transform 'reaching' into 'teaching', distance education must marry these technologies with effective instructional design on the one hand and learner support mechanisms on the other. The further transformation of 'teaching' into 'facilitating learning' requires designers and implementers to pay close attention to the learners for whom the programme is being designed. As already noted, distance educators have been emphasising for decades that learners and their needs are at the core of distance education provision. For example, Hilary Perraton, in an address to a conference on 'correspondence tuition' in June 1973, made the point that 'our tutors' central role is to discover the educational needs which our courses are going to meet, and to relate our teaching material to the local, and even individual needs, of particular students' (Perraton 1974: 59).

Conceptualising and identifying these needs, however, is far from straight-forward. The aim of this chapter is to explore this issue of learners and their needs in basic education: first, by outlining the characteristics of the potential audiences for basic education; second, by presenting some examples of actual audiences and their characteristics; and finally, by looking at two ways of conceptualising learners' needs in basic education and what these conceptual-isations imply for the ways in which distance educators design and deliver their programmes.

Characteristics of basic education audiences

Basic education is a complex area to define, as the authors of the introduction to this book point out. For the purposes of the book, they settle on a definition which includes all those programmes which are equivalent to primary and in many countries junior secondary education, as well as those programmes with alternative curricula, including areas such as basic health, nutrition, family planning, literacy, agriculture and other vocational skills (chapter 1: p. 7). This definition raises similar complexities for the task of characterising the audiences for these programmes.

Some of the actual audiences, primarily children, are in classrooms, enrolled in what we think of as conventional, formal schooling. Far more of the audiences, however, especially the potential audiences, are out of school, having lost out on the opportunity for education with their peer group, for whatever reason. These out-of-school audiences present a set of characteristics which is far more complex to describe than that of the more captive, bounded audiences found in school classrooms. These characteristics vary along a number of dimensions, some of the more significant ones being age and formal educational experience, gender, physical location, health, and ethnicity, culture and language.

Age and formal educational experience

In terms of age, basic education audiences include both children and adults, as well as members of that indeterminate middle category, 'youth'. All three terms are a matter of social and cultural definition. Depending on the social and economic circumstances of the societies in which they live, children may move very quickly from infancy to adulthood. The latter category tends to be bounded at the lower end by puberty, but even this is by no means a hard and fast rule. Those labelled 'children' in society 'A' are in society 'B' given tasks such as child tending or street hawking, which would be classified as 'adult' in society 'A'. The UNDP, in their series of *Human Development Reports*, use the age of 15 and above to define the category 'adult', a demarcation line which seems appropriate given its midway point between the biological age of puberty and the legal age which many societies set as an 'age of majority'.

In terms of formal schooling, members of any of these age groupings may have had no formal education at all. They may have had some formal schooling, but have dropped out or been pushed out before completion. There are a variety of factors which either prevent school attendance altogether for these audiences, or preclude completion of basic education. For example, there may be no schools available. In Mozambique, more than half the primary school infrastructure was destroyed during fifteen years of civil war; in the sparsely populated hinterland of Guyana children may have to travel impossible distances to school. Parents may lack the money needed for uniforms and books, even though they want their children to attend school. Parents may choose not to spend scarce resources on schooling, because they do not perceive the school curriculum as relevant or advantageous to their children's lives. They may need their children as labour in the household, to care for younger children, to care for livestock, to work on subsistence plots, or, in the case of urban households, to work the streets, for example as petty traders. There are also children who have no parents, because they have been abandoned by adults who can no longer care for them, or because they have been orphaned, by war or by the devastation of diseases such as AIDS. Or the children themselves may be physically or mentally disabled, so that they cannot be accommodated within the classrooms which are available.

Gender

For girl children in many parts of the world, there are a number of additional 'push-out' factors at work in their being denied opportunities to go to school. These include early marriage; parents' fears for daughters' safety when travelling considerable distances to school; the lack of appropriate facilities, such as toilets, for girls in the schools which are available; the lack of female teachers or of girls-only classes, factors which are especially important in faith communities in which sex segregation is mandated from an early age. There may also be a particular need for girls to remain in the household to care for younger children and to carry out domestic tasks for the extended family. And, when household resources are scarce, boys are likely to be favoured over girls for education, because it is the boys who will eventually be the major breadwinners for their own households and responsible for caring for their ageing parents.

The consequence for basic education audiences of these additional barriers posed by gender is a population of the marginalised and underserved which is overwhelmingly female. At the adult level, of the more than 840 million adults (those aged 15 and over) in the developing world who can neither read nor write, 538 million are women (UNDP 1997: 30). At the child level, UNICEF estimates that two thirds of out-of-school children are girls (Bellamy 1997: 52).

Location

Access to basic education clearly varies by gender. Equally clear is the effect of physical location. If one lives in a country classified as 'industrial', one is more likely to be living in an urban area, and far more likely to be described as 'literate', than if one lives in a country classified as 'developing'. In developing countries, in the year 2000, close to three out of five people are likely to be classified as 'rural', whereas in the industrialised world, the corresponding number is one in four (UNDP 1997: 193). In terms of basic education, those living in a country categorised as 'industrial' in the Human Development Index (HDI) are probably literate. By contrast, with the index set at 100 for countries of the 'north', i.e. industrial countries, according to the HDI the index for all developing countries for adult literacy in 1994 was 64 and for sub-Saharan Africa 56. In the developing world, rural-urban differences in literacy are stark: according to the UNDP figures, in developing countries 43 per cent of rural men are illiterate, more than twice the share in urban areas, and for women the shares are 66 per cent and 38 per cent (UNDP 1997: 42). Those populations displaced by war within their own countries, or who have fled as refugees to other countries, represent a special case of 'location' as marginalising. UNHCR oversees the work of providing education to people in these situations, which for the most part is carried out by international and national NGOs, but with an estimated 40 million refugees worldwide, and at least thirty currently active conflicts generating still more, the task is a massive one (see Thomas 1996).

Health

Ill health or physical disability is another factor contributing to educational marginalisation. People suffering from debilitating illness are not likely to be taking advantage of those educational opportunities on offer, and only the most affluent countries are able to make special educational provision for the ill or physically disabled. Again, the disparities between developing and industrial countries are marked. For example, in 1995, reported AIDS cases in sub-Saharan Africa numbered 22.2 per 100,000 population, compared with 5.6 in industrial countries. In 1994, in sub-Saharan Africa, tuberculosis cases numbered 93.6 per 100,000 population, compared with 27.2 in developed countries. And in 1992, in all developing countries, there were 206.4 cases of malaria reported per 100,000 population, whereas the number of cases reported in industrial countries was negligible (UNDP 1997: 177). As for people with disabilities, the same table indicates that 2.6 per cent of the population of developing countries are classified as disabled; comparative figures for industrial countries are not available, but are certainly very much lower.

Ethnicity, culture and language

Disparities among ethnic groups in any given society are also marked, overall in terms of human poverty and likewise in terms of basic education. There is no global index possible for such disparities, but the situation in various countries can be considered indicative. For example, in South Africa, about 8 per cent of whites lack an education, contrasted with 16 per cent of blacks. In Bolivia and

Mexico, indigenous children receive on average three years less education than non-indigenous children. And in Guatemala, the majority of indigenous people have no formal education – only 40 per cent are categorised as literate. In industrialised countries there are equivalent gaps. For example, in the United States 31 per cent of hispanics aged 25 to 65 have not completed ninth grade, whereas only 6 per cent of whites have not (all figures are cited in UNDP 1997: 43). Differences in language and culture are contributing factors in these disparities. Those who speak a language other than one designated as 'official' are likely to be disadvantaged in terms of access to basic education, as are those whose cultural practices, values and world view mark them as out of the mainstream population for whom educational systems and programmes have been designed. The effects of this type of marginalisation are described elsewhere in this volume, for example, in chapter 10.

Actual basic education audiences: some examples

It is not possible for two or three – or even two or three hundred – examples of the kinds of learners involved in actual basic education programmes to be representative of the total, or do justice to the range which that total represents. Nonetheless, examples do help put flesh on the bones of an otherwise skeletal set of characteristics. The following examples are all programmes which involve distance education approaches, and are drawn from three continents: from Africa, the work of the Sudan Open Learning Organisation (SOLO) and INADES-Formation (Institut Africain pour le Développement Economique et Social); from Asia, the FEPRA programme in Pakistan (Functional Education Project for Rural Areas); and from the Americas, the Pre-University Education Programme offered by the Institute of Distance and Continuing Education at the University of Guyana.

Sudan

The Sudan Open Learning Organisation (SOLO) has been operating since 1984, for its first ten years as an international NGO affiliated with IEC and other organisations, and since 1995 as a Sudanese NGO. Over these years SOLO has been providing a number of educational programmes, among them several basic education programmes, to many thousands of adult refugees and displaced Sudanese, using the methods of distance education and open learning. SOLO's aims are:

- to enable refugees and displaced people to improve the quality of their lives through participation in these educational programmes
- to provide whatever support services are necessary to increase participants' involvement in and contribution to the development of their own educational activities

SOLO runs three programmes at the basic level. The first is a literacy programme which runs for three cycles of five months, for close to 5,000 participants a year. The second is a primary health care course, which involves over 600 participants per year. The third is a teacher assistance course, a one-year course aimed at training basic-level teachers employed within the refugee schools, plus some teachers from the displaced camps, and involving some 3,500 participants a year. In terms of age, the participants tend to be adults in their twenties and thirties. In terms of gender, they tend to be mostly women, especially in the literacy programme. In terms of location, participants are in camps on the outskirts of Khartoum and in a number of other provinces of Sudan. In terms of health, there are no special provisions made for the ill or disabled, and active participants tend to be able-bodied. Finally, in terms of ethnicity, culture and language, the refugee participants come from Ethiopia and speak Tigrinya, whereas the displaced participants come from southern Sudan and tend to speak the languages of that area. This poses special problems for SOLO, since the official – and mandated – language of education in Sudan is Arabic (Mutalib 1997).

INADES-formation, west Africa

INADES-formation has been operating primarily in the francophone countries of west Africa, and also as far afield as Tanzania, for close to three decades. The target audience is small farmers. The purpose is

> to enhance the construction of a rural world in which farmers are organised and have genuine socio-economic power which enables them to actively participate in the process of their own development; be recognised and respected as farmers, men and women; master and control agricultural networks; have a reasonable degree of autonomy and properly manage and control community resources; and contribute to the construction of a state of law and social peace.
>
> (Ngang 1997)

Provision is made for both group and individual study. Although print is used extensively, along with radio and audio media, local facilitators assist the non-readers among the participants to take advantage of the programme. In terms of age, participants tend to be relatively young farmers, in their twenties and thirties. In terms of gender, participants are predominantly male, although special efforts are made to reach out to women farmers; INADES staff make a point of noting, for example, that most of the non-literate participants are women. In terms of location, participants live in a number of countries in west Africa, and all are rural. In terms of ethnicity, culture and language, participants come from a wide range of ethnic and language groups; one of the factors organisers use to explain the success of the programme is that course materials are translated into more than fifty local languages. The intake of participants has been declining over recent years (6,844 in 1992 compared with 2,987 in 1996), which programme organisers have taken as a sign that the interest of the target population in agri-cultural production techniques is declining, and that the programming focus needs to be shifted to other areas, such as financial management, marketing and group management and networking, a shift which is currently under way (Ngang 1997).

FEPRA, Pakistan

The Functional Education Project for Rural Areas, offered by Allama Iqbal Open University, started in 1982 and ran as a pilot project for three years. The 'test bed' location – the Gujrat District of northern Punjab – was chosen with care, so as to be truly rural but not too remote or inaccessible. The aim was to offer functional courses in topics which would be of direct and immediate relevance to the lives and livelihoods of the villagers. Anyone over 15 years of age was eligible to register, and over the project period 126 learning groups of about 2,000 learners were involved. Of these, thirty-seven were women's groups and eighty-nine were men's. This was a function mostly of the decision to use the course on livestock raising as a basis for expanding the programme (a programme which because of its inclusion of information on reproduction was considered inappropriate for women), rather than an indication of any inherent reluctance of women to involve themselves in the project. FEPRA was concerned to help the poorest and most vulnerable members of rural society. However, the majority of participants were from the higher-status, Gujar families, and were aged mostly in the middle years (20–45), a little under a third being younger than 20 and a much smaller proportion being older than 45. In other respects, however, course participants were fairly typical of the rural communities in the area, in terms of the proportion of those with little or no formal education and the proportion involved in farming (Warr 1992). The project eventually took on a more permanent if somewhat different shape, and is still operating (see chapter 4, p. 79–80).

Guyana

The Pre-University Programme run by the Institute of Distance and Continuing Education (IDCE) of the University of Guyana started in 1992, offering remedial courses in English language and mathematics. These subjects are considered basic routes to the acquisition of knowledge and skills in a range of technical, vocational and academic subjects, and are areas in which the performance of most Guyanese students has been deemed unsatisfactory. Outside the narrow coastal plain of the country, educational provision is both quantitatively and qualitatively limited, making remedial adult education, offered by distance means, a dire necessity. The audience for this programme comprises mainly Guyanese from these hinterland regions who have had some formal schooling (64.5 per cent of those enrolled have had some exposure to secondary-level, albeit poor-quality, education), but who have failed in their efforts to progress to higher levels of education. Despite its secondary-level thrust, the Pre-University Programme fits clearly within the definition of adult basic education offered by Griffith (1996), that is, programmes aimed at improving basic reading, writing and computation skills and designed to enable undereducated adults to function more effectively in the workplace, at home and in the community. Over 70 per cent of the participants are women, a pattern typical of educational participation in Guyana. They are relatively young, around 60 per cent aged between 21 and 55. Interestingly, in one remote area, nearly 95 per cent of the intake were younger than 21, and 50 per cent were younger than 17. In addition, the participants are geographically and economically disadvantaged, and would find regular travel to conventional classes prohibitive. Finally, participants tend to be unable or reluctant to attend conventional classes, because of responsibilities such as parenting and hours of work (although the unemployment rate among the basic education students is higher than that among their counterparts in other, more advanced-level, programmes offered by IDCE).

As already stated, no set of examples can be representative of all audiences for basic education world-wide. Nonetheless, the examples provided do illustrate two of the major conclusions which have been reached in the research literature on non-formal education programmes for adults, a broad category within which adult basic education is usually included. The first is that those most likely to succeed in non-formal programmes are those who already have some level of formal schooling, and who are relatively young. An IEC monograph (IEC 1983) pointed out in 1983 that there is little experience of successful education projects at the most basic level for those who have never been to school at all. Close to a decade later, the picture remained basically unchanged, as documented in Carron and Carr-Hill's 1991 study:

> Every household survey of participation in adult education, admittedly above the basic literacy level in general, has made it abundantly clear that the major beneficiaries of non formal education are those who have already reached a level of formal education.
>
> (Carron and Carr-Hill 1991: 58)

The second conclusion from the literature is that, in addition to already having some education, participants in adult basic education programmes tend also to be young. In the same study, Carron and Carr-Hill point out that in developing countries and developed countries alike, the majority of participants in adult education are in the 15-to-24 age range. This is indeed the case in our four examples, all of which are doing valuable work, but none of which is reaching the most marginalised populations.

Conceptualisations of basic education learners and their needs

Adult basic education

The majority of the participants in the basic education programmes described above share another characteristic: whatever schooling they may have had, they have been underserved or poorly served by it. They have been denied the basic skills of reading, writing, and computation, skills which are universally considered basic to full participation in the 'modern' world, whatever one might mean by the term 'modern', and which are the focus of what is termed 'adult basic education'.

Providers of this basic education for adults generally subscribe to what are acknowledged as the principles of adult education. Brookfield's description of the characteristics of adult learners is fairly representative (Brookfield 1986). One, adults are a highly diversified group of individuals with widely differing preferences, needs, backgrounds and skills. Two, adults maintain the ability to learn, despite the gradual decline they experience over time in physical and sensory capabilities. Three, the adult learner's experience is a major resource in learning situations. Four, adults tend to be life-centred in their orientation to learning; in other words, they prefer to learn things which are directly relevant to their lives. Five, adult learners have a number of commitments – for example, keeping a family, growing food, finding enough resources on which to get by – with which learning in structured situations must compete. Six, adults are motivated to learn by a variety of factors, which must be discovered and taken into account in designing effective situations for learning. Seven, adults learn most effectively if they are active participants in their learning. And finally, adults learn most successfully in a comfortable and supportive environment.

Adult educators have derived lists such as these from years of experience with and research among audiences of adult learners. This does not mean, however, that there is a uniform approach to acting on these characteristics. Adults may well be a 'highly diversified group with widely differing needs', but how does one determine what those needs are? How does one use the learner's experience as a resource in learning situations? How is 'relevance' determined? Or motivation? What does it mean to be an 'active participant' in one's learning? What constitutes a 'comfortable and supportive environment'?

'Deficit' and 'difference' conceptualisations

Answers to these questions differ, depending on how educators conceptualise their audience, the adult learner. One can base one's answers, for example, on a 'deficit' notion of one's audience. 'Deficit' notions assume a group of learners who are deficient or lacking in some set of skills, knowledge and attitudes which, if they were to acquire them, would result in a change in these learners. This change in turn would lead to better – i.e. more socially concerned – decisions, and hence ultimately to a changed and more 'developed' society. Typically, policy makers and programme designers work to identify learners' needs and proceed to design and deliver a programme which they believe meets those needs. This programming is usually generalised in nature, designed to meet needs which a wide swathe of learners are believed to share. It is customised to meet the needs of specific groups or individuals, where necessary, by study groups or other tutorials. The kind of education programming which results has been described at times as operating on a 'transmission' model (Freire's 'banking' model): the teacher as expert transmits, or deposits for later withdrawal, a fund of knowledge and expertise, which learners then receive or draw out, in order to fill in the gaps in their own knowledge and skills.

Another, quite different, possibility is to emphasise the differences which characterise learners, rather than any 'deficits' which they may share. This way of conceptualising the learner, and the audiences for basic education, is characteristic especially of work inspired by approaches like that of Paulo Freire and his colleagues. It emphasises the varying social and political contexts in which learners live and work, their unique, lived realities. Rather than focusing on what learners may lack, educators operating with this concept place the emphasis on what learners can already do. As Freire argued, adults must already have a substantial measure of basic competencies and knowledge, otherwise they could not be coping with the exigencies of adult life. They bring these with them to any educational programme, and it is incumbent on the programme organiser to find out what the learners bring with them, so that the learning experience can use these indigenous skills and knowledge as actual materials. Freire's main emphasis was on offering adults reading and writing capabilities which build on their existing knowledge, and offer them a way of 'reading their world' which enhances their ability to reflect on their particular world in the context of wider worlds. The ultimate hope is that these new tools enable learners to act together on the world in order to change it for the better, to make it more equitable. Learners, in this conceptualisation, become agents rather than recipients, fully empowered to and capable of acting on their worlds (Freire 1972, 1974).

Each of these conceptualisations has implications for the way in which basic education is designed and delivered, and in particular for distance modes of delivery. First, in terms of needs assessments, those operating with a 'deficit' conceptualisation tend to assume that they know what participants' educational needs are, usually on the basis of 'top-down' needs assessments which they or others have conducted. These assessments may be very thorough. The intent, nevertheless, is to arrive at a set of needs which can be addressed by a programme of training or education. The challenge then becomes to design the programme so that it will appeal to whatever generalised group of learners has been bracketed as 'needing' the programme, to recruit learners to it, and to keep learners motivated long enough to complete it. In sum, deficit notions of the adult learner lead educators to generalise adult learners' needs and then devise universalised programmes to meet them. In so doing, educators tend to put the educational task first, and then find situations in learners' lives to use as examples of development tasks to which the educational point can be applied.

'Difference' notions of the learner, in contrast, tend to work from the opposite direction, putting some concrete, real-life task first and helping learners to do that task through enhancements of skills and knowledge. So, for example, a group of women in a village might identify their greatest need to be safe and accessible water. At the moment they or their children must walk two miles to a neighbouring village to use its well, a privilege for which they must pay. They decide that they should dig their own well, and ask a development agency which is active in their area for assistance. Operating from a 'development' model of the learner, the agency worker helps them obtain the tools and plans they need and determine where they should dig the well. Along the way the worker may well incorporate in the work some help with reading and computational skills, as the need arises. If so, locally generated or 'found' materials, such as a manual on priming and maintaining a water pump, will be used rather than pre-prepared and prescribed primers. The worker may also prompt discussion of the socio-economic aspects of the task, thereby widening the horizons of the participants and supporting them in making connections between their lives and the wider forces at work in configuring their lives. For example, what difference will the well make to the lives of the women and their families? How might they use the time which is freed up? Who controls water supplies in their region? How is this related to control over other aspects of village life? And so on.

Rogers (1994: 36) terms this a 'sociocultural' approach, since it puts the emphasis on the sociocultural context of adult learning tasks and assumes competencies in the learners – competencies such as problem identification and abstract thinking – rather than deficits. It could also be termed a 'constructivist' approach, since it involves learners working together to construct meanings within real learning situations, rather than having those meanings imposed on them from outside their context. This notion of the learner also fits well with the participatory approaches to development which have become normative. Such approaches take as their first principle the involvement of communities and their members in decisions about their own development, as opposed to more 'top-down' methods (see Chambers 1993).

Whatever the label, the approach appears to be aligned with a number of principles of adult learning. The first is the importance of 'starting where they are'. Adults learn when such learning meets their immediate or longer-term intentions. Adults are normally accustomed to making decisions about their lives, and effective approaches to adult learning start with participants' current motivations and competencies, rather than trying to motivate them to learn things they do not wish to learn. The second is the importance of learning by doing. As long ago as 1973, the UNESCO report *Learning to Be* contrasted adult or lifelong learning – 'learning to be' what you are – with the formal education of younger persons, which it characterised as 'learning to become' something which you are not yet. Adults learn best through their daily life experiences. They are already autonomous learners, are already engaged in experiential lifelong learning.

The approach also accords with contemporary feminist approaches to adult education. Walters and Manicom, in the introduction to their edited volume on gender in popular education, set out a number of themes in feminist educational practice which emerge from the various contributions to the volume (Walters and Manicom 1996: 12ff.). These include:

- starting from where women are – not only geographic settings but social locations and emotional contexts as well
- taking women's experience and expertise as the point of departure for educators
- breaking the silence and giving women voice – closely allied to ending what Freire termed 'the culture of silence'
- enabling empowerment – whether this means achieving social and political objectives, gaining greater decision making capacity, or deepening one's understanding of the conditions configuring one's life and the controlling conditions of one's life
- working with and across differences – in class position, race, and gender
- finding the balance between facilitation and control – acknowledging the tension between allowing a spontaneous and creative process to emerge and directing the process to complete an agenda
- and finally, creating space, time and places for learning, acknowledging that, given the responsibilities of most women for family care and household management, a place away from 'the everyday' and from home is often a catalyst in an empowering education process

Implications for open and distance learning

The 'difference' notion of the audience for basic education thus appears to accord more closely than does the 'deficit' approach with the principles of adult learning and feminist education, as well as with contemporary development discourse and its rhetoric of participation. This, of course, does not guarantee that such approaches will be any more effective than the more traditional approaches to adult basic education, especially in terms of the statistics on successful completions so dear to the hearts of policy makers and their need for accountability. As a recent monograph on post-literacy programming points out, 'It is difficult to point to many examples of the new approaches … making notable achievements' (EFD 1998: 63). The general conclusion is one it cites from Benton (1996: 95): 'Although it is possible to point to some particularly compelling experiments, no single strategy has gained a solid reputation for effectiveness.'

The point here is not to pass judgement on these approaches, however. Rather, it is to assess the implications for the use of open and distance learning methods of putting these approaches or models into practice. The appeal of these methods is that they offer possibilities for expanding the populations reached by a particular programme of adult basic education, by using a mix of media (such as print, radio, audio, and face-to-face study groups or learning circles). The question is, to what extent are these mixed media approaches helpful, appropriate, or even feasible, for helping educators reach more basic adult education audiences? The answer differs, depending on the notion of the learner/audience on which the programming is based.

So-called deficit notions of the learner lend themselves relatively readily to delivery by distance learning methods. Programmes such as the four examples described earlier demonstrate how distance approaches can be used to good effect in extending to regional or even national level the reach of programmes based on generalised curricula. The more localised and context-specific nature of the learning activities arising out of 'difference' notions of audience poses greater challenges for open and distance learning methodologies, however. In the EFD monograph, for example, the authors raise the issue of whether it is possible to build a nationally valid post-literacy programme on the basis of myriad local or micro-literacies, which derive their materials from the experience of particular sets of learners. Can programmes be scaled up, while still remaining sensitive to local literacies? These authors' answer is that this is possible. They suggest that there are no generally applicable methodologies, given the diversity of needs and interests of adult students. They do, however, suggest a number of practical approaches, based on the principle that all basic education programmes should begin by exploring what tasks a specific group of learners wants to accomplish and then help them to do so.

What do these principles mean for the use of distance learning approaches? There appears to be little place in this model for generalised curriculum materials; local and 'found' materials from within the learners' own environment are more likely to be relevant to the learning tasks. There is perhaps a place, however, for such generalised materials in the training of the post-literacy facilitator or trainer. One could envisage developing a set of materials, using print, audio and video media, which teach and demonstrate such skills as the following: how to assist learners in their basic education activities, such as literacy; how to conduct contextualised and specialised needs assessments; how to assess and use locally generated or 'found' materials for learning; and how to help learners transfer to their lives outside the classroom the skills they are learning within it.

Indeed, given the huge number of facilitators who would be needed in such a national scheme – student-facilitator ratios will have to be kept relatively low for the approach to be effective – distance education methodologies would seem an essential feature of their training programme. Perraton draws a similar conclusion regarding non-formal education at a distance, which he describes as having been successful in localised contexts but for the most part non-sustainable on a large scale:

> One conclusion … is that non-formal education can be strengthened by using distance education to raise the capacity of field staff … It may turn out that the most effective use of the mass media is not to run programmes of adult

education of the kind envisaged a generation ago but to work in concert with the agents of various government extension services.

(Perraton 2000: 30)

Paraphrasing the closing sentence of Perraton's argument, adult basic education may not belong in Cinderella's cupboard, housed in an outbuilding of the ministry of education, but amongst adult educators and trainers themselves, whether in the rural health post, agricultural office or NGO headquarters. This would constitute yet another audience for adult basic education at a distance, and one which merits further attention and exploration.

References

Bellamy, C. (1997) The State of the World's Children 1997 – Focus on Child Labour, New York: UNICEF.

Benton, L. (1996) 'Post-literacy', in International Encyclopaedia of Adult Education and Training, Oxford: Pergamon.

Brookfield, S. (1986) Understanding and Facilitating Adult Learning, San Francisco, Jossey-Bass.

Carron, G. and Carr-Hill, R. (1991) Non-Formal Education; Information and Planning Issues, Paris: IIEP.

Chambers, R. (1993) Rural Development: Putting the Last First, Harlow: Longman.

EFD (1998) Changing Post-Literacy in a Changing World, report presented to DFID, August, Education for Development.

Freire, P. (1972) Pedagogy of the Oppressed, London: Penguin.

Freire, P. (1974) Education: The Practice of Freedom, London: Penguin.

Griffith, L. (1996) 'Adult basic education', in Grolier Multimedia Encyclopedia, New York: Grolier Electronic Publishing.

IEC (1983) Basic Education for Adults, Cambridge: International Extension College.

Mutalib, R. (1997) Sudan Open Learning Organisation: Information Note, Presentation to an international workshop on Affordable Communication Technologies for Non-Formal Distance Education, Namibia, December 8–11.

Ngang, F. (1997) 'Distance non-formal education: The INADES-Formation experience', presentation to an international workshop on Affordable Communication Technologies for Non-Formal Distance Education, Namibia, December 8–11.

Perraton, H. (1974) 'Is there a teacher in the system?', Teaching at a Distance, 1, November 55–60.

Perraton, H. (2000) Open and Distance Learning in the Developing World, London: Routledge.

Rogers, A. (1994) Women, Literacy, Income Generation, Reading: Education for Development.

Thomas, J. (1996) Distance Education for Refugees, Cambridge: International Extension College.

UNDP (1997) Human Development Report 1997, Oxford: Oxford University Press.

Walters, S. and Manicom, L. (eds) (1996) Gender in Popular Education, London: Zed Books.

Warr, D. (1992) Distance Teaching in the Village, Cambridge: International Extension College.

Chapter 4

Basic education curriculum

Contexts and contests

Richard Siaciwena and Jennifer O'Rourke

This chapter examines the content of non-formal basic education programmes which apply distance learning methods in different geographical and socio-economic contexts. It also identifies the determinants of the distance non-formal basic education curriculum and discusses some issues pertinent to the nature and scope of the programme content.

Background: the rationale for basic education

In the 1960s, strategies to universalise primary education provision in developing countries were based on the hope that the formal school system would serve as the main channel for providing basic education for school-aged children, and would produce a steady improvement in the education levels of the whole population. But by the 1970s it became evident that the socio-economic strategies in which the formal education system was expected to play a central role were not bringing about the desired and expected socio-economic transformation in Africa, Asia and Latin America. The reasons related to both the capacity and the appropriateness of the formal system.

Formal education systems simply have not been able to accommodate the needs of growing populations, especially with the severe limitations on public education imposed by structural adjustment policies. As UNESCO (1992) noted, hundreds of millions of school-aged children worldwide, a larger number of whom are girls, have no access to education. In addition, every year several millions of children, the majority of whom are girls, leave school before they acquire essential knowledge and skills necessary for a healthy and productive life.

Moreover, as Coombs and Ahmed (1974) observed, an increased emphasis on development of the rural areas in poor countries required the adoption of fresh approaches to meeting the educational needs of rural populations. This line of thought, and the many social and economic factors which limited the growth of formal school systems, generated interest in non-formal education. This new interest was strengthened and operationalised, especially, by the newly pronounced strategies which called for a stronger, more integrated community-based approach to rural development to meet the basic needs of the poor, the children, youth and adults.

At the same time, there were a number of initiatives to develop larger-scale, centralised strategies which would compensate for the lack of instructional resources in the formal school system. A number of these strategies used broadcast media to deliver the formal school curriculum to children in the school system, as well as programmes to provide this curriculum to children, youth and adults who were out of school.

Basic education curriculum and context

As Article 5 of the World Declaration on Education for All states, the diversity, complexity and changing nature of basic learning needs of children, youth and adults necessitate constantly redefining the scope of basic education. The development of non-formal basic education has been anchored in the widely and increasingly accepted view that basic learning needs are diverse and therefore require diverse curricula and a variety of delivery methods. Non-formal basic education is therefore heterogeneous, principally because it applies to many fields, many activities, diverse clientele, and is provided by different agents (Hallak 1990).

Like other forms of education, basic education tends to reflect a spectrum of political, social and economic standpoints, based on underlying belief systems about the nature of the individual, the role of the individual in society, and the relationship between political, social and economic roles. At one end of the spectrum, the individual is regarded in terms of her/his potential contribution to the economy, as a producer and consumer. In this view, education is designed to enable that person to become an efficient member of the economic system, by generating wealth and requiring the minimum level of public support. At the other end of the spectrum, the individual is regarded as someone with rights to food, shelter, security and a livelihood. Education should enable the individual to claim those rights and act on them, as an individual, as a member of a group, and as part of the larger society; if necessary, challenging the systems and structures which constrain those rights. At some point between these two ends of the spectrum, the individual is seen as someone with potential for self-realisation, as well as multiple roles and responsibilities to her/himself, family, community and the broader society. In this view, education should equip the individual to realise his/her own potential and to carry out these roles effectively in ways that suit her/his goals.

Alongside this spectrum, there are a range of perspectives on the appropriate balance between education as a social good, whose purpose is to build society as a whole, and education as an individual benefit, whose purpose is to support individual growth and self-realisation. Broadly speaking, policy makers in many developing countries (notably in Africa and Latin America) tend to support the former view, while those in Western industrialised countries tend to emphasise the latter view.

Curriculum: the dynamic relationship between content and methods

A broad definition of curriculum provides a framework for analysing the factors which shape basic education. Curriculum is made up of both content and methods; it includes all the planned experiences to which learners may be exposed in order to achieve the learning goals (Rogers 1996). Indeed, curricula are dynamic and evolving entities which comprise, broadly, 'all the experiences for learning which are planned and organised by a given educational programme in which policy and decisions are put into practice' (Ouane 1989: 423). Ouane further states that the principal features of this process are 'the aims and objectives, the planned and guided learning experiences and intended learning outcomes, teaching-learning methods, materials and evaluation' (Ouane 1989: 423).

In the formal education system, the curriculum is usually centrally developed and locally delivered. The degree to which local instructors can have input into the curriculum they teach depends on a number of factors: the context, structure, and policies of the educational system, the general ethos of the local school administration, and the confidence and abilities of local teachers in customising curricula to meet the specific needs and circumstances of their learners.

The content, structure, dynamism and delivery methods of the non-formal basic education curriculum are a result of the interplay of a number of factors, including political structures, economic systems, and the context, nature and size of the target participant group. The discussion of curriculum must include how these factors influence what is taught, how and to whom, and how they determine who makes these choices.

The increasing use of various media in non-formal education and the development and practice of open and distance learning (ODL) have had a major impact, particularly on the structure of non-formal education curricula. ODL has the potential to provide flexible curricula which meet the learning needs of different social and cultural sub-groups in many countries.

By reaching people who would otherwise find it difficult to access education ODL also has the potential to counter some of the structures which marginalise some groups of people and limit their ability to participate more fully in the society and economy. For example, ODL can be used to serve women and girls who, because of local customs, cannot leave home to study; people living in remote communities; those in occupations which preclude attendance at classes (for example farm workers or shift workers); and those responsible for the care of children or elderly members of the community.

We shall examine the extent to which mediated learning, including ODL, has realised its potential to provide appropriate, accessible learning opportunities which enable participants to acquire the levels of basic education they want and need for their goals and roles in their particular context. In other words, to what extent has the curriculum met learners' needs and addressed the broader social issues that shape their immediate context?

The relationship between open and distance learning, curriculum and control

Besides offering the potential for improving access to basic education ODL changes the relationship between content, learner and context. Content presented by direct classroom instruction carries a certain authority: it is difficult to challenge the 'rightness' of content in a didactic situation. In the formal education system, the curriculum is planned by a central authority, but the teacher usually has some flexibility in choosing the most effective instructional methods, and in some cases, the opportunity to select from among curriculum options.

In a genuinely non-formal setting which enables dialogue and affirms the learners' experience, content is ideally linked to and shaped by the learners' context. Mediated learning presents an additional challenge. Some media, for example, print and radio, may reinforce what has been termed 'the givenness of knowledge' (Haughey 1995); the learner feels she or he cannot challenge what has been delivered somewhat impersonally by an authority from afar. On the other hand, well-designed flexible learning resources used in a supportive environment can enable learners to consider and discuss content and its relevance to their lives.

Open and distance learning can use the authority of media to provide content and teaching strategies which support existing social and economic structures, or it can be used to enable active participation in learning which leads to a critical examination of these structures. In either case, ODL tends to be more visible and subject to scrutiny than education in a formal classroom, because its content is captured in media (print, radio, audio cassette, video) which can be readily reviewed by anyone who is interested. This means that, in politically authoritarian contexts, there may well be a reluctance to design ODL materials which challenge the status quo. Instead, as in a striking example provided by a Polish educator, ODL may be carried out by those with the courage to be 'the speaking syllabus', who devise methods to reach learners in a way which encourages them to question the state-sanctioned curriculum. As she described the situation prior to the 1989 change of government: 'My aim was to create students' [capability for] criticism, to stop making a fetish of the curriculum "baked" by the department of education in the socialist government given out for obedient realisation' (Potulicka 1991).

As well, curriculum delivered directly into the formal education system by a central agency, such as a broadcaster, can supersede the local teacher and eliminate the capacity for local adaptation of curriculum to meet specific learners' needs. There are examples of radio or television programmes which are broadcast directly to students in the classroom, which, by eliciting students' responses directly to the radio or television, effectively diminish the teacher's role to that of a classroom monitor, who is responsible for turning on the radio or television and sending in the students' assignments to be marked.

The applications of open and distance learning for basic education

In the formal education system, open and distance learning is used for several distinct purposes, both within conventional schools and outside the classroom context. Within the school system, ODL programmes are used to supplement classroom teaching and to expand the range of programmes available in schools with limited resources. Outside the conventional system, ODL programmes provide a substitute for face-to-face instruction for learners who cannot attend school, and also offer the official curriculum to those who are beyond the school system but want formal qualifications.

Many ODL programmes delivered in schools focus on basic academic skills: literacy, mathematics, science, and topics related to everyday life, such as health. As well, ODL is used to provide access to academic subjects which would not otherwise be available, for example, in small schools where there may be no teachers qualified in that subject. In some cases, programmes are delivered to the classroom with the teacher present, and in other situations, programmes are offered directly to groups of students, sometimes with a monitor present.

Where provided as open schooling in place of classroom instruction, ODL programmes usually cover the entire required curriculum, as is noted in the examples given by Jenkins and Sadiman in chapter 12 of this volume. The variety of ODL arrangements for out-of-school youth and adults seeking formal qualifications usually includes open learning materials, local or distance delivered support or tutoring, and some flexibility for learners in pacing and selection of priorities. In many cases, the ODL materials are designed specifically for these older learners and reflect their context. For example, the National Extension College in the UK offers a full range of programmes from basic literacy to school completion, designed to be used by adult learners in local open learning schemes or at a distance.

Although non-formal education programmes initially used face-to-face interaction, many developing countries in Africa, Asia and Latin America also have a long history of using media and distance education for non-formal education. In Africa, for example, there were a variety of experimental projects using radio and some simple printed materials in agriculture, health and community/civic education for adults, often with little or no formal schooling, as far back as the 1960s. Dodds' survey (1996) shows the increasing and wide use of various media, particularly print, in non-formal education across geographical areas. As well, it shows extensive use of combined media: the combination of radio/print/study group is the most common. Dodds notes there is a 'widespread recognition in non-formal education of the added effectiveness of using more than one medium'.

From the practical to the political: the range of curricular directions in basic education

Programmes in formal education

As described by Jenkins and Sadiman in chapter 12, the curriculum provided by open schooling in the formal education system tends to match that of the conventional classroom-based system, although methods of teaching and learning may differ. In these situations, the challenge is reconciling a centrally planned curriculum with the needs of local learners, especially if there are few opportunities for local intermediaries to adapt the curriculum or introduce locally significant content. In situations in which mediated basic skills programmes are delivered directly into the conventional school system, there is still the issue of reconciling the mediated curriculum with local needs, but there is also the risk that the centrally produced broadcast programme may overshadow the rest of the curriculum, making it more difficult for the local teacher, with limited resources, to present the other components of the curriculum as equally important and interesting.

Several examples of the use of ODL to provide the formal curriculum offer valuable lessons in balancing multiple needs for relevant content, and appropriate methods which enhance rather than displace local educational providers.

In Côte d'Ivoire (Ivory Coast), educational television was introduced in 1971 to reform a primary school system facing a drastic shortage of qualified teachers, low enrolments, and low student success rates. Television was used as the principal medium for a programme which began with the first grade, and was intended to be supplemented by printed teacher guides, pupil materials, animation guides and wall charts. Radio was used for in-service teacher education in the schools receiving the television broadcasts. The programme was ultimately unsustainable, due to limited resources and infrastructure, high costs, and few options for incorporating the programme into the conventional system. Nonetheless, the positive outcomes included an increase in the number of children in primary schools and in ETV classes, some signs of improvement and equalisation of quality in schools, and indicators that children in ETV schools performed better academically (Kaye 1976).

Another early educational television initiative took place in Niger, where television was used to address the low participation rate in primary school. Instead of being delivered into the conventional classroom with a teacher present, this programme provided direct instruction to groups of children, supported by monitors: young, untrained primary school graduates. The programme began in 1964 with 800 children in twenty-two pilot classes; by 1972, 510 of the participants had graduated from primary school without ever having a face-to-face lesson from a trained teacher.

Also remarkable was the children's attitude to learning. In traditional society in Niger the elders have authority, and children are expected to ask no questions; these children were taught to question, to find out for themselves, and were soon doing so enthusiastically. One of the things which made this possible was that the curriculum was closely tied to the children's environment. Although the project got off the ground very quickly, time was allocated for a careful study of local village life, including an analysis of the agricultural cycles, so that the themes of the television programmes fitted in with what was actually happening in the villages. The role of the monitors was particularly interesting, pointing to a new pattern for distance teaching. Most of the monitors were young, about 20 years old, and they were not seen as threatening authority figures; their job was to organise the children's activities throughout the day. They were helped by their own television programmes before the start of each day in the classroom, and a manual which laid down procedures for that day in very great detail (Young *et al.* 1991).

The significance of the monitor's role was shown by an experiment conducted in 1971. For one week, the children were left to run the classes on their own: older children came early to watch the monitor's programme, and they followed the day's instructions in the manual. But, although everything was apparently functioning normally, at the end of the week, the children showed signs of fatigue and stress. There is no reason to suppose that the children were less competent than the monitors in following the day's instructions: some of the monitors had difficulty in doing this well all the time themselves, while some of the brighter, older pupils by this time knew more than their own monitors. What this finding points to is the importance of the adults' presence for motivation and support. Perhaps the children would not have continued coming for much longer without their guide. As one child commented, 'The television set doesn't breathe' (Young *et al.* 1991).

Although the programme demonstrated considerable success, plans for expanding the programme to include 30 per cent of primary age children were never implemented, due to a number of systemic problems. The complete lack of integration of the television programme with the existing facilities in the country prompted opposition from both the broadcasting and educational systems. Problems within the project itself included tension between expatriate staff and Niger staff, high production costs and logistical difficulties which prevented expansion of coverage to serve the whole country. Yet the Niger scheme's educational success points to some useful strategies: using local monitors and enabling them to relate centrally produced curriculum materials to the children's own experience, and the design of programmes so they are relevant to the learners' context. These strategies can address some of the issues of reconciling the centrality of curriculum and the reality of local context.

Some of these successful strategies were used in a very different part of the world to expand educational opportunities for children in schools with limited resources. In at least three different provinces in Canada, ODL is used to provide programmes which would not otherwise be available in local schools. In Newfoundland and in Manitoba, conferencing technologies (audio or video) and print are used to provide mathematics, science and some specialised courses to students in remote or small schools where there are no teachers for these subjects. In both cases, the technology is used to link a viable 'class', composed of multiple sites with a qualified teacher at another location, through real-time interaction. Although the programmes provide the conventional curriculum content, and are modelled on classroom teacher-learner interaction, the use of ODL changes the dynamics in significant ways, requiring the learners to become more actively engaged and to take more responsibility for the learning process at their site (Boone and Keough 1994, Bilan and Henderson 1994). In British Columbia, where ODL is also used to provide courses for small schools, the local school must designate a part-time teacher-facilitator for on-site technical help, student support, and liaison with the central delivery agency. However, this model has proven to be quite costly (Fryer and Gregg 1997).

Another example demonstrates how a centralised medium and methodology can supersede the prevailing educational approach and diminish the classroom teacher's role. A methodology termed Interactive Radio Instruction (IRI), originally developed by a Stanford University team for teaching mathematics in Nicaragua in 1975, delivers lessons by an 'audio teacher' over broadcast radio to students in the classroom. The programmes are not, as might be implied by the term 'interactive', a two-way radio communication between students and a remote teacher. Instead, they include a one-way radio broadcast presentation and questions, followed by pauses in which the students are expected to say aloud their responses to the radio (rather than to the teacher present in the classroom). IRI has been primarily developed and implemented internationally by a Washington-based agency, Education Development Center (EDC), with funding from USAID.

Many of the articles about IRI have been written by EDC staff and associates. In one such article, the author comments,

> IRI is distinct from other forms of distance education because its primary goal has been the improvement of educational quality ... IRI began as a tool to use in the classroom to counteract low levels of teacher training, poor achievement among learners, and limited resources.
>
> (Bosch 1997: 1)

Bosch also notes that, while early versions of IRI were designed to be '"teacher proof"', this concept has largely been discarded, and more recent versions are designed to serve as a guide or tool for the teacher, and in some cases, for teacher training' (Bosch 1997: 5). A recent initiative in South Africa 'had a particular interest in developing constructivist programmes and attempted to make English and math more open to individual discovery and analysis'. Although the proponents of IRI state that this method has moved away from its behaviourist beginnings to a more constructivist approach, the example still provides a useful lesson in how a particular educational philosophy and methodology, combined with a valuable ODL medium, radio, can prevail over indigenous approaches to teaching and learning.

These examples provide some useful lessons about the necessity for balance between centralisation and customisation of both the content and methodology of curriculum in formal education. The combined weight of a centralised curriculum and a powerful one-way medium, such as broadcast radio or television, can bypass the local classroom and de-skill the local teacher. While these strategies are sometimes used when there is no other way to provide mass basic education, it does not necessarily help to build a local infrastructure or work within an indigenous tradition of teaching and learning. There may be more long-term benefits to be gained by balancing good-quality programmes with local support and customisation which offers a meaningful role for school staff. Rather than expect that curriculum material designed for schoolchildren will also serve to train the teachers in place, it seems more appropriate to develop appropriate training materials specifically for teachers, as is currently underway with the Science, Technology and Mathematics Programme in southern African countries, sponsored by the Commonwealth of Learning.

Some examples of formal education programmes delivered flexibly to out-of-school learners show it is possible to provide a formal, accredited curriculum using methods and content which are appropriate for youth and adults.

ACPO (Acción Cultural Popular) operated from 1974 to 1998 with the aim of providing Colombian peasants and their children with basic skills of literacy and numeracy, embracing all aspects of community development, such as health, family care, and agriculture. ACPO used educational radio, supported by books, pamphlets and charts, to serve about 150,000 students in 22,000 informal radio schools or listening groups in rural areas. The groups were led by a monitor trained to use the materials and guide the discussion. There were also local overall organisers in charge of monitors and schools. ACPO offered adult basic education and primary school equivalency out of school, as well as formal primary school equivalency for rural children. Through the monitors and field organisers of radio schools, participants were encouraged to engage in cultural and sporting activities and to maintain correspondence with the centre. They were also encouraged to read the weekly newspaper El Campesino. ACPO was also instrumental in initiating a series of action campaigns to improve health, housing, agriculture and local communities (Coombs and Ahmed 1974).

In Canada, Australia and the UK, open and distance learning materials and local support systems are used to offer programmes which combine the flexible delivery of formal education with preparation for a career change or specific job training. By framing the formal education content within the context of adults' goals (e.g. job preparation, family and community life), and by providing local support, completing the formal curriculum is no longer a matter of 'finishing school', but one of taking active steps to prepare for one's current and future life stages. As such, the model shifts from one of compensating for a deficiency to becoming a proactive learner, acquiring skills and knowledge which are relevant to one's life choices. Examples include the Community Skills Centres in British Columbia, Canada, the Tuggeranong Flexible Learning Centre in Australia, and local colleges participating in the National Extension College's FlexiStudy programme in the UK (Calder 1993, Crellin and Graham 1996, Heath 1998, MacPherson and Dekkers 1997, O'Rourke *et al*. 1999, Withers and Pogliani 1996).

These hybrid programmes which provide a formal curriculum in a non-formal setting, although evidently quite effective, raise their own issues about jurisdiction, quality control and adequate funding. Competing public agencies may claim participants as 'their' learners; there is often a reluctance to fund local support on the grounds that the investment in developing 'self-contained' ODL materials was intended to obviate the need for additional support; and there may be a suspicion that local customisation of content or methodology will diminish the programme's quality.

Alternatively, non-formal programmes can provide basic education which directly addresses learners' needs without the constraints of multiple policy guidelines and conflicting agendas, but often without the benefit of consistent mainstream funding. We turn now to this area.

Non-formal basic education curricula

Concern about the inadequacies of the formal school system, and the irrelevance of the school curricula to the immediate needs of out-of-school children, youth and adults, contributed to the growth of non-formal education programmes tailored to suit specific objectives and emphasising practical demonstration rather than theory (Sheffield and Diejomaoh 1972). In general, the curricula of non-formal basic education programmes respond to these educational and developmental needs and are radically different from school-based education (Sheffield and Diejomaoh 1972, Coombs *et al*. 1973, Coombs and Ahmed 1974, Dodds 1996). The programmes demonstrate that non-formal basic education principally aims to help people in various communities and societies to make practical changes to their daily lives in accordance with their goals (Bates 1984).

Social and personal development

Coombs *et al*. (1973) established that there was a great diversity of non-formal education approaches in developing countries aimed at broadening and enriching the educational opportunities of rural young people. Their study showed four main categories of programmes in terms of purpose and subject matter. These were:

- agricultural
- artisan and craft vocational and pre-vocational preparation
- leadership and civic service
- general education, multi-purpose and miscellaneous, including literacy training and school equivalency programmes

In an unprecedented worldwide survey of distance non-formal education, Dodds (1996) assembled information on seventy-three non-formal education initiatives in fifty-six developing countries and seventeen industrialised countries (covering both Commonwealth and non-Commonwealth countries). Of the fifty-six programmes in Africa, Asia and Latin America, forty-six provided programming in the social field which includes health and family education, society and community education, environmental education and personal self-realisation/ self-improvement education; forty-one programmes offered topics in the economic field: agriculture, income-generating skill training, running and managing a business and para-professional training. Basic education and educational equivalency programmes, i.e. literacy, numeracy, and post literacy, adult basic education and primary school equivalency, were offered in twenty-seven programmes.

In Asia, Africa and Latin America, the two most common subjects in the social field were health and family (offered by twenty-four programmes); addressing the broader social context, twenty-three programmes included community development, social development or political organisation. In the same regions, the most common topic in the economic area was agriculture (offered by twenty-two programmes), while fourteen programmes included other income-generating occupations, including crafts, computers and para-professional training and eleven programmes included entrepreneurship and business management.

Topics in personal self-realisation or self-development were offered in eight programmes in these regions, as Dodds observed, somewhat surprisingly, since these topics are 'normally thought to be the exclusive interest of non-formal education in industrialised countries'.

Dodds cautions that the information collected for this survey is not necessarily comprehensive; nonetheless, this broadly based sample does provide some interesting indicators about curriculum content and context in non-formal adult basic education. One of the most striking common features is that a range of topics dealing with many aspects of personal and community life are covered in one programme: there are many cases in which agriculture, family health, community health, literacy and income generation are offered at one site. The programmes which reported specialising in just one area are the exception rather than the rule. The trend seems to be that basic education is woven into the whole fabric of learning about issues which are of immediate importance to oneself, family and community, as opposed to a school-based approach, which tends to treat literacy and numeracy as skills to be developed in isolation from their application to life.

Also notable are the areas in which there are gaps. Dodds comments on the paucity of programmes which include environmental issues (seven if water management topics are included), despite the evidence from offering agriculture topics that practical hands-on subjects can be addressed by open and distance learning. This shortfall is equally apparent in developing and industrialised countries, and it raises a question about whether topics which address conflicting interests (economics and health in this case) can be readily included in non-formal programmes.

Another apparent gap is that there are only two specific references to HIV/ AIDS education in all of the programmes surveyed, although it is possible that this topic is included under the more general area of health education. Even though the widespread problem of HIV/AIDS in Africa and other developing countries is profoundly affecting the socio-economic fabric of these countries, it is not clear whether it has yet become an integral part of the non-formal basic education curriculum. If it is not generally included in the many programmes which offer health education, this raises questions about how curriculum is selected, and how it is decided to treat a topic such as HIV/AIDS which at once involves sexuality, family life, health care provision, broader social issues and religious and moral codes.

On the whole, the content areas and educational strategies in the programmes in these regions seem to respond to the educational and developmental needs of the people and communities they serve; these examples also demonstrate that open and distance learning can be used for a very broad range of topic areas and learner groups. Programmes including health and family education, agriculture, vocational training, literacy and community education address some of the most critical socio-economic problems affecting these regions, namely poverty, disease, illiteracy and unemployment. Most countries in these regions have high rates of adult illiteracy, especially in rural areas (many school-aged children drop out too early to acquire literacy skills or lapse into illiteracy), high and rapidly increasing populations, large rural populations, underdeveloped rural areas, large numbers of urban poor and inadequate health services. Many small-scale, peasant or subsistence farmers need knowledge and skills to increase agricultural production substantially, to meet the food requirements of the increasing population and allow for modest improvements in health and living standards. For example, in Zambia, for most of the subsistence farmers who produce 60 per cent of the country's agricultural output, particularly the country's staple food, maize, distance education is the only realistic way of accessing agricultural extension services.

Clearly the curriculum for non-formal basic education, especially in developing countries, is directly related to the socio-economic activities of the people and is aimed at improving the living standards of the poor or marginalised segments of the countries' population. As Dodds observed, most of the programmes surveyed offered a curriculum which dealt with subject matter of immediate practical life-related topics.

In industrialised countries, lack of basic education is often concomitant with economic and social marginalisation. For example, many participants in adult basic education programmes in Canada are facing poverty, unemployment, home-lessness and poor health, and adult basic education includes topics designed to enable learners to cope with these issues. As well, many programmes also provide some element of self-realisation, although at present this tends to be more focused on personal development than on collective action. This is not surprising in a society where education is regarded as an individual gain, and where poor people are a minority (although an increasing one) in a materially wealthy environment. Those who are poor and undereducated tend to be regarded as responsible for their situation, and many basic education programmes are designed to enable participants to compensate for personal and social deficits so that they can make a contribution to society: whether this is achieved in a manner which genuinely respects the individual is contingent on those providing the programme and their context.

There are examples of flexibly delivered adult basic education programmes which incorporate values of inclusiveness and co-operation rather than contributing to marginalisation and isolation.

In 1999, a Canadian pilot project to provide web-based literacy training for francophone and anglophone participants demonstrated that it is possible to design a curriculum which enables learners to weave in their own life experience, to select content which is appropriate for their own skill level and interest, and to decide whether and how to work with others. Sponsored by several government agencies, the Alpharoute programme was developed by adult basic educators and instructional designers who, despite their different perspectives, shared values about learner independence and curriculum relevance. Designed to serve a range of learners, from minimally literate to mid-secondary school level, the programme covered basic language content, such as vocabulary, grammar and usage, as well as everyday life issues, such as health, employment, and leisure activities. In addition, learners were able to access an area of the website which presented broader social issues, such as the question of euthanasia, and to discuss these issues with other participants, using e-mail and conferencing. A number of learners began to share their own personal writing with each other, and eventually asked for, and were assigned, their own conference area as a 'writers' forum' by the programme managers.

The pilot programme was offered at six different locations widely distributed across Canada, and it became clear that local site support was essential. Site co-ordinators provided help and support so that learners could acquire the basic computer and navigational skills which they needed to get into the website and to work within it. Despite the logistical difficulties in acquiring computer skills, and occasional problems with the web programme, most learners felt that the computer methodology enhanced both their skills and their self-esteem; in addition to their literacy development, they acquired keyboard and site navigation skills, and were able to tell their friends they were 'working on computers'.

The pilot programme was designed for out-of-school young adults; a subsequent phase is now underway to provide basic education programmes for the deaf community and for aboriginal learners. What is particularly notable about this initiative is that these next phases will have their own curricula and design, rather than using the programme already developed for a different learner cohort. This curriculum customisation is based on two factors. Alpharoute and its funders are committed to creating a curriculum relevant to identified learner needs and their context. As well, web developments which have expanded the technical possibilities for customisation have also broadened instructional design approaches and placed greater value on enabling learners to be more proactive by charting their own path through the content (Larocque 2000). These developments, although emerging from a new technology, are equally applicable to 'older media', as is shown in the next example.

One situation which clearly demonstrates the inadequacy of a 'one size fits all' approach to basic education and open and distance learning is that of aboriginal education. In Canada and in Australia, many aboriginal people live in remote communities, and many have limited opportunities to complete their basic education. Attempts to provide distance education programmes designed for solitary learners were unsuccessful. In consultations with aboriginal people, educators came to recognise that both the content and methodologies of conventional distance education were inappropriate for aboriginal learners. The typical no-nonsense, let's-get-on-with-it, goal-oriented approach did not allow time for considered thought, much less accommodate other valued aspects, such as personal, spiritual and emotional dimensions of learning. As Spronk (1995: 92) notes, 'for people for whom one to one relationships are central to learning, the decontextualised nature of correspondence learning materials renders them alien in the extreme'. Spronk also identifies the strategies which contribute to the development of more successful approaches. These include: establishing a genuine partnership with the aboriginal community, enabling collaboration on content and on methodology so that both are culturally appropriate; providing local support which meets learners' social and academic needs; recognising the need for group learning and interaction; respecting aboriginal approaches to communication and discourse.

A recent initiative to provide mathematics education to aboriginal learners in remote areas highlights some of the challenges. The Math Readiness Programme was started in Saskatchewan to address a series of situations which effectively prevented the mainly aboriginal residents of remote areas from working in local resource industries. Many of these jobs required training in technical, science and engineering subjects, which in turn required completion of secondary school mathematics. However, this was difficult to achieve in smaller, remote schools. A web-based mathematics readiness programme was initially designed to be used by out-of-school adults working independently, using computer communications to keep in touch with a mentor, but it was recognised that, ideally, aboriginal learners should have local tutors and the opportunity for in-person discussion and interaction. However, it emerged that many prospective tutors, mostly local teachers, also had incomplete math skills and knowledge. Consultations with teachers, learners and other stakeholders have resulted in a plan to use the web materials for resource-based learning at local sites, with reliable equipment and technical help, and supported by staff who themselves had used the materials to enhance their knowledge of the content. This series of adaptations reflects the need to be aware of and responsive to the impact of curriculum on learners, and for flexibility in designing and adapting content and methodology to meet the needs of specific groups of learners (Wong 1999).

Practical outcomes of basic education programmes

The Pakistan basic education project described by Dodds (1996) and Saif (1997) provides an example of a programme which enables participants to take more direction over improving their lives and their social and economic situation. It operated as an experimental Functional Education Project for Rural Areas (FEPRA) between 1982 and 1985, and then became the regular Basic Functional Education Programme (BFEP) of the Allama Iqbal Open University (AIOU) Faculty of Mass Education, as a somewhat unusual example of university-sponsored basic education.

The target audience comprises illiterate and neo-literate men and women in villages in different language/cultural communities in the country. Between 1983 and 1985 there were 126 village groups (thirty-seven for women and eighty-nine for men) in which about 2,000 learners participated in three courses offered under FEPRA. In the BFEP period there were 230 village groups with over 9,000 participants. The majority of the FEPRA/BFEP learners are small landowners, more than half (55 per cent) of whom lack schooling of any kind (Saif 1997). In a country where women are historically 'victims of social and economic restraint' (Saif 1997), it is significant that about one-third of the learners are women.

The programme content includes practical topics related to occupations (child care, knitting, poultry keeping, livestock management, agriculture), and topics related to the well-being of society as a whole (village electrification, civic education, sanitation, women's health, environment and population education).

The teaching system is based on self-study printed materials (flip charts, picture handouts, group-leader manuals), audio cassettes and study groups (Dodds 1996). Materials are designed to be used by group leaders who are neither trained teachers nor subject specialists, and can be adapted for use in different regions and by different language groups. Course materials are structured to encourage learners to relate new information to their own circumstances and to take some collective action whenever and wherever possible; they contain both discussion exercises and practical tips. There is minimal use of lectures: dialogue and feedback between learners in the villages and AIOU staff are encouraged.

A study which focused on two villages (Kharian and Uch) showed that very few learners (5–10 per cent) dropped out between the first and last study meetings of each cycle. The course design and instructional methods are considered to be significant reasons for the high and sustained interest in the functional education courses. Since the programme began, there is evidence of change in how the participants deal with life situations and their occupations. There is more frequent monitoring of women during pregnancy; increased use of oral rehydration therapy (both home mixes and packets) in the treatment of diarrhoeal diseases, increased immunisation of infants and children; and improved livestock breeding techniques (Saif 1997).

The Faculty of Mass Education also offers literacy and numeracy, primary, middle and secondary school equivalency for adult and young adult women. The target audience are in villages and rural towns, and have not been able to go to school or to complete basic schooling. The functional literacy and secondary programmes are regular university activities; the middle level project is currently being developed and tested (Dodds 1996).

Social and political dimensions

In many societies, basic education provided through families, local communities, and religious groups is designed to reproduce rather than transform existing social structures and is essentially intended to lead to conformity. By the same token, basic education provided through the state can also be used to support compliance with existing structures. Alternatively, it can enable learners to help to transform them.

The advent of political independence and social movements for economic self-determination in Asia, Africa and Latin America provided opportunities and the necessary motivation for new, nationalist governments to develop political and socio-economic systems in which educational reforms became prominent. Education reforms were instituted to make education relevant to and of benefit for the majority of the people. Since then, socio-economic policies which are the products of diverse political systems have had a profound influence on the basic education curriculum, both within and outside formal school systems. Such policies also shaped the development and provision of non-formal and adult education, and the curriculum frameworks and institutional arrangements for provision of the curricula. A few examples illustrate how political systems have provided guiding principles for curriculum development in non-formal basic education.

In South Africa the demise of apartheid and the advent of a democratically elected government created a new political environment in which new policies on all aspects of the socio-economic life of the country were developed, including policy guidelines for the development of flexible adult education and training curriculum. Recognising the fact that basic education for youth and adults is a prerequisite for a truly democratic society, the adult education and training curriculum framework sets out a philosophy and includes all aspects of teaching and learning (South African Department of Education 1997a). After a government-commissioned review of ODL in South Africa (International Commission into Distance Education in South Africa 1995), plans were developed to overhaul the ODL system of South Africa to make it more responsive to the needs of a range of learners, including those in basic education. The South African Institute for Distance Education (SAIDE), which has a significant role in this plan,

> views learner-centredness as a key principle for any open learning approach. Independent learning is about learners taking responsibility for what and how they learn, rather than an emphasis on individual students working by

themselves, 'banking' the content handed down to them by the teaching institution.

(Glennie 1995: 3)

ODL, combined with a network of community learning centres, was envisaged as a primary means of providing adult basic education to the large numbers of people who required it. ODL was also planned as an essential approach to providing teachers with an opportunity to improve their skills and qualifications.

An example of an open learning initiative designed for practical learning, social and political development is Radio Ada, a new, innovative community education project in Ghana. Established in 1998, it is situated at Ada, the capital of the Dangme East district in the Greater Accra region. It was designed as a development-oriented community-based radio station whose goal is to 'encourage, promote and contribute to informed dialogue and reflective action' among the one million Dangme-speaking people within this region of Ghana.

Radio Ada was designed to facilitate the participation of the Dangme-speaking people, including disadvantaged groups such as women, in planning and evaluation of development activities. It was also intended to enable communication within and between all sections of the community, so that Dangme people could direct their own development. In addition, the project will contribute to non-formal education initiatives in agriculture, environment, population, and health.

Although the radio station is officially owned by the Ghana Community Broadcasting Services, there is a strong sense of community ownership by the Dangme-speaking people, in terms of programme production and patronage, participation of community members in the various activities of the station, and its day-to-day management and operation. The station is operated by a core group of fourteen Dangme-speaking volunteers; community development officers, health educators, public health nurses, agricultural extension officers, teachers and literacy promoters produce programmes which use radio to extend further knowledge about activities they promote at face-to-face meetings.

Four hours of the 17-hour broadcast day are devoted to development-oriented programmes, which focus on non-formal basic education activities designed for the main socio-economic groups in the area. There are programmes for women, for occupational groups such as fishmongers, drivers and traders, and community-related programmes on the environment, health, sanitation, culture and functional literacy. The radio station also uses many of the teaching/learning methods used in functional literacy, such as plays, drama and participatory techniques (Siabi-Mensah 1999).

Issues in determining the non-formal basic education curriculum

Providing a learner-centred curriculum which takes into account the characteristics, needs and context of potential participants is becoming an important issue in non-formal basic education. But developing a suitable, and responsive, learner-centred curriculum is a complex matter. The contextual analysis entails a careful study of a given country's national development goals and its educational policy, as well as an inquiry into the educational needs at the community level where a specific programme is to be implemented. Identifying the social, demographic, political, cultural, economic and physical factors which characterise the resources and potential of specific situations enables the customisation of programmes so that they address the particular features of that community (de Armengol 1992: 3).

It is, however, not always possible to match national socio-economic policies and goals with the basic needs of potential participants in non-formal basic education programmes. This is because different social groups have particular needs and people's ability to identify their own needs should be recognised and acknowledged (de Armengol 1992). It should be possible to link the national socioeconomic developmental goals and the needs of various communities by identifying common areas among needs, resources and issues. However, this activity can be time-consuming and its financial and human resources requirements are in many cases beyond the capacities of developing economies.

If educators and policy makers determine the curricula and methods without input from the learner group, it may lead to an authoritarian style and a one-way transmission of knowledge and skills. On the other hand, if learners select curricula and methods without input from educators, the resulting programme may not be sufficiently coherent and comprehensive to achieve its goals.

Arriving at a consensus between educators and learners, while ideal, may not be easy. The educator or curriculum developer may not be willing and able to relinquish part of his/her traditional role as an expert in curriculum development. And communities of learners may not be able to participate in the design and development of the curriculum, if they have not had the opportunity to develop skills in identifying needs, consensus building and community animation. There is always the danger that significant elements of the community may be left out of the discussion, especially in a stratified or segmented community. Narrow community self-interest, which may be influenced by short-term perspectives and aim at short-term benefits, may dominate the process of community participation in curriculum development. Such interests could ignore longer-term socioeconomic implications for a given community, and may contradict more general socio-economic goals of national development and integration. The local powers that be may reinforce popular community traditions, which may impede development in such areas as health, nutrition, family planning and agriculture (de Armengol 1992).

The scope of a non-formal education programme appears to be an important factor in the process of curriculum development. When, for example, a curriculum is being developed for a small-scale project at community or local level, it is easier to develop content and methods which respond directly to the needs of learners. However, many large-scale programmes offer nationally developed curricula, which tend to be standardised and do not always sufficiently respond to the varying needs and conditions of learners in different geographical, cultural, social and economic environments (Siaciwena 1991).

As stated above, there is a need to reach a compromise between national or regional developmental goals and the concrete needs of groups of learners at the community level. This implies that non-formal basic education should be dynamic, responding to the changing needs of communities. This can be achieved by, among other things, ensuring that an on-going curriculum should be periodically evaluated. This evaluation should discern the gaps between the original purpose or objectives of the programme and the actual practice, and should assess how well the original/revised proposal fits with the present social, political and cultural conditions, and how it is actually used by teachers/facilitators and learners (de Armengol 1992: 7). Without regular assessment and review, non-formal basic education programmes, particularly in developing countries, will not adequately respond to new socio-economic problems, for example that of HIV/AIDS.

Conclusion

For both formal and non-formal education, it is clear that neither the content nor the methodology are value free. Even when the curriculum content is centrally planned, as in most formal education, the methodologies chosen can effectively emphasise some elements at the expense of others. Reading about a topic will be less memorable than discussing its relevance to our lives. Watching a television programme or video will overshadow what the teacher says in a lecture. Media which directly engage the learner, such as video- or computer-based programmes, can include or exclude other elements in the learners' context: their school, their community, their life experience.

In non-formal education, there is potentially much more leeway in choosing both content and approaches. Content can reflect the political, social, ethnic or religious majority, or can accommodate diverse perspectives and local realities. Methodologies can establish a closed system, which does not allow for any input at the 'delivery' end by local teachers, facilitators, or learners, or they can be designed to enable learners and facilitators to participate in creating the learning process. These design decisions, like many other structural decisions, are value-based.

Values are articulated in response to the question, 'What do we want education to achieve?' Value statements encompass both the benefit to society as well as benefit for the individual, as if these two goals can always be compatible. For example, Coombs articulates the 'education for informed citizenship' tenet. Although Coombs' commentary is directed towards science education, it is pertinent to education in general,

> Its aim is not solely to produce more scientists and technologists but also to produce a new generation of citizens who are scientifically literate and thus

better prepared to function in a world which is increasingly influenced by science and technology.

(Coombs 1985: 246)

A government statement includes both goals:

> Curriculum for adults (worldwide) is mainly concerned with the acquisition of knowledge and skills necessary for them to live a productive life and to respond to the dictates of their physical, cultural, political and socio-economic environment. In South Africa it includes both the educational base which individuals require for improving their life chances and the essential income-generating or occupational skills which individuals require for improving their living conditions. But it also refers to a wide range of skills and expertise which includes technical skills such as plumbing, dress making and the like, through specialised skills such as conflict management and negotiation, to creative skills such as dance and praise poetry.
>
> (South African Department of Education 1997b: 14)

Adult basic education and training also provides fundamental skills required for further learning to those individuals who have been unable to gain, or have been denied, access to basic education.

Basic education curriculum requires balancing the need for coherence and consistency (and cost effectiveness) with the need for appropriateness and relevance to the learners. Although the social and political goals of basic education are to enable citizens to become productive members of society, this is realised on an individual and community basis which entails understanding the learner and his or her context. In the words of J. Roby Kidd:

> It means understanding the needs and interests of the learner, understanding the situation in which he lives, and the kinds of content which may serve his needs. It means a careful statement of objectives in a form which sets out the desired changes as well as the subject matter. It means selection of the precise learning experiences which may best accomplish these objectives. It assumes the fullest possible participation by the learner in curriculum building.
>
> (Kidd 1983: 77)

References

Bates, A. (1984) *Broadcasting in Education: An Evaluation*, London: Constable.

Bilan, S. and Henderson, L. (1994) 'Manitoba Telephone and Evergreen School Division demonstration of interactive television network', in *Proceedings of 1994 Conference of Canadian Association for Distance Education*, Vancouver: Canadian Association for Distance Education.

Boone, W. and Keough, E. (1994) 'The challenge of providing equality of educational opportunities for secondary students in small schools in rural Newfoundland and coastal

Labrador', in *Proceedings of 1994 Conference of Canadian Association for Distance Education*, Vancouver: Canadian Association for Distance Education.

Bosch, A. (1997) 'Interactive Radio Instruction: Twenty-three years of improving education quality', in *Education and Technology*, 1,1, posted on website of Education Development Center, Inc. Available HTTP: *http://www.edc.org*

Calder, J. (ed.) (1993) *Disaffection and Diversity: Overcoming Barriers for Adult Learners*, London: Falmer Press.

Coombs, P. (1985) *The World Crisis in Education: The View From the Eighties*, Oxford: Oxford University Press.

Coombs, P. and Ahmed, M. (1974) *Attacking Rural Poverty: How Non-Formal Education Can Help*, Baltimore: Johns Hopkins University Press.

Coombs, P., Prosser, R. and Ahmed, M. (1973) *New Paths to Learning: For Rural Children and Youth*, New York: International Council for Educational Development.

Crellin, I. and Graham, J. (1996) 'The delivery of distance education and other community services through multi role public access facilities in rural communities: Australian experiences', in *Open Learning 96, Proceedings of the Second International Open Learning Conference*, Brisbane: Queensland Open Learning Network.

de Armengol, M. (1992) *Curriculum Evaluation with Special Reference to Literacy and Non-Formal Basic Education*, Paper presented at the Orientation Seminar on Monitoring and Evaluation, 15–20 June, Hamburg: UNESCO Institute of Education.

Dodds, T. (1996) *The Use of Distance Learning in Non-Formal Education*, Vancouver/ Cambridge: Commonwealth of Learning/International Extension College.

Fryer, A. and Gregg, D. (1997) 'The Nechako electronic busing program: An alternative model for distance education', in *Proceedings of 1997 Conference of the Canadian Association for Distance Education*, Saskatoon: Canadian Association for Distance Education.

Glennie, J. (1995) *Towards Learner-Centred Distance Education in the Changing South African Context*, Presentation to the 1995 Cambridge Conference on Open and Distance Learning, Cambridge.

Hallak, J. (1990) *Investing in the Future: Setting Educational Priorities in the Developing World*, Oxford: UNESCO and Pergamon Press.

Haughey, M. (1995) 'Distinctions in distance: Is distance education an obsolete term?', in J. Roberts and E. Keough (eds), *Why the Information Highway?* Toronto: Trifolium Books.

Heath, G. (1998) 'Responding to the client: learner support and management', in *Open Learning 98, Proceedings of the International Conference on Open and Distance Learning*, Brisbane: Queensland Open Learning Network.

International Commission into Distance Education in South Africa (1995) *Open Learning and Distance Education*, Manzini: Macmillan Boleswa.

Kaye, A. (1976) 'The Ivory Coast Educational Television Project', in R. Arnove (ed.), *Educational Television: A Policy Critique and Guide for Developing Countries*, New York: Praeger.

Kidd, R. (1983) 'The learning transaction', in M. Tight (ed.) *Education for Adults*, London: Croom Helm.

Larocque, D. (2000) *AlphaRoute (Phase 2) A Research Report*, Toronto: Alpharoute. Available HTTP: *http://village.ca/eng/projects/Alpha2_english.pdf*

MacPherson, C. and Dekkers, J. (1997) 'Open learning centres: The perception of distance education students', in J. Osborne *et al.* (eds), *Open, Flexible and Distance Learning*.

Education and Training in the 21st Century, Thirteenth Biennial Forum of the Open and Distance Learning Association of Australia, Launceston, Tasmania: ODLAA.

Ministry of Education (Zambia) (1996) *Educating our Future: National Policy on Education*, Lusaka: Ministry of Education.

Moulton, J. (1994) *Interactive Radio Instruction: Broadening the Definition*, LearnTech Case Study no. 1, posted on Educational Development Center website Available HTTP: *http://www.edc.org*

O'Rourke, J., Schachter, L. and Zuckernick, A. (1999) *Creating an Inclusive Learning Environment: Distributed Learning and Community Skills Centres*, Victoria, BC: Consortium of Community Skills Centres of British Columbia.

Ouane, A. (1989) *Handbook on Learning Strategies for Post-Literacy and Continuing Education*, Hamburg: UNESCO Institute for Education.

Potulicka, E. (1991) 'The student, community and curriculum: Their integration: Polish perspective and the case of the comparative education course', in *Proceedings of the Cambridge International Conference on Open and Distance Learning*, Cambridge: Open University East Anglia.

Rogers, A. (1996) *Teaching Adults*, Buckingham/Philadelphia: Open University Press.

Saif, L. (1997) 'Role of Allama Iqbal Open University, Pakistan, in distance education at the basic level', in *Workshop Papers: The Potential of Open Schooling for Increasing Access to Basic Education for Girls and Women*, Islamabad: Allama Iqbal Open University.

Sheffield, J. and Diejomaoh, V. (1972) *Non-Formal Education in African Development*, New York: African American Institute.

Siabi-Mensah, K. (1999) *The Use of Radio in the National Literacy and Functional Skills Project in the Volta and Northern Regions (Ghana)*, Unpublished research report.

Siaciwena, R. (1991) 'Innovative approaches for developing non-formal education', in M. Kelly (ed.), *Conference Papers: National Conference on Education for All: Issues, Challenges and the Way Ahead for Zambia, 7–8 March, 1991*, Lusaka: National Task Force on Education for All, Ministry of Education.

South African Department of Education (1997a) *Policy for Adult Basic Education and Training*, Final draft, Pretoria: Directorate of Adult Education and Training.

South African Department of Education (1997b) *A National Multi-Year Implementation Plan for Adult Education and Training: Provision and Accreditation*, Pretoria: Directorate of Adult Education and Training.

Spronk, B. (1995) 'Appropriating learning technologies: Aboriginal learners, needs and practices', in J. Roberts and E. Keough (eds), *Why the Information Highway?*, Toronto: Trifolium Books.

UNESCO (1992) *Education for All: An Expanded Vision*, Roundtable Themes II, World Conference on Education for All, Jomtien, Thailand, 5–9 March, 1990.

Withers, G. and Pogliani, C. (1996) 'Tuggeranong Flexible Learning Centre: A case study', in *Open Learning 96, Proceedings of the Second International Open Learning Conference*, Brisbane: Queensland Open Learning Network.

Wong, A. (1999) *Promoting the Effective Learning of Mathematics Among Aboriginal Adults: A Community Based Adaptation of the MRC Package for the Internet*, Canada: Research report submitted to the Office of Learning Technologies.

Young, M., Perraton, H., Jenkins, J. and Dodds, T. (1991) *Distance Teaching for the Third World: The Lion and the Clockwork Mouse*, Cambridge: International Extension College, second edition.

Chapter 5

Organisational and delivery structures

Tony Dodds and Palitha Edirisingha

The audience for basic education delivered through open and distance learning is diverse. It includes people of all ages, from young school children to ageing adults in literacy classes. The curriculum through which it is delivered is also diverse. It covers what is taught in traditional early childhood education as in initial primary school classes: reading, writing, counting and stories which reflect in simple terms the values of society. It includes adult literacy and numeracy, community education such as health and civics education, economic and income-generation skill training, and religious and moral education. Distance and open learning methods have been used for all these audiences and for all these curricula. They have been used both in school and out of school, and a wide variety of organisational and delivery approaches have been used.

This chapter examines these diversities of organisation and delivery: are there common patterns of organisation and delivery which emerge from such an examination? Are there at least any discernible trends? Do such patterns or trends, if there are any, relate mainly to the different categories of audience or to the curricular divisions? What can we learn from a survey of experience to date about how to organise and deliver basic education using these methods for different audiences and to present different curricula?

What do we mean by organisation? We mean the agencies involved in arranging that such learning can take place, the administrative structures through which it is made possible, including the actual arrangements for learning, the ways in which those arrangements are managed and the relationships between such agencies. And what do we mean by delivery? We refer to the media, the methods and arrangements through which students are given access to the learning opportunities, the materials they need to study and the contact with their teachers and tutors which enables or facilitates their learning.

We hope that our survey will give us some indication of what works effectively and what does not, and of the extent to which organisational and delivery patterns determine effectiveness. If we can point out some organisational and delivery trends which seem to make for effectiveness, we can suggest some guidelines for future activities and programmes in this field. We can help practitioners to capitalise on the successes of the past and avoid the mistakes and constraints experienced to date.

Categories of basic education by open and distance learning

In chapter 1 some clear categories of basic education by open and distance learning were identified. We are treating these under two headings: audiences and curricula. As regards audiences, three very clear, almost self-evident, categories can be identified:

Children, i.e. those of normal school-going age.   Here we must recognise that normal school-going age varies from country to country. For example in Tanzania in the 1960s and 1970s, children did not start school until they were at least seven years old. Similarly in the Scandinavian countries children started school older than in Britain.

Adults, however defined in any particular country or region.   In many countries today adulthood is defined by the age at which people are eligible to vote or to do military service. Traditionally, in many African countries for example, adulthood started when people got married, assumed the responsibilities of social management or went through traditional initiation ceremonies. For our purpose here we are talking about people who were unable to benefit from formal education when they were children and, as they move into broader social responsibilities, wish to benefit from educational opportunities.

Mixed audiences of adults and children, i.e. programmes in which this distinction between adults and children does not apply and in which learning opportunities are provided for both at the same time and in the same place.

Most programmes for mixed audiences, however, are actually based on the primary school, or basic education, curriculum and therefore bear more resemblance to programmes for children than to those organised specifically for adults. We shall therefore look at the organisation and delivery structures commonly applicable in programmes for children and mixed audiences as a single category and at those for adults as another. We shall then attempt to assess to what extent audience characteristics affect the way in which the education is organised and delivered.

In relation to curriculum, less clearly and simply definable differences emerge, but we can identify three reasonably distinct categories:

*   *curricula which are applied in formal and conventional schools,* including literacy and numeracy, basic sciences, social sciences and religious and moral education

- *non-formal, life-related subject matter,* often not organised in pre-prepared curricula, but responsive to the needs of the students as they arise and are articulated
- *mixed basic education as taught in schools and non-formal life-related subject matter*

Under the non-formal category we can recognise various sub-categories, namely home/community subjects such as health, family and civics education; general interest subjects such as religious and moral education, cultural studies, leisure and personal self-realisation studies; and income-related, skill-development, job-related concerns and studies.

One other division or categorisation which we must take into account is the in-school/out-of school divide (see chapter 1). Clearly in-school provision relates almost exclusively to programmes for children and for mixed children/adult audiences, where the curriculum is largely a replica of that offered in primary schools. It is therefore, by definition, a predominantly formal curriculum. Out-of-school programmes include those for children who are unable to attend formal schools, but predominantly relate to programmes for adults and mixed-age audiences. They cover mostly non-formal, life-related subject matter, however organised into curricula, but can include formal content as well.

The history of the use of open and distance education methods for basic education, for all these categories, is outlined in chapter 1. New information communications technologies (NICT), and their potential for expanding basic education, are discussed in chapters 7 and 8.

Programmes for children and mixed audiences

Open and distance learning programmes for children and mixed audiences fall into the two broad categories defined above. In-school programmes are for children of school-going age, and are provided within school alongside normal classroom instruction. The aim is to raise the quality of teaching and learning in schools. Out-of-school programmes, on the other hand, provide opportunities for those who do not have access through conventional means, for geographical, economic, and social reasons. This audience may consist of children, adolescents and adults, hence the term 'mixed audience'.

In-school programmes

Experience suggests that young children need a formal institution like a school in order to learn a formal curriculum effectively (Perraton 1992). Therefore programmes for children rely heavily on face-to-face teaching. Within this commonality, the organisational and delivery structures vary between developed and developing countries. In Australia, New Zealand and Canada, children have facilities to learn at home under the supervision of parents, supported by teachers at a base school of the air operating at a distance. An interesting experiment is currently in hand in Zimbabwe to adapt the schools of the air originally introduced for the children of white settler farmers in remote areas, for the needs of black children in rural areas, where schools and trained teachers are scarce. This involves supporting institutionalised and communally supervised learning, rather than home-based learning. In developing countries such models are rare. Instead, for children of school-going age, open and distance learning methods have mostly been used to improve the quality of instruction in schools.

Numerous in-school radio and television programmes have been tried, as mentioned in chapter 1. One survivor among these is the Interactive Radio Instruction model, a well researched and well-documented approach pioneered by Stanford University in 1974 (see chapter 1, pp. 12–14). A high proportion of these IRI projects, after successful testing at pilot stage, failed to be incorporated into the national schools system. However, a recent experiment, in South Africa, seems to be surviving for a longer period. Here we present the experience of the IRI programme in South Africa.

Interactive radio instruction in South Africa

Status and governance: The South African IRI programme was launched in 1992 by the Open Learning Systems Educational Trust (OLSET), an NGO based in Johannesburg. Initially USAID provided the funds and LearnTech provided technical support. Currently funding for the running of the programme comes from foreign donors, the main source being Norwegian aid.

Audience: The audience for the South African IRI programme comprises black children in Grades 1–3 of primary school.

Teaching methods and media: The programme provides daily, half-hour English lessons, either through radio broadcasts, or using audio cassettes, to Grade 1, 2 and 3 classrooms of black primary schools. The teachers receive support and training on IRI methodology through a network of co-ordinators. The original design was based on the IRI model pioneered by Stanford University. Soon the curriculum and instructional design changed, reflecting the needs of democratic South Africa (Naidoo 1998, Potter and Leigh 1995). The programme tries to increase teacher involvement and peer interaction among the learners.

Cost advantages and disadvantages: Programmes for improving the quality of teaching and learning in schools usually add costs to existing educational budgets. The cost of running IRI programmes is also a cost additional to regular educational expenditure. The recurrent cost of IRI in South Africa in 1998 was US $1.8 per learner per year.

Outcomes: The outcomes of the South Africa IRI programme can be measured in four ways: the number of learners enrolled, their learning gains, the kind of audience served, and teachers as secondary beneficiaries. First, the enrolment figures show a phenomenal growth over its six-year history. There were about 500,000 learners in all three grades during the school year 1999, compared with 13,000 in 1993, when the programme was first launched on a pilot basis. Second, there has been a significant increase in the test scores of the students who learned from radio programmes, which is consistent with evaluations of IRI programmes elsewhere (AID n.d.). Test scores have shown a 20-per-cent increase for IRI learners over a control group. Improvements in test scores have been higher for learners in rural schools than in urban schools (Potter and Leigh 1995, Leigh and Cash 1999, Bosch 1997). The third outcome measure is that the programme serves a seriously disadvantaged section of the community. South African IRI was initiated when black people were discriminated against by educational policy, and even after the democratic elections in 1994 most schools in black areas are still under-resourced. IRI in South Africa reaches a very important audience, as do other IRI programmes in developing countries. Finally, there were about 12,000 teachers using the programmes in their classes. Evidence suggests that these teachers, as secondary beneficiaries of IRI, acquire better communicative skills in English, and become better at teaching.

Out-of-school programmes

Out-of-school programmes exist to increase educational opportunities for children and mixed audiences. In affluent countries, such as Australia, Canada, and New Zealand, such programmes provide educational opportunities for disadvantaged population groups in dispersed locations where conventional schools are not viable, providing a choice for students, and their parents, as to what they choose to learn (Mukhopadhyay 1995). In developing countries, however, the picture is more complex. Out-of-school education is expected to solve a variety of problems: the existence of a proportionately large adult population who have missed out on general education; inequality of access due to social, economic and geographic conditions; and high drop-out rates in conventional schools. To illustrate how developing countries attempt to provide education out of school, table 5.1 presents six organisational and delivery structures and their main features. These programmes are: Telesecundaria in Mexico, supervised study centres in Zambia and Malawi in central Africa, open schools in Indonesia, the National Open School in India, the Department of Non-Formal Education in Thailand, and radiophonic schools in Latin America.

We can refer to these programmes as 'models' (Perraton 2000), because most of them, or their adaptations, are available within a particular geo-political region, rather than a particular country. For example, supervised study centres are common in southern Africa; open schools in Asia, with variations in India, Indonesia and Bangladesh; and radiophonic schools in Latin America. Programmes offered by Departments of Non-Formal Education of ministries of education are common in most countries, with varying degrees of success.

Table 5.1 The main features of out-of-school programmes in developing countries

Organisational structure	Telesecundaria	Supervised study centres	Open schools	National Open School	Department of Non-Formal Education	Radiophonic schools
Region/Country	Mexico	Zambia and Malawi	Indonesia	India	Thailand	Colombia and other Latin American countries
Date started	1966	1987, following National Correspondence College in 1964 in Zambia and 1972, following merging of Malawi Correspondence College and School Broadcasting Unit (established 1964) in Malawi	1984, after 5-year pilot	1989, following a ten-year pilot project	1979, following non-formal education since 1938	1947
Status and governance	Ministry of Education	Ministry of Education	Ministry of Education	Autonomous within the Ministry of Human Resources Development	Independent department within the Ministry of Education	Church-based organisations, NGOs
Audience	Primary school leavers	Primary school leavers and secondary school 'dropouts'	Primary school leavers	14+ year-olds	14+ year-olds	No age limit
Curriculum	Formal: junior secondary (7th–9th grades)	Formal: junior secondary and senior secondary	Formal: junior secondary	Equivalent to formal primary, junior and senior secondary, vocational and life-related	Equivalent to formal primary, junior and senior secondary, vocational and life-related	Non-formal, literacy, numeracy, combined with life-related skills
Teaching media and methods	Television programmes, print, and classroom sessions	Print, some radio, daily 3-hour supervised study at local centres, tutor-marked assignments	Printed material and face-to-face teaching	Printed study material, weekly tutorials	Printed material, radio and television programmes, weekly tutorials	Radio programmes, print materials supported by auxiliars in radio schools

Outcomes						
Total enrolment	767,696	11,138	197,000	400,000	2,547,664	160,000–220,000
Graduation rate	93%	35%	92%	43%	39%	n.a.
Female enrolment	n.a.	44%	n.a.	33%	53%	n.a.
Cost Cost per learner	$554	n.a.	$31	$10	$26	n.a.
Cost per graduate	n.a.	n.a.	n.a.	$92	$66	n.a.
Comparative figures: graduation Lower secondary	74%	n.a.	n.a.	70%	87%	n.a.
Upper secondary	n.a.	n.a.	n.a.	76%	84%	n.a.
Comparative figures cost Per learner	n.a.	n.a.	$178	$27	$286	n.a.
Per graduate	n.a.	n.a.	n.a.	n.a.	$324	n.a.

Notes

n.a. = not available.

All cost figures are in US dollars.

$1 = 37.12 Indian rupees (average conversion rate 1.4.1997 – 31.3.1998).

$1 = 42.02 Thai baht (average conversion rate 1.10.97 – 31.09.1998).

$1 = 5.53 South African rand (average conversion rate 01.01.1998 – 31.12.1998).

$1 = 2,200 Indonesian rupiahs at 1995 rates.

Supervised Study Centres: the figures are for the Open Secondary Classes in Zambia, 1990 figures.

DNFE, Thailand: all figures are for the fiscal year 1997/8.

Open schools, Indonesia: Enrolment figure is for fiscal year 1996/7, graduation rate for 1993, cost for 1997/8 and comparative figures for 1995.

NOS, India: enrolment figures are for the fiscal year 1998/9; outcomes and cost figures are for fiscal year 1997/8.

Te esecundaria, Mexico: enrolment and cost figures for 1996/7.

NOS's 'total number of graduates' figure consists only of the secondary and senior secondary levels. Enrolments for vocational and bridge courses constitute only 2 per cent of total learners.

The graduation percentage for DNFE is calculated based on the total number of learners in the system during the year. This is compared with the rate of transition of the formal system for various levels.

STATUS AND GOVERNANCE

Four of the programmes presented in the table operate in a ministry of education (MOE), with varying degrees of autonomy. The only programme which is outside government control is that of the radiophonic schools in Latin America, which are church-related organisations. The governance of the programmes which have links with the MOE varies, with implications for the curriculum offered and the number and diversity of the learners served.

The first three programmes presented in the table, Telesecundaria, supervised study centres and open schools in Indonesia, are part of the ministry of education of the country, and are governed by the rules and regulations of the ministry. The National Open School (NOS), on the other hand, is an autonomous body within the ministry responsible for education. NOS can set up courses, prepare its own curriculum, conduct national examinations, and conduct assessments and certifications, within ministry guidelines. The NOS has administrative and financial autonomy. The DNFE in Thailand is a separate department within the MOE. The organisational structure of the MOE, and the history of non-formal education in Thailand, are such that the DNFE enjoys considerable autonomy. The radiophonic schools in Latin America are non-government organisations, mostly initiated and controlled by the Christian church.

AUDIENCE AND CURRICULUM

Telesecundaria, supervised study centres and the Indonesian open school offer the formal curriculum to primary school leavers unable to enter formal secondary school. These organisational structures provide 'the alternative' to the formal schools.

The reason for establishing these organisational structures seems to be the difficulty of expanding post-primary education through conventional schools. The Mexican Telesecundaria was established in 1966 with a pilot group of 6,500 as a response to the lack of secondary schools in rural areas, and attracted the poorer and more remote students (Perraton 2000). In central Africa too, many countries felt unable to cope with the demand for education by expansion of schools, even over the time span of a generation or more (Perraton 1982). Distance education was chosen as the alternative method, and the study centre model was the organisational structure established in Malawi and Zambia. The governments of the newly industrialised nations in east Asia, such as Indonesia, saw secondary education as a necessary factor for industrialisation, and the expansion of primary education created a huge demand. Shortages of qualified teachers and school buildings were obstacles to the expansion of secondary education through conventional means. Open schools for mixed audiences were started in the late 1970s. Indonesia piloted its system from 1979, and expanded its open schools in 1984 (Perraton 2000). Learners in open schools are mainly from poor and rural families, and have to work for the family. The open school is part of the formal school system so that the students follow the same curriculum and take the same examinations.

The other three programmes (National Open School in India, DNFE in Thailand and radiophonic schools in Latin America) offer a different type of curriculum and serve a different kind of audience. As we move towards the right of the table, the curriculum becomes more flexible and the audience more diverse. At both NOS and DNFE, the learners can choose a combination of subjects which enables them to gain an equivalent formal qualification, or alternatively they can choose a combination of vocational or community-related subjects. They also can choose subjects from both categories. Learners can migrate to formal schools if they obtain relevant qualifications. To be eligible to study, learners ought to be more than 14 years of age. Formal qualifications are not required, and they can start at the foundation or primary equivalent levels. Successful learners can work their way up the ladder to junior secondary and senior secondary levels, where formal entry qualifications are required. (For more about open schools, see chapter 12.) The third organisational structure, the radiophonic schools, offers learning opportunities completely independent of any formal curriculum, and does not impose an age limit.

TEACHING MEDIA AND METHODS

There are two main features of the delivery structures in all six examples: first, the teaching and learning approach recognises that the learners need considerable face-to-face support, and second, regardless of other media used, print seems to be the dominant medium. In Telesecundaria, students attend classes, usually in premises provided by local authorities, and have thirty hours of television lessons per week, helped by co-ordinators, who are mainly primary school teachers. In supervised study centres, students meet every day at a local study centre and study under supervisors who are either primary school teachers or reasonably well-educated adults. They may get an opportunity to listen to the radio or taped instruction (Curran and Murphy 1992). Open schools in Indonesia are attached to a regular junior secondary school (a base school), where students receive fifteen to eighteen hours of supervised study a week, with teachers from the base school (Perraton 2000).

The other programmes presented in table 5.1 differ slightly in teaching approach, in that there is more flexibility in terms of attendance at face-to-face sessions. At the NOS, students attend tutorials and counselling sessions conducted by teachers at a local study centre, which is a regular school, usually at the weekend. These sessions are not compulsory. Learners at DNFE Thailand have a choice of three types of learning: totally face-to-face (evening classes during the week), distance (monthly tutorials for two to three hours) and mixed (weekend tutorials). Printed course material is the main carrier of content in all programmes, with DNFE offering some radio and television programmes. In the radiophonic schools a group of learners, usually members of a single family, both adults and children, learn together with the help of an *auxiliar* (or monitor), who may be a better educated member of the family, using print and radio broadcasts.

COST ADVANTAGES AND DISADVANTAGES

Several studies (Jamison, Klees and Wells 1978, Perraton 1982, Murphy and Zhiri 1992) show that distance education has the potential to be more cost-effective than comparable conventional education. Where comparative figures are available, the programmes presented in our table also show this to be the case. In conventional education recurrent costs rise more or less in line with student numbers. Teachers' salaries, which usually account for a high proportion of total recurrent costs, are beyond the control of school managers. In conventional education, therefore, while the costs of teaching students can be predicted with a high degree of accuracy, the measures which managers can take to control unit costs are quite limited (Curran and Murphy 1992).

Early analysis of Telesecundaria suggested that it was cost-effective compared with conventional schools, but more recently its relative costs have risen (Perraton 2000). The supervised study centres in Malawi, Zambia and Zimbabwe show that the system can work and be less costly per student enrolled than the conventional alternative (Perraton 1992). In Malawi, the cost of educating a student in the study centre system is between one-fourth and one-fifth of the cost of a student in a day secondary school (Curran and Murphy 1992). The Thai DNFE and Indian NOS also show favourable cost figures, according to table 5.1.

OUTCOMES

All the programmes reach large numbers of learners in absolute terms, except the supervised study centre model. Although the figure for the study centres is the lowest of the examples presented, in terms of the population and of total enrolments at secondary level, the percentage is impressive (Siaciwena 1995). In Zambia, fewer than 20 per cent of primary school leavers are able to enter the conventional secondary system every year, and enrolment in the study centres constitutes 8 per cent of the primary school final year enrolment and more than 40 per cent of total secondary level enrolment.

Telesecundaria started with a pilot group of 6,500 in 1967, rose to 29,000 by 1971 and had nearly 600,000 students in more than 9,000 schools by 1993, more than 15 per cent of the total junior secondary school population (Murphy 1995: 65). It attracts the poorer and more remote students (Perraton 2000). Its numbers have grown in pace with the expansion of secondary education generally. By 1997/8 there were 756,000 students in 12,000 centres.

Indonesian open schools also show successful growth and enrolment (Perraton 2000). In the pilot stage there were only eight schools in five provinces, later increased to fifty-nine throughout the country with a total of 17,478 students. Expansion accelerated after 1994 with the formal introduction of universal basic education. Currently there are 376,620 students in 3,773 locations (chapter 12, p. 211).

The National Open School enrolled 130,000 learners for the year 1998/9, whereas in 1990/1 the figure was little over 40,000, and during its first years at the pilot stage, the figures were only about 1,000. Sixty-three per cent of students follow secondary courses and 33 per cent follow senior secondary courses. While the school has students of all ages, 68 per cent are aged between 14 and 19. About two-thirds are male, reflecting the balance in secondary education generally. The school has had some success in attracting disadvantaged students: 23 per cent of 1996/7 enrolments were from scheduled castes or scheduled tribes or the disabled (Edirisingha forthcoming). Most students were from families on less than the average income (Gaba 1997: 44).

The DNFE programme reaches larger numbers of learners than NOS does. The total number enrolled during the academic year 1998/9 was over 2.5 million. The figure ten years earlier was a little over a half a million. DNFE has a long history of providing out-of-school education (twenty years since its formal inception, but a lot longer under various initiatives), which suggests that it is successful in reaching large numbers. DNFE makes efforts to enrol members of communities which are socially, physically and geographically disadvantaged, such as women, girls, street children, drug addicts, prisoners and hill tribes.

The Latin American radiophonic schools also attract large numbers of learners. The ACPO programme in Colombia had, at any one time, 20,000 radio schools, with enrolments which normally ranged from 160,000 to 220,000 people (Fraser and Restrepo-Estrada 1998). In its first twenty years, more than 2.25 million peasants participated in its radio schools (McAnany 1976).

Where comparisons can be made, programmes offering out-of-school education usually show lower graduation rates than the formal system. In the Indonesian Open Schools it is reported that 92 per cent of students passed the national junior secondary examination and that there was no significant difference between the academic achievement of open school and regular school graduates (Sadiman 1994: 97). But pass rates in secondary and senior secondary levels at NOS in 1998 were 26 and 23 per cent respectively. Figures for the formal system were 70 per cent and 76 per cent for the year 1994 (Gaba 1997). DNFE completion rates for 1998 were 64 per cent for functional literacy, 40 per cent for primary, 26 per cent for lower secondary and 23 for upper secondary. The higher pass rates for functional literacy may be because the course is taught face-to-face. This kind of comparison with the formal system, however, needs to allow for the characteristics and backgrounds of students studying at a distance (Murphy 1992). Students may study only part of the course, and do not always sit for examinations. Distance study requires discipline and commitment on the part of learners, and the time they can spend studying on their own may be limited by other commitments.

Programmes for adults

All the examples described and used as the basis for our discussion in this section are predominantly focused on adults and all are organised out-of-school. Let us start by giving thumb-nail sketches of several such programmes. The sketches which follow are drawn from a documentary survey carried out by the International Extension College for the Commonwealth of Learning (Dodds 1996). The conclusions which follow are therefore also heavily based on the 73 projects, mainly but not exclusively from within the Commonwealth, covered in that survey, it being the widest study of such projects carried out in recent years. In addition, readers are referred to the descriptions elsewhere in this volume of the AMREF programme (chapter 11, p. 197), the Gobi Women's Project (chapter 6, p. 112) and the work of AIOU's Faculty of Mass Education (chapter 4, p. 79).

Programmes

Ghana: Ministry of Education Non-formal Education Division (and collaborating agencies)

Content: Functional literacy and numeracy and post-literacy programmes – farming, fishing, forestry, health education etc.

Audience: Illiterate, semi-literate and neo-literate adult men and women

Distance education methods used: Radio series; audio cassettes; rural newspapers and reading clubs; self-study training manuals for supervisors, facilitators etc.

Governance: Ministry of Education NFED collaboration with NGOs and district and local authority structures

History and impact: Nationwide coverage, distance education methods concentrate on mobilisation (radio), staff training, support for study of development functions, post-literacy activities

(Source: Mensah and Yates 1996)

Sudan: Sudan Open Learning Organisation (SOLO) (incorporating SOLU: Sudan Open Learning Unit)

Content: Adult literacy (functional) in Tigrinya and Arabic, primary health care, income-generating and small business management skills for women

Audience: Ethiopian and Eritrean refugees living in Sudan, southern Sudanese displaced people living in northern and eastern Sudan, special project for women in displaced communities in Khartoum and Omdurman

Distance education methods used: Self-study print materials, printed pictorial visuals, flipcharts, audio cassettes, group leader and primary health worker training from self-study manuals, study groups, briefly trained study-group leaders

Governance: SOLU was created in 1984 to establish formal and non-formal education programmes for refugees, with support from the Sudanese government, UNHCR and international distance education and funding agencies. NFE programmes have consistently been an important part of its activities, including literacy and primary health care (PHC). These programmes continue with the remaining population of refugees from Ethiopia and Eritrea who are seeking settlement in Sudan. SOLO/SOLU is increasingly developing and adapting programmes to meet the needs of displaced southern Sudanese and other Sudanese educationally disadvantaged groups. The NFE programmes have reached and continue to reach significant proportions of the refugee groups. SOLO is currently running two new pilot projects: a PHC campaign and a Women's Development Project.

(Source: SOLU reports 1995)

India: Yashwantrao Chavan Maharashtra Open University (YCMOU) extension, community education and non-qualification programmes

Content: Agriculture and crop production; marital adjustment, personality development, ageing; child care, nutrition, first aid; vocational skills, entrepreneurship development
Audience: Illiterate adults; new literates; less-educated adults; earthquake victims; unemployed youth; leprosy patients etc.
Distance education methods used: Self-study printed materials, including visual materials; audio-vision; study groups (or Prayog Parivars); practical demonstration programmes
Governance: State open university often working with local government agencies and local NGOs
History and impact: The YCMOU, established in 1989, was India's fifth open university. It was the first in India to develop and implement a deliberate policy of mass education of a non-formal nature with strong emphasis on grass roots vocational skills and social linkages

(Source: Takwale *et al.* 1994)

Namibia: University of Namibia, Centre for External Studies: Action research pilot project on the use of affordable media for farmer education in northern Namibia

Content: Education about best cattle husbandry practices including immunisation, avoidance of cross-border grazing, common diseases in cattle and how to prevent or cure them, marketing etc.
Audience: Small-scale cattle farmers in the four north-central regions of Namibia, both men and women
Distance education methods proposed to be used: Radio, simple post-literacy printed hand-outs/pamphlets, study groups, visits by extension officers, audio cassettes
Governance: Project being set up as an action research pilot project by the Oshakati office of the Centre for External Studies of the University of Namibia in collaboration with the Faculty of Agriculture and Natural

Resources and the Department of Information and Communication Sciences; close co-operation with and involvement of the local extension services and the traditional authorities of the regions; overseen by a steering committee consisting of representatives of all these bodies
History and impact: The project was developed from a course project prepared for the IEC/University of London postgraduate diploma in distance education by the late Shondili Aijambo, and has been worked up into an action research project by Haaveshe Nekongo-Nielsen, following the workshop in Namibia in December 1997 to try to take further the research and proposals for additional research arising from the Dodds (1996) survey; the base-line survey for the project was being carried out at the time of writing and the actual media education project was due to take place in the middle of 2000.

Conclusions and generalisations

Perhaps the most obvious conclusion to be drawn from this survey, which reinforces long-held general impressions of many authors about non-formal education, is that there is a vast variety of organisational structures and of governance. It is much more difficult to generalise about such programmes for adults than it is for more formal programmes for children, whether they be in school or out of school. What follows is an attempt to draw some general conclusions, using the same sub-headings as in the previous section.

STATUS, GOVERNANCE AND ORGANISATION

Those reviewing this kind of education provision often comment that it is underfunded, held in low esteem by governments, run only on a small scale and usually only as pilot projects, often at the initiative of NGOs or under pressure from international humanitarian funding agencies (Dodds 1996, Spronk 1999). Our conclusions from revisiting the projects surveyed do not contradict these somewhat depressing conclusions. However, a closer look at the organisation of the projects suggests that this is not the whole truth, as indicated in the following conclusions.

- Fifty-six (or 77 per cent) of the projects listed were long-term programmes, and seventeen (23 per cent) were limited-time projects; some have survived for many, often more than ten, years.
- The following list shows the agencies with prime responsibility for the organisation of the programmes or projects:

broadcasting stations	21	(29 per cent)
other government departments	13	(18 per cent)
NGOs	12	(16 per cent)

universities	10	(14 per cent)
parastatal/autonomous bodies	8	(11 per cent)
trade unions/co-operatives	4	(6 per cent)
international agencies	5	(7 per cent)

If we recognise that many of the radio stations listed, all parastatal bodies and most universities are themselves predominantly state-funded, government involvement in the programmes and projects covered is of a very high order.

• About 70 per cent of the programmes and projects covered make clear that inter-institutional collaboration is a keynote feature of their organisation. In many cases a broadcasting station makes its facilities and expertise available to an educational body which may be government, non-government or parastatal; the initial initiative may have come either from the broadcasting station or from the educational body. Also in very many cases the providers will have sought co-operation or consultation with local community organisations, especially in the setting up of study groups or other kinds of face-to-face contact sessions; this broad co-operation may be one reason for the long-term weakness and failure to grow to scale which is a characteristic of many non-formal education programmes.

• Often the relationships between the various agencies involved are, perhaps inevitably, ad hoc, set up for the project and hard to maintain if it becomes a regular programme of the initiating agency.

• Finally, in many cases the original project managed to raise external aid funds to get going. Such funds are provided for a limited period and when they run out it is very difficult to find core funding for the long-term maintenance of the programme. Almost by their nature, such programmes have limited ability to raise their own finance on a scale which allows strength and long-term growth.

AUDIENCE AND CURRICULUM

The audiences for the programmes in this section are all adults who are seeking education, not in order to progress up the formal education ladder, but for its own sake, with the aim of improving the quality of their lives. In developing countries such audiences are usually characterised by low levels of previous formal education. Many will have had no formal education at all and will be illiterate or neo-literate. They have enrolled to achieve a particular learning purpose and want to progress towards achieving that purpose as quickly as possible. These characteristics largely determine the nature of the curricula for such programmes. Most of the programmes surveyed (59 per cent) come under the classification of non-formal curricula; the other 41 per cent can be classified as formal or school-equivalency curricula, if we include adult literacy and numeracy. Most of those which have non-formal curricula are mixed: they include subject matter from several categories: 66 per cent include social and community education topics, of which about half relate to health and family matters; 63 per cent include economic or earnings-related education, about 44 per cent agricultural topics. Most do not lead to assessment by examination or to the award of certificates other than attendance certificates.

TEACHING MEDIA

The overwhelming majority of the projects surveyed, probably more than 85 per cent, use a combination of media or methods of delivery. The following lists their use of each of those media.

- About 90 per cent used some form of printed media; 30 per cent combined their printed materials with an element of correspondence.
- About 85 per cent made use of broadcast or recorded media to communicate with their audiences; 67 per cent broadcast their materials (55 per cent radio, 7 per cent television); 37 per cent made use of audio cassettes and 15 per cent video cassettes.
- About 84 per cent included in their delivery approach some form of face-to-face contact; 63 per cent organised study groups or study circles; 18 per cent arranged face-to-face tutorials and the same number made arrangements for contact between the learners and local extension services; 10 per cent set up seminars or public meetings as part of the programme; finally, one project, the Gobi Women's Project in Mongolia (see chapter 6), included home visits by tutors to learners.
- It is perhaps worth mentioning that the information collected referred to only two projects where telephone contact was used, and to only two using any form of computerised contact. This may simply indicate the limited vision of the researcher; more recent information (for example several case studies in the collected papers prepared for the Pan-Commonwealth Forum in Brunei in March 1999) suggests that there is a growing recognition, mainly in industrialised countries, of the potential of new information technology for this neglected and usually technologically backward form of education. There is certainly evidence of some small, determined, but as yet very limited, attempts to set up telecentres to give rural people access to computers and thereby to e-mail and the Internet (for example, the Canadian Alpharoute Project referred to in chapter 4 above). These may eventually, when the adult population has had the chance to break through to literacy in whatever languages the computers are using, provide valuable support in non-formal learning.

MEASURES OF ACHIEVEMENT

The issue of costs did not figure in Dodds (1996). It is thus extremely difficult to generalise about the costs of these programmes. Costs per participant are also very difficult to calculate because of their flexible nature. There is, moreover, usually no parallel programme delivered in a conventional manner with which to make comparisons. From a recent study of six projects in Africa (Siaciwena forthcoming), though the costing details are also somewhat sketchy and uneven, it would appear that costs per student are generally low by comparison with formal in-school education.

It is similarly difficult to measure the impact of such programmes in a way comparable to the measures of achievement normally applied to formal school programmes. There are usually no examinations; no concepts of passing and failing; often there are no fixed time limits for study; there are no fixed structures for curriculum or student progression from one stage to another. Again, the purpose of the study (Dodds 1996) was not to calculate attendance or completion rates, but to identify existing programmes. To measure achievement for the purposes of this chapter, we can only draw on the forthcoming Siaciwena study of six African projects. Five of these (the results of the sixth study are not yet available) have enrolled a total of more than 25,000 learners in the past few years, even though many are operating in quite limited areas of their countries. The surveys of learners, tutors and supervisors show that the participants themselves believe they make very significant learning gains as a result of their studies, and that what they learn has a direct impact on the quality of their lives, by increasing either their agricultural skills and productivity, or their social effectiveness as health workers. There are many significant statements quoted about changes in attitudes to family planning, to modern agricultural methods or to traditional patterns of social organisation, such as the roles and status of women in local communities (Siaciwena, forthcoming). Such achievements are almost impossible to express in economic value terms. If replicated on a large enough scale, however, they would contribute immensely to improving the quality of the lives of communities and nations in comprehensive terms. Such improvement is an important purpose of educational expansion. Our studies suggest that the technical capacity exists to bring about such change on a large scale through non-formal education using open and distance learning methods.

Effectiveness and sustainability of programmes

Many projects using media for education, both in and out of school, in developing countries have died or stagnated before they reached full-scale implementation. There have been too many examples of the same historical cycle: 'great enthusiasm, early research support, later research showing failure and the eventual discarding of the technology' (Cuban 1986, cited by Klees, 1995: 398). The high-profile ETV programmes and many of the IRI programmes are illustrations of this cycle. Some of the adult non-formal programmes discussed show evidence of much longer survival, though not of nation-wide expansion. Their survival or expansion, however, does not seem to be correlated with their technical effectiveness. Let us try to identify some common and some contrasting factors, which seem to have a bearing on the sustainability of organisational and delivery structures.

Political context and support

There is convincing evidence that political support is a crucial factor in long-term sustainability and growth to scale. Many of the IRI projects have failed because they were unable to attract political support to ensure national funding and integration into national education structures, as they tried to pass from USAID-funded and expatriate-managed projects into national programmes. The South African IRI project, which was nationalised in its leadership much earlier in its life and has been able to diversify its funding base, may hopefully prove to be one of the few exceptions. The ACPO radiophonic schools programme, after a sustained period of dramatic success, with both church and governmental support, died after forty years, when the church and the politicians turned against it (Fraser and Restrepo-Estrada 1998). Two programmes which seem to continue to command political support and to have survived and grown to scale are the DNFE programme in Thailand and the Indian NOS. Both have had firm national political support from their inception. The political will to make resources available is the main factor determining effectiveness and sustainability in adult and non-formal programmes using open learning media. Many of the programmes we have surveyed have survived long after the end of the pilot projects, but few have achieved large-scale implementation and therefore large-scale social and economic impact.

Integration into mainstream education

Many programmes, particularly those started with external funding, fail to pay adequate attention during the pilot stages to the issue of institutionalisation, and as a consequence are poorly integrated into the administrative and professional fabric of the educational system (Dock 1999). The IRI project in Kenya, for example, failed due to a lack of consultation with the MOE on how to make the project's and the MOE's goals consistent (Helwig, Bosch and Dock 1999). In contrast, the NOS in India, Thailand's DNFE, Telesecundaria in Mexico and the Indonesian open schools are all examples of healthy integration into national mainstream educational systems. Non-formal education programmes, as their name implies, are not dependent on such integration into the formal system. They depend on a recognition by the target audience, education officials and the politicians, as well as the general public, that they are educationally and socially important and effective. Their survival, however, does depend on their incorporation into the regular programmes of a permanent institution, and their effectiveness often depends on inter-institutional co-operation.

Cost of the programme

The costs of such programmes clearly vary according to their nature. Those of in-school programmes, which set out to improve the quality of the learning, are obviously add-on costs. The ETV programmes appear to have been too expensive for the national governments to take over when external funds dried up. The same was claimed for the IRI programmes, though political and integrational problems probably outweighed cost concerns in most cases. The costs of running out-of-school programmes, whether school equivalency for mixed audiences or non-formal programmes for adults, are different. They are not add-on costs, except to the national budget. The evidence we have reviewed suggests that they are usually significantly cheaper than their conventional alternatives, though the cost per student will vary with the size of the audience and therefore with the coverage of the programme. They are, however, programmes which have to be paid for: the more students covered the bigger the budget required, even if the cost per student comes down. It comes back to political will: only if they are considered politically important will sufficient funding be found for them.

Funding regime

Programmes can use a combination of four kinds of funding regimes: external grants, government budget, fees charged to students and private sponsorship. Many media projects, as we have seen, start their lives on external grants, particularly at pilot project stage. This is one of their major constraints. It appears vital that from the outset there is local financial commitment and investment, and a clearly stated and agreed programme for the replacement of external by local funds. These local funds can, as shown in the Indian NOS and the Thailand DNFE, be a mixture of government subsidy and student fees. The latter, however, raise the question of equity: the programmes are often aimed at students who, for economic reasons, have not been able to use the formal system. NOS and DNFE have found ways of admitting students who cannot afford the fees. These same points apply to non-formal programmes for adults: those which have survived are those which, from an early stage, were able to match and eventually replace external funds with local budgets. One important difference lies in their ability to charge economic student fees. Such programmes, like basic primary schools, must rely heavily on government subsidies. If government or international agencies wish to insist on student funding of such programmes they cannot survive on any scale in developing countries.

Independence and flexibility of organisation

Many of the organisations which we have studied are parts of government ministries. They operate within the guidelines, regulations and administrative structures of their parent ministry. Such bodies have little freedom or self-control in matters of staffing, programme initiatives or finance. Decisions are taken according to criteria which are not sensitive to the needs and characteristics of open learning. This often constrains their development. Organisations such as the NOS and the DNFE have flourished because in different ways they have enjoyed freedom of operation and internal self-management. Flexibility is probably the keynote of successful non-formal education programmes. Flexibility and innovation, almost by definition, require a high degree of autonomy in day-to-day management. Most of the surviving and successful NFE programmes we have surveyed are run by parastatal bodies or NGOs.

Flexibility of the curriculum

We have seen three kinds of curricula: those which follow formal school curricula exactly; those which combine school curricula with subjects and approaches specially designed for their out-of-school audiences; and those which are almost entirely non-formal. Those which are tied to school curricula have been criticised, either for giving their students a programme irrelevant to their lives, or for encouraging them to leave the rural areas where they live and are needed, for urban areas where they have great difficulty getting jobs. Organisations like the NOS and the DNFE appear to have successfully combined formal, vocational and life-enrichment curricular concerns, to allow their students to receive equivalency recognition with formal school graduates and to prepare for living and working successfully in their own environments. The curricula of adult NFE programmes correspond with our third category. Some NFE purists would see the absence of a structured curriculum as a prerequisite for a non-formal definition. We believe that flexibility and the ability to respond to the immediate learning needs of the audience are a major strength of non-formal education. The challenge is to provide this flexibility through open learning media and to give the students something which they and their communities recognise as worthwhile.

Access to broadcasting infrastructure

Broadcasting appears to be central to most ODL basic education systems. To date, clearly radio is the lead medium. Access to broadcasting facilities is therefore crucial. There are no clear guidelines as to whether the educational body should have its own or use public broadcasting facilities. Where public broadcasting is run by a government ministry other than education, it can be difficult to put together the expertise on the side of the educators and the recognition of educational priorities on the side of the broadcasters. On the other hand few of the agencies which we have examined can justify or manage the expenditure of running their own transmission facilities. There are examples, such as the DNFE in Thailand, where a strong working agreement is in place between the educational and the public broadcasting institutions, to ensure proper resources are available to the programme. Insofar as it is the responsibility of the state to provide education, including adult education, to its citizens, it is logical to assume that a tool as powerful as radio should be made available at a subsidised rate to educational bodies. This includes access both to the air waves and to the facilities and expertise to utilise the medium to its best effect.

Quality of learner support

Evidence suggests that the quality of learner support has a strong effect on pass rates. The quality of the supervisors is the single most important factor. It is also clear that younger learners are more dependent than mature students on such support. Quality support depends on training for the supervisors or tutors, especially in tutoring distance students. While the nature of the support and the ways of delivering it may differ for non-formal education, the need for it does not.

Collaboration with other government and non-government organisations

A centralised organisation has limited capacity to reach distance students in remote corners of the country, especially with quality support services such as we have just mentioned. The programmes which are successful in reaching large numbers of learners, especially those from educationally disadvantaged communities, are those which forge successful partnerships with other bodies, including NGOs. Such collaboration, as we have seen, is an essential feature of non-formal education programmes. If adult non-formal programmes are to use open and distance learning effectively and with quality over extended periods of time and to achieve maximum outreach, such collaboration is an essential feature; structures to ensure it works must be established.

A final word

It is our belief from what we have seen and studied in this review that the techniques and structures for organisation and delivery exist, have been tested and found potentially effective to use open and distance learning approaches:

- to improve in-school basic education for children
- to increase the scope and effectiveness of out-of-school provision of formal or alternative equivalent learning at basic education level for children and mixed-age audiences
- to provide much larger-scale adult non-formal education programmes than have as yet been achieved

The techniques are there, the organisational structures exist, the costs are reasonable by comparison with their formal school equivalents. The achievement of significant inroads into the unmet backlog of education for all by these approaches depends on the political will of governments both as direct providers and as international funders.

References

AID (n.d.) *Interactive Radio Instruction: Confronting Crisis in Basic Education*, Newton, Massachusetts: Agency for International Development and Education Development Center.

Bosch, A. (1997) 'Interactive Radio Instruction: Twenty-three years of improving educational quality', *Educational Technology Notes*, 1, 1, Washington, DC: World Bank.

Cuban, L. (1986) *Teachers and Machines: The Classroom Uses of Technology Since 1920*, New York: Teachers College Press.

Curran, C. and Murphy, P. (1992) 'Distance education at the second level and for teacher education in six African countries', in P. Murphy and A. Zhiri (eds), *Distance Education in Anglophone Africa: Experience with Secondary Education and Teacher Training*, Washington, DC: World Bank.

Dock, A. (1999) 'Success and sustainability', in A. Dock and J. Helwig (eds), *Interactive Radio Instruction: Impact, Sustainability, and Future Directions*, Education and Technology Notes Series 4, 1, Washington, DC: USAID/World Bank.

Dock, A. and Helwig, J. (1999) 'An overview of IRI experience to date', in A. Dock and J. Helwig (eds), *Interactive Radio Instruction: Impact, Sustainability, and Future Directions*, Education and Technology Notes Series 4, 1, Washington, DC: USAID/World Bank.

Dodds, T. (1996) *The Use of Distance Learning in Non-Formal Education*, Vancouver: Commonwealth of Learning, and Cambridge: International Extension College.

Edirisingha, P. (forthcoming). *Open and Distance Learning for Basic Education in Developing Countries*, Final report of a two-year research project, Cambridge: IRFOL.

Fraser, C. and Restrepo-Estrada, S. (1998) *Communication for Development: Human Change for Survival*, London: I.B. Tauris.

Gaba, A. (1997) 'Open schooling in India: Development and effectiveness', *Open Learning*, 12, 3: 43–9

Helwig, J., Bosch, A. and Dock, A. (1999) 'Brief case studies of six IRI initiatives', in A. Dock and J. Helwig (eds), *Interactive Radio Instruction: Impact, Sustainability, and Future Directions*, Education and Technology Notes Series 4, 1, Washington, DC: USAID/World Bank.

Jamison, D., Klees, S. and Wells, S. (1978) *The Costs of Educational Media*, Beverly Hills: Sage.

Klees, S. (1995) 'Economics of educational technology' in M. Carnoy (ed.), *International Encyclopaedia of Economics of Education*, second edition, Oxford: Elsevier Science Ltd.

Leigh, S. and Cash, F. (1999) 'Effectiveness and methodology', in A. Dock and J. Helwig (eds), *Interactive Radio Instruction: Impact, Sustainability, and Future Directions*, Education and Technology Notes Series 4, 1, Washington, DC: USAID/World Bank.

McAnany, E. G. (1976) *Radio's Role in Development: Five Strategies for Use*, Washington, DC: Clearinghouse on Development Communication.

Mensah, E. and Yates, R. (1996) 'Case studies on Ghana functional literacy campaigns', in MA and Diploma in Distance Education for External Students, *Course 7: Non-Formal and Adult Basic Education at a Distance: A Reader*, London: Institute of Education, University of London/International Extension College.

Mukhopadhyay, M. (1995) 'Open schooling: An introduction', in M. Mukhopadhyay and S. Phillips (eds) *Open Schooling: Selected Experiences*, Vancouver: Commonwealth of Learning.

Murphy, P. (1992). 'Effectiveness of full-time second-level distance education in three African countries', in P. Murphy and A. Zhiri (eds), *Distance Education in Anglophone Africa: Experience with Secondary Education and Teacher Training*, Washington, DC: World Bank.

Murphy, P. (1995) 'The challenge of open secondary education: demands and models', in S. Anzalone (ed.) *Multichannel Learning: Connecting all to Education*, Washington, DC: Education Development Center.

Murphy, P. and Zhiri, A. (ed.) (1992) *Distance Education in Anglophone Africa: Experience with Secondary Education and Teacher Training*, Washington, DC: World Bank.

Naidoo, G. (1998) Personal communication, Johannesburg: OLSET.

Perraton, H. (1982) (ed.) *Alternative Routes to Formal Education: Distance Teaching for School Equivalency*, Baltimore: Johns Hopkins University Press.

Perraton, H. (1992) 'Post-primary distance teaching', in P. Murphy and A. Zhiri (eds), *Distance Education in Anglophone Africa: Experience with Secondary Education and Teacher Training*, Washington, DC: World Bank.

Perraton, H. (2000) *Open and Distance Learning in the Developing World*, London: Routledge.

Potter, C. and Leigh, S. (1995) *English in Action in South Africa 1992–1993: A Formative Evaluation*, Internal document, Johannesburg: OLSET.

Sadiman, A.S. (1994) 'The Indonesian Open Junior Secondary Schools', in M. Mukhopadhyay and S. Phillips (eds) *Open Schooling: Selected Experiences*, Vancouver: Commonwealth of Learning.

Siaciwena, R. (1995) 'Zambian open secondary classes', in M. Mukhopadhyay and S. Phillips (eds) *Open Schooling: Selected Experiences*, Vancouver: Commonwealth of Learning.

Siaciwena, R. (ed.) (forthcoming) *Case Studies of Non-Formal Education by Distance and Open Learning*, Vancouver: Commonwealth of Learning and Cambridge: International Extension College.

Spronk, B. (1999) *Nonformal Education at a Distance: A Framework for Discussion*, Round table discussion paper presented at the Pan-Commonwealth Forum on Open Learning Empowerment through Knowledge and Technology, Bandar Seri Begawan, Brunei Darussalam, 1–5 March.

Takwale, R. *et al.* (1994) *YCMOU: Status and Innovative Developments*, Unpublished paper presented to conference on Open Education Achievements and Challenges, New Delhi.

Chapter 6

Evaluation and quality

Judith Calder and Santosh Panda

Is distance education any good? How can we ensure our project will achieve its aims? These are surely the first questions which come to mind for many people when introduced to the idea of promoting a basic education project using distance education. Many will be aware of the problems of varying levels of quality associated with many correspondence courses, or, more recently, with on-line courses. In previous chapters, we have seen examples of the different ways in which distance education can be used to promote basic education. While some projects are successful, others have more difficulties in achieving their aims. The evaluation findings from these projects contribute to the pool of knowledge upon which policy makers, planners and educationalists draw when designing and developing their own distance education systems for this type of education. Unfortunately it is often the case that there is inadequate information about what was actually achieved, the process by which it was achieved and which aspects worked well and why. The process of drawing upon the lessons of one's own experience and the experience of others is what we term evaluation. While we use informal evaluation all the time in our decision making, the need for formal evaluation is often not recognised until rather late in the day. The reasons for this can range from lack of awareness of the benefits of systematic and rigorous data collection to a simple lack of concern about those benefits.

The need for accountability has driven the design of many evaluation studies of national and international projects. There are many different stakeholders in distance education projects. By stakeholders we mean individuals and groups who are affected by distance education (DE), and who in turn may have influence on it – that is, people whose interests are linked in some way with DE. These may include

- politicians
- governmental agencies
- international agencies
- international/national/local education providers
- employers

- media organisations
- wider academic/teaching communities
- DE academics/teachers
- DE regional/local staff
- DE specialist technical staff
- community leaders
- learners/target groups

Each of these stakeholders will have their own particular concerns, lines of accountability and criteria against which their judgements will be set. The number and range of stakeholders in distance education projects is large. Learners used to traditional classroom-based methods of learning have to be prepared to undertake an unfamiliar form of study which uses a range of different media, is not classroom-based, and may not be teacher led; community leaders may need to give it their support; teachers, assessors and inspectors have to try to achieve high standards using unfamiliar methods; instructional designers need to select appropriate media and produce distance teaching materials; managers have to co-ordinate the design, production, testing and distribution of the teaching material. At the same time, policy makers and planners have to take decisions about whether to support the introduction of new DE projects, or to continue funding an old one. They may have to choose between different projects, or they may have to justify to their paymasters the earlier decisions they made. Realistically the criteria which policy makers and planners use for such decisions will be a mix of political, economic and ideological considerations. They and the other stakeholders need to know what sort of approaches work in what sort of conditions, with what sort of groups, and what sort of outcomes might be expected.

Formal evaluation processes then can be used to inform many different types of decisions – from assessing the outcomes of initiatives; the potential target groups; the effectiveness and quality of different types of approaches or procedures; the identification of barriers to implementation; cost implications; the illumination of complex processes; the selection of media; through to the monitoring and assurance of the quality of the provision and the sustainability of the project. In spite of the clear benefits of evaluation for management and decision making, there is little literature which records the experience of non-formal education projects. The lack of such literature means that individual projects are unable to benefit from the experience of similar past projects, and the lack of systematic project evaluation which should underpin project decision making means that projects also lose the benefit of appropriate and timely information on which to base their planning and decision making.

In this chapter we aim to show that a well-planned evaluation programme is an essential component of any project and especially of distance basic education projects. We identify some of the different evaluation approaches which have been used in basic education projects through DE. The advantages and disadvantages of different evaluation options will be explored, together with their implic-ations for quality, and ways forward for planners and policy makers.

A Mongolian case study

> With the disintegration of the former Soviet Union, Mongolia was abruptly severed from its exterior financial and technical support. Rebuilding the country's human resources became a top priority with self-sufficiency and the creation of employment matters of urgency ... In 1991 with the support of UNESCO, the Government of Mongolia launched a non-formal distance education programme. Its mandate was to respond much faster and more efficiently than traditional formal education to the population's learning needs. The women of the Gobi desert were identified as being most at risk, and by 1996, 15,000 nomadic women were taking part in education activities offered through radio, printed materials and the support of visiting teachers ... Learning, in many instances, became a family affair with many members of settlements, including men and children, being drawn into listening to radio programmes.
>
> (Robinson 1997)

In the report of the Mongolian basic education initiative detailed above, attention was also drawn to the importance of the high literacy levels (96 per cent), and relatively high status of Mongolian women in comparison to so many Asian women, to achieving the aims of the project. The decisions to focus initially on nomadic women in the Gobi desert, to use a non-formal education approach, and to use DE as the means to achieve the desired ends was a response to the challenges set by the need to meet rural women's needs for information, know-how and skills and having to reach large numbers of learners scattered over vast distances with limited transport and a weak communications infrastructure (Robinson 1999). A non-formal approach usually means that face-to-face learning takes place in settings other than the traditional classroom; with teachers who are not necessarily education professionals, but who may have some other expertise. The decision to use distance teaching rather than face-to-face teaching represented an additional challenge. The project had two main aims:

> (1) to develop national capacity in non-formal education and ODE, and (2) to assist Gobi women to survive the sudden changes in their lives (through providing access to information and knowledge, changing attitudes and developing skills for self-reliance and income-generation).
>
> (Robinson 1999)

A range of formal data collection and research approaches were used as part of the evaluation strategy for the Mongolian initiative. An initial needs analysis identified the most urgent learning needs of the women who were being targeted. A formative evaluation of a five-month-long pilot course was then undertaken in order to investigate the feasibility of the distribution and teaching systems and to identify where improvements were needed. Questionnaires were used to gather feedback, together with field visits and reports. The pilot study having established the feasibility of the project, the main project, involving 15,000 women, was launched. Monitoring activities took place throughout the project, but focused on inspection of activities rather than on collection of data. The formal evaluation took place at the end of the project, with its findings being used to inform the development of the follow-on project.

Evaluation approaches

The CIPP approach

The report of this project not only highlights the urgency of the situation faced by the decision makers in Mongolia, but also details the key features of the socio-economic and geographical context driving the need for an innovative educational programme. The selection and development of a DE response, its implementation and the quality of the outcomes from the project are also detailed. In other words, the key information components of an evaluation approach similar to that known as the CIPP (Context-Input-Process-Product) approach are there.

Context: the national, regional and local socio-economic-political situation in which the project is being introduced

In the example above, the precipitating causes leading to the need for the project were established (the withdrawal of exterior financial and technical support leading to economic and social crises), together with information about key attributes of the target group (high literacy rate and relatively high status and independence of women, equal rights to employment and education).

Input: the financial and human resources invested in the project; its status; and the quality of the planning, the infrastructure, the learning media and the operational, administrative, support and evaluation systems

The range of stakeholders involved in the project (government, UNESCO, Danish government aid, teacher trainers, provincial and district officials and community leaders, local people as instructors, print and radio production groups, producers and technicians, international consultants) were identified, as were their attitudes to and knowledge of non-formal education and of the DE approach used for the project. The lack of knowledge of some of the key stakeholders and their concerns about non-formal basic adult education were identified, and the steps taken to address these problems made explicit. Other inputs, such as planning and co-ordination of materials production and distribution, the learning media – print and radio – and the support systems provided were also included, and the problems experienced identified.

Process: the actual operation of the system including interactions between component parts

Details of the way the system was designed to operate were given, together with an indication of the need for improvement in some of the components of the system as it eventually operated. So, for example, the need to improve co-ordination of schedules for producing and distributing written materials with those for the radio programmes to which they were linked was identified. So was the development of teamwork skills, not only for co-ordinating and scheduling materials production, but also for training and supporting those responsible for the initial development and testing of materials. In particular, the need to define standards for self-study texts, in relation to learner activities, language levels and pre-existing knowledge, was stressed. Student assessment strategies, as well as monitoring and the development of a common data-base, were also identified as areas for development.

Product: the short-term and long-term outcomes emerging from the study including unanticipated outcomes

The report concluded that, certainly in the short term, there was substantial movement towards the stated aims of the project – 'to help nomadic women survive the many rapid changes affecting their lives':

> Skills that seemed lost were revived and improved the quality of life. Income-generating facilities imparted through radio have meant that small crafted objects, camel saddles, cheese and fuel from dung have become part of a wide system of exchange and bartering in the desert.
>
> (Robinson 1997)

At the time the report was written, it was clearly too early to see what the longer-term outcomes would be. Issues arising out of the project included the question of sustainability and finance, with the need to institutionalise non-formal education through staffing and resource allocation identified, together with the parlous nature of the financing, with much being dependent on the goodwill and voluntary efforts of visiting teachers. Certain unanticipated outcomes were also identified. One which was particularly noted was that, although the project was designed for women, the wider family became involved. Men have learned skills as well as the women, and local economic activity is growing. Another outcome was that a decentralised education programme has been shown to be successful in a country accustomed to centralised provision and control.

This case study illustrates well the complexity of setting up a completely new non-formal DE project in a country with no history of either approach. It is also a clear exposition of the contribution which evaluation can make to the recording of the experience of setting up such a project, so that further improvements can be made and future developments can be guided by what has been learned. In particular, although the evaluation approach used was not explicitly labelled, the advantage of using what was in reality a CIPP approach was clear: that is the importance of paying attention to the context in which the project is operating, in order to get a better understanding of factors which may enhance or inhibit the successful introduction and operation of an innovation.

The 'classical' approach

The CIPP approach to evaluation is only one of a number of possible approaches. A more traditional approach to the evaluation of educational programmes is the 'classical' approach, in which student performance is measured through the use of standardised tests. The assumption behind this approach is that the gains from the introduction of a new programme can be explicitly measured, with greater gains being seen as greater success for the project. In other words, the target population are seen as the experimental 'subjects', to whom a 'treatment' is applied, and the 'effect' of that treatment is measured. This 'cause and effect' perception of how social interventions were seen as operating underlay the popularity of this approach in the USA during the 1960s and 1970s. At a time when major educational programmes had to 'prove' their worth to funding bodies, and justify their often considerable costs, classical experimental designs appeared to carry with them the certainty of the traditional scientific method.

This view of educational programmes as an intervention whose effect can be measured through student performance is one which still plays a part in DE provision, although probably more so for higher level education than for basic education. However, there are arguments for using aspects of this approach with some types of basic education programmes. For example, a key experiment was carried out in Poona in India in the late 1950s involving the use of radio forums for non-formal rural education (Rogers et al. 1977). The aim of this initiative was 'to improve the livelihood of the villagers' by creating interest, facilitating learning and increasing village-based economic activity. In each case, a number of villages were selected for 'experimental treatment'. That is, they were given full support and funding for participation in the radio forums project. Control villages were also selected, being given radio receivers but with no participation in the forums. Pre-tests and post-tests were given to participants in the ten-week experiment, and it was claimed, both by the researchers and by the external experts who subsequently assessed the research, that these data provided clear evidence of the success of the radio forum approach. The Indian government subsequently extended the scheme nationwide, with 12,000 village radio forums enrolling a quarter of a million villagers by 1965 (Schramm *et al.* quoted in Rogers *et al.* 1977).

Literacy is another area where simple literacy tests have often been used as 'before' and 'after' measures when new programmes are introduced. The aim is to measure the effect of the initiative (see, for example, World Bank 1979, UNESCO 1990, Skyers 1994). However, while this approach provides clear and explicit data about the literacy levels of those tested, it does have limitations, in that it does not provide any explanation or context for the outcome measures. So, for example, when the national radio forum initiative in India began to experience fluctuations in the numbers of forums, with a clear decline in numbers during the 1960s, other data had to be sought in the attempt to explain the phenomenon. One explanation was that the changes nationally in the levels of transistor radio ownership meant that there was no longer any need for people to gather together to listen to broadcasts. Similarly, the Jamaican Movement for the Advancement of Literacy (JAMAL) was initially hailed as a success over the first fifteen years of its life. Using radio and television, together with non-formal face-to-face provision using voluntary teachers, the illiteracy rate was reduced from over 40 per cent in 1972, when the project started, to 18 per cent in 1987 (Skyers 1994: 171). Subsequently, however, it became apparent that illiteracy was again on the increase, particularly among the 15- to 24-year-olds. The lack of formal evaluation data meant that many fell back on 'common sense' and 'speculation' to explain this state of affairs. Other observers have undertaken a more detailed analysis of statistics related to the national context against which these changes have occurred, and have identified a number of possible explanations which would be worth further investigation. For example, continuing problems in the formal primary school system include attendance levels of only 80 per cent, high drop-out rates, low resources, poorly qualified teachers and over-sized classes (Skyers 1994). Skyers also quotes the Statistical Yearbook of Jamaica as stating that JAMAL 'was established in 1974 to take over the functions of the former National Literacy Board, established in 1972 with the major objectives of not only eliminating literacy from Jamaica, but also of maintaining functional literacy through the prevention of illiteracy by the concept of continuing adult education' (Skyers 1994: 167). Clearly any evaluation of the JAMAL initiative would need to take account of changes in context – that is, within the formal system.

Similar occurrences of initial apparent success, followed by fluctuations in fortune and then decline, have been reported elsewhere and with other types of initiative. For example in Tanzania, correspondence courses for rural community-based co-operatives were introduced in 1964 to help raise the literacy level among co-operative members and particularly among rural members. Starting with around 857 co-operatives, they reached their apogee of 8,970 co-operatives in 1990, thereafter decreasing to 2,525 in 1996 (Donge 1999). In the discussion about the problems of this DE programme, the explanation for the decline is placed primarily on contextual issues: the Tanzanian economic environment, changes in government policies on co-operatives and lack of funds are identified as key features.

While some recognition of the increasing inadequacy of the actual learning materials through 'ageing' is made, the responsibility for this is placed firmly with the lack of funding and the resultant lack of resources to enable updating to take place.

Qualitative approaches

How is an understanding of the very complex and often idiosyncratic distance education initiatives reached? Radically different research approaches are needed in order to achieve understanding of complex structures and behaviours. For this, we turn to qualitative research approaches. Qualitative research has been referred to as 'multi-method in focus, involving an interpretative, naturalistic approach to its subject matter. This means that qualitative researchers study things in their natural settings, attempting to make sense of, or interpret, phenomena in terms of the meanings people bring to them' (Denzin and Lincoln, quoted in Dall'Alba and Hasselgren 1996: 8–9). Such approaches are popular among those evaluators who are particularly concerned with, for example, drawing on or understanding the learner's experience. Researchers in Sweden, Australia and, to a lesser extent, the UK have attempted to achieve a deeper level of insight into the process of learning from the learner's perspective, in order to identify ways of guiding learners in their approach to their studies, and to motivate and support them more appropriately. Much of this work, focusing explicitly on what is called a 'phenomenographic' approach (the investigation of how phenomena appear to people) has been undertaken on learners studying at a higher education level through DE means (see, for example, Morgan 1993, Evans 1994, Roberts 1993). Certainly the greater emphasis on what and how the learners learn, rather than on how much they learn, is aimed at improving the quality of both the teaching and the learning which takes place (Calder 1997).

Different kinds of qualitative approach are widely used in primary level and basic education projects, for a variety of purposes. For example, the Allama Iqbal Open University in Pakistan established what was seen as a 'major programme of non-formal education for rural learners'. Using distance education methods, groups studied subjects like electricity, looking after livestock and child care, using a combination of audio cassettes, flipcharts and handouts. Key features of the project were the careful training of group leaders; the choice of media suitable for both literate and non-literate villagers; thorough action research to determine subjects for study and messages to be carried; and close collaboration with relevant development agencies. In a report on the project, David Warr reports how action research 'plays a vital part in course production, providing information about the needs, capabilities and limitations of rural adults in the area concerned' (Warr 1990). Key to the idea of action research is the group. The group undertakes collaborative decision making and makes a commitment to improvement. In effect, action research is 'a form of *collective* self-reflective enquiry undertaken by participants in social situations in order to improve the rationality and justice of their own social or educational practices, as well as their understanding of those practices and the situations in which those practices are carried out' (Kemmis and McTaggart 1988).

The role of observation in the collection of data is an important one. Jenkins and Perraton made use of existing studies of INADES-formation's work and a detailed analysis of its costs. They also undertook an intensive three-week visit to INADES-formation, commenting that: 'As far as the evidence goes, INADES-formation is effective in teaching farmers and extension agents. We have quoted the evidence of our eyes, and of what INADES-formation students told us about its value for their work' (Jenkins and Perraton 1990: 33). While the report produced by Jenkins and Perraton drew upon studies which had used a range of different data collection techniques, they draw attention to the importance of their own understanding of the project, gained from direct interviews with local farmers participating in the project, and observation of the environment in which learners met 'to fill out the description of the correspondence studies'. As they point out: 'Conclusions based on visits to these and other students are bound to be subjective. Some impressions are, however worth recording' (Jenkins and Perraton 1990: 13).

Benefits and disadvantages of different approaches

Some of the benefits and some of the disadvantages of the different evaluation approaches which can be used will have become apparent already. The need for accountability by decision makers means that projects need to be shown to be credible, of appropriate quality, and (usually) sustainable. The advantages of the classic approach are that quantitative measures can be used to test the effect of different types of intervention, and statistically valid conclusions may then be drawn. Its disadvantages are that when interventions do not take place in the controlled conditions of a laboratory, but in the real world, there is little control over extraneous events, conditions, contexts, methods of operationalising the treatment and so on. Thus there is considerable likelihood of causes other than the one being measured intervening in the experiment. The need also to under-stand the what and the why of what is happening, has already been mentioned. The move to other types of approach, using such methodologies as statistical surveys for monitoring and feedback purposes, is another way of gaining such quantitative information directly from learners. Areas of difficulty with support, with administration, with receipt of materials, with their use, can all be identified. The advantages of the survey approach are that surveys retain strong credibility as objective statistical tools from which generalisations can be drawn. Their weakness is their need for a consistent structured framework and for limiting the range of individual responses, even where one person's interpretation of what is happening may differ substantially from another's. There is also the issue that the survey tradition is one which has grown rapidly in the developed world, while there is as yet little tradition or experience of it in many developing countries.

Basic education which uses open and distance approaches involves the operation of a complex set of social and organisational structures. In addition, different stakeholders will have different perceptions of what is happening. In order to understand the processes which are taking place and the outcomes which are occurring, some form of qualitative method has to be used. However, the weaknesses of such methods are that the conclusions drawn are not necessarily generaliseable or replicable.

The way forward

What then is the approach to adopt? As we have seen, many of those DE projects used to provide basic education which have reported their experiences have adopted a mixed approach. However, it should be noted that the literature on which we have drawn is all in English, and is overwhelmingly authored by people from Western countries who are not resident in the countries in which the projects have been based. This means that, inevitably, there will be a Western perspective in what has been seen as important to report and in the emphases given in the reports. With this *caveat* in mind, a number of points can be made which those thinking of introducing a distance-education-led project might find useful to reflect upon.

There has been considerable speculation about the reasons for fluctuations in the fortunes of initially successful projects – some of it well grounded in reliable data and some less so. Evaluation can be used as a tool to address issues such as this. For example, examining the contexts for these projects shows a common factor in that there is a background of diminishing resources. Inevitably, the funding initially made available for new projects was generous, and subsequent funding became considerably less reliable.

Another explanation, the 'Hawthorne effect', originates from the 'Hawthorne experiments' which took place in the USA during the 1920s and 1930s. These showed the danger of attributing improvements in performance to a particular intervention rather than to the effect of measuring changes resulting from participation in a new activity, *regardless of what that activity was*. In other words, it provided strong research evidence both that the act of measurement itself may have an effect on people's behaviour and that people's membership of informal groups can have an important effect on their behaviour, in that there is pressure on them to conform to group norms. Their performance and attitudes can be influenced more by their need for recognition, and by the desire to belong to informal groups, than by the intervention itself (Burnes 1996: 48). The 'Hawthorne effect', as it has become known, can therefore often be mistaken for a 'real' effect which has been caused by a particular treatment or intervention, rather than the temporary effect of measurement and of conformity to expected group norms.

Thirdly, there are both short-term and long-term outcomes. Particularly with issues such as functional literacy, the same people who are tested as literate on one occasion may well test as illiterate on a later occasion, if they have not been using their literacy skills.

An understanding of the issues which act as barriers to the success of projects, or which facilitate their success, can come only through the use of a wide range of evaluation activities and research methodologies. There are very few references in the literature to the setting up and use of data-bases. With modern information and communication technology, the hardware and the software are now easily available for setting up the type of data-base which allows different data-sets to be entered. Increasingly, qualitative as well as quantitative data can be handled in this way, facilitating the use of a range of systematic and rigorous methods of data collection. Finally, the question of the stage at which evaluation is introduced within a project needs to be addressed. We have seen examples of evaluation activity at every stage of a project – from the initial needs analysis with target groups, through to outcomes assessment. Only by designing evaluation in from the earliest stage in a project can it be used to its full potential, as a tool for planning, programme and materials development, quality assurance and quality control.

An eight step evaluation programme is therefore recommended (Calder 1994):

1   *Identify an area of concern* – Either through formal monitoring or through informal anxieties and concerns.
2   *Decide whether to proceed* – Not all problems are of sufficiently high priority to justify further investigation.
3   *Investigate identified issues* – Appropriate data-collection methodologies need to be identified and used.
4   *Analyse findings* – The amount of effort and detail will depend on the technical competence available and the needs of the decision makers who are using the findings.
5   *Interpret findings* – The more complex the research, the more important is this phase. The same set of analyses can be interpreted in very different ways.
6   *Disseminate findings and recommendations* – The timing of the dissemination, the people who receive the findings and recommendations and their perceived relevance will be crucial in ensuring that the evaluation findings are used.
7   *Review the response to the findings and recommendations and agree any corrective action* – an essential final stage for the evaluation work.
8   *Implement agreed action.*

The question of whether the evaluation should be undertaken internally or by external experts, or by some combination, does depend on the availability of personnel and other resources. Certainly any evaluation has to be authorised and put in place by someone with sufficient authority and seniority to elicit the confidence of those who will be contributing to it. That person acts, in effect, as a guarantor of the use to which the findings will be put. An overall commitment to the raising of the quality of any basic education does carry with it an explicit commitment to plan, implement and use a systematic programme of evaluation.

References

Burnes, B. (1996) *Managing Change: A Strategic Approach to Organisational Dynamics*, London: Pitman Publishing.

Calder, J. (1994) *Programme Evaluation And Quality: A Comprehensive Guide to Setting Up an Evaluation System*, London: Kogan Page.

Calder, J. (1997) *Deliberate Change in Adults and Their Use of Media-Based Learning Material*, 18th ICDE World Conference, Pennsylvania State University, USA: ICDE/Pennsylvania State University.

Dall'Alba, G. and Hasselgren, B. (eds) (1996) *Reflections on Phenomenography: Toward a Methodology*, Goteborg Studies in Educational Sciences 109, Goteborg, Sweden: Acta Universitatis Gothoburgensis.

Donge, L. (1999) *Distance Education for Rural Community Based Organisations: Correspondence Courses for Rural Co-operatives in Tanzania*, Pan Commonwealth Forum on Open Learning, Bandar Seri Begawan, Brunei Darussalam: Commonwealth of Learning.

Evans, T. (1994) *Understanding Learners in Open and Distance Education*, London: Kogan Page.

Jenkins, J. and H. Perraton (1990) 'Institut Africain pour le Développement Economique et Social-Formation, Cameroon', in B. Koul and J. Jenkins (eds) *Distance Education: A Spectrum of Case Studies*, London: Kogan Page.

Kemmis, S. and McTaggart, R. (eds) (1988) *The Action Research Planner*, Australia: Deakin University.

Morgan, A. (1993) *Improving your Students' Learning: Reflections on the Experience of Study*, London: Kogan Page.

Roberts, D. (1993) *Distance Education in the South Pacific*, 11th Biennial Forum of the Australian and South Pacific External Studies Association, Underdale: University of South Australia.

Robinson, B. (1997) *In the Green Desert*, Paris: UNESCO.

Robinson, B. (1999) 'Open and distance learning in the Gobi desert: Non-formal education for nomadic women', in *Distance Education*, 20, 2: 181–204.

Rogers, E. M., Brown, J. R. and Vermilion, M.A. (1977) 'Radio forums: A strategy for rural development', in *Radio for Education and Development: Case Studies*, volume 1, Washington, DC: World Bank.

Skyers, R. (1994) 'A case study of distance education and development', in *Jamaica: A Study of Three Distance Education Organisations and their Contribution to Development*, Milton Keynes: IET, Open University.

UNESCO (1990) *Education for All: Purpose and Context: World Conference on Education for All – Meeting Basic Learning Needs*, Jomtien, Thailand: UNESCO.

Warr, D. (1990) 'Functional Education Project in Rural Areas, Pakistan', in B. Koul and J. Jenkins (eds) *Distance Education: A Spectrum of Case Studies*, London: Kogan Page.

World Bank (1979) *International Study of the Retention of Literacy and Numeracy*, Washington: World Bank Research Programme, Abstracts of Current Studies.

Chapter 7

The use of technologies in basic education

Keith Harry and Abdul Khan

We begin with a brief overview of the range of technologies which are available for distance education today, then look at some examples drawn from distance education at basic education level and/or from developing country experience to illustrate the diversity which exists in practice. After reviewing some of the successes and failures which have been reported in previous years in using technologies specifically for basic education, we identify some commonly encountered problems. Drawing on the examples and case studies documented earlier in the chapter, we conclude by considering some implications of applying technologies.

Regarding terminology, we follow Bates's distinction between media and technology (Bates 1995: 29–31). Bates defines the term 'medium' as describing 'a generic form of communication associated with particular ways of representing knowledge'. He uses the example of television as a medium which may be carried by a number of different 'technologies', such as satellite, cable or video cassette.

In this chapter it is important to bear in mind the fact that the principal teaching medium in the vast majority of distance taught courses is print, particularly in the form of specially prepared correspondence materials. Student support, whether or not using some form of technology, may also be a critical element in retaining students on the course. Technologies are therefore most commonly used to supplement other distance teaching components. They are also very frequently employed for administrative functions.

The current range of technologies in distance education

The recent enormous expansion of distance education (DE) has occurred in parallel with the revolutionary development of information and communication technologies, and has in many instances been inspired by it. Khan (1996: 41) identifies some of the positive educational implications associated with using technologies in DE. He cites:

- the availability of a greater variety of learning resources
- improved opportunities for individualised learning

- the possibility of greater control for students over their learning
- more extensive coverage via technologies and therefore greater access to them
- greater flexibility offered by the wide range of technologies
- the characteristic fall in cost of new technologies as they become established
- a higher degree of interactivity as convergence occurs between old and new technologies
- the emergence of more powerful cognitive tools

What technologies are currently used in DE? Bates's list (Bates 1995: 30), which assumes the pre-1980 development of teacher, book, postal service, radio, film and television, comprises:

- audio cassettes
- video cassettes
- telephone teaching
- computer-based learning
- cable television
- satellite television
- computer-based audio-graphics systems
- viewdata
- teletext
- video discs
- computer-controlled interactive video
- video conferencing
- electronic mail
- computer conferencing
- the Internet
- computer-based multimedia
- remote interactive databases
- virtual reality

Bates has indicated in a personal communication (1999) that the obvious omission from his 1995 list is the Web, although he had included all of its main functions, such as databases and conferencing. In 1995, he also classified one-way and two-way technology applications in distance education, and states in 1999 that he would probably include new technologies such as RealAudio and RealVideo, products which enable real-time lectures on a global basis, as one-way applications.

No institution uses all of the technologies listed by Bates, and many use only one, or else two or more in combination. In practice, the patterns of technology use among institutions across the world are extraordinarily varied, and are commonly influenced by many non-pedagogical factors, such as cost, access and availability, as much as by pedagogical factors. The ways in which different institutions employ any one particular technology are also subject to great variation.

Along with the increase in numbers of types of technology, there has been a marked change in the style of communication which they make possible. Nipper (1989: 63–73) describes the evolution of a 'third generation' of DE, a generation which enables greater communication with learners and among learners. The third generation is based on the emergence of computer-mediated communication, whereas the first generation is identified with correspondence teaching, and the second with multiple media systems combining print with broadcast media, cassettes and a limited use of computers. Taylor has postulated the emergence of a fourth generation, 'the Flexible Learning Model, [which] promises to combine the benefits of high quality interactive multimedia …, with access to an increasingly extensive range of teaching-learning resources and enhanced inter-activity through computer mediated communication … offered by connection to the Internet' (Taylor 1998: 56–7), and Khan and McWilliams (1998) provide an overview of interactive technologies and their possible DE applications.

The task of selecting technologies has become extraordinarily complex. In recognition of this fact, a number of attempts have been made to guide those who have the task of making such a selection. Bates has evolved the ACTIONS model based on considerations of Access, Costs, Teaching functions, Interactivity and user-friendliness, Organisational issues, Novelty, and Speed (Bates 1995: 1–12). He attempts to provide a universally applicable solution to the selection problem. In 1996, a team commissioned by the South African Minister of Education was given a more localised task. This was to develop a policy document on the use of technologies in education and training, sketching out a broad framework for mak-ing decisions about which technologies to use to support education and training in the South African context. In 1998, the South African Institute for Distance Education was commissioned to turn the framework, the Technology-Enhanced Learning Investigation document, into a digital tool. Butcher (1999: 6) describes the tool as comprising four components or steps, each designed as a self-contained unit 'to allow different starting points for people, depending on their needs'.

How are technologies currently employed in DE programmes and projects round the world? The following examples reported in 1999 demonstrate current practice at a variety of points on the spectrum, either in developing countries, or at basic education level, or sometimes both.

Donge's report on the Tanzanian Co-operative College (Donge 1999) provides a stark reminder that government funding for educational programmes at basic education level is a scarce commodity in many countries, and that access to technology to operate DE programmes may also be very limited. Donge describes a well-established programme operated through first-generation DE methods, such as printed correspondence materials, radio, and tutorial support, to promote member education in co-operatives in Tanzania. Although the Co-operative College contributed towards a significant rise in the literacy level amongst the rural population (from 20–30 per cent in the 1960s to 55–90 per cent in the 1980s/1990s), government funding has ceased, with the catastrophic results for the college that new materials have not been created since 1989, radio programmes have ceased, and enrolments are falling.

In complete contrast, it is reported from the South African Institute for Distance Education (SAIDE) that the Departments of Communication and Education in South Africa have commissioned SAIDE to undertake a feasibility study on the establishment of a dedicated educational broadcasting service in South Africa. This will involve more than just a new application of an old technology. SAIDE will explore the potential for the support of education and training in the country through telecommunications networks and information technologies (TAD 1999). This example is a reminder of the critical importance of political support, with the accompanying availability of resources which this implies, for the promotion and sustainability of projects and institutions.

Aguti (1999) describes the potentially revolutionary access to global electronic resources to students in countries whose indigenous knowledge resources, and whose information and communications technology infrastructure, are negligible. She reports on the first year of involvement of Makerere University in the African Virtual University project. For Makerere, this involves Ugandan students studying using satellite television supported by one-way video and two-way audio and via the Internet, and by local staff members. The concept of students receiving programming via satellite television is not a new one – the National Technological University, for example, has been making courses available in this way inside and outside the United States for many years. This application of an older technology is new in Uganda, however. Most of the courses transmitted are north American in origin, but there is some local curriculum development input.

One feature of particularly great potential is student access to electronic library facilities, including access to full-text online journals. This is an extraordinary facility in an institution whose conventional library resources are as depleted as those of Makerere. This particular facility may not be of especially great value to those studying at basic education level, and the African Virtual University project may or not prove successful; the important point which we can draw from this project is that it is now technologically possible for students in any country in the world to have access to the full panoply of electronic knowledge resources. It would, however, be naïve in the extreme to assume that anything approaching universal access will be achieved in the foreseeable future. A vast range of issues relating to the desirability and feasibility of such developments remains to be addressed and resolved.

Granites and Holt (1999) describe the work of the Tanami Network, a seven-site aboriginal-owned video-conferencing network, in creating educational and social opportunities for remote central Australian desert communities. High-speed digital narrow band video-conferencing, using both satellite and integrated services digital network (ISDN), was used to provide access to additional secondary education and community programming. Following the initial project phase, the Tanami Network has become involved in the Outback Digital Network, which is designed to introduce not only video-conferencing but also telephony, electronic banking, telemedicine, radio broadcasting, and Internet/e-mail services. Granites and Holt report problems in obtaining funding for the Tanami Network beyond the initial three-year allocation from the Australian Federal Department of Education, and difficulties in negotiating the introduction of a new technology into the course delivery profile of an existing institution.

Past successes and failures in using technology for basic education

There are a number of long-term successes to report in Australia, Canada and New Zealand, all wealthy countries with extensive and effective telecommunications infrastructures. Here the problem of school-age students not being able to attend conventional schools – because of distance, illness, disability, or other reasons – has been successfully addressed for many years through DE. More recently, provision has also been extended to adults. In Australia and Canada, provision is made at provincial level, whereas a national body, the Correspondence School, is the provider in New Zealand. In all these institutions, the principal teaching medium has always been printed material, sometimes used through the medium of parents in a tutorial role. Emerging technologies have also been employed in a pragmatic way, as in the early use of radio by schools of the air, in the pioneering use of fax in the 1980s, and most recently through the opening of opportunities via information and computer technologies. Recent developments are described in the next section.

Evaluative accounts of individual distance-taught programmes and projects are hard to come by, but there are several in the area of basic education. The first example is from Tanzania, a country possessing relatively few resources and relatively poorly developed infrastructure. The national radio campaigns of Tanzania have been most extensively written up by Hall and Dodds (1974). The best documented is probably the 1973 health education campaign, *Mtu Ni Afya*, which reached almost 2 million people. This was the first mass campaign in Tanzania, building on the experience of earlier, smaller campaigns associated with the 1970 election and the 1971 tenth anniversary of independence. The campaign, organised through the University College of Dar-es-Salaam Institute of Adult Education and the Co-operative Education Centre, Moshi, was based on radio broadcasts to groups, followed by discussions based on two specially prepared books and by group health-related actions. There were problems associated with the campaign – particularly with the size of groups, the shortage of textbooks and group leaders' manuals, and with a shortage of tools with which to undertake the actions – but in general the campaign was regarded as a success.

As the result of a European Commission-funded project, the work of Radio ECCA has been documented in English as well as in Spanish (Kaye and Harry 1982). The Jesuit-funded institution has been remarkably successful in providing basic education in the Canary Islands and to a lesser extent in mainland Spain, and has also extended its activities into Latin America, where there is a long history of radiophonic schools, often operating at basic education level. ECCA's web site confirms that the instructional system has not undergone significant changes over the last twenty years, even though new technologies such as audio and video cassettes are now used, along with computer software. Radio transmissions are followed by students in their own homes and are closely linked to specially prepared printed materials. The third component is regular face-to-face meetings with tutors. Students have traditionally been mainly adults with limited education from conventional schools. ECCA offers both formal and non-formal courses.

Documentation of failures is extremely scarce in the literature of distance education, but the demise of the Programme for Educational Television in the Côte d'Ivoire has been reported by Koné and Jenkins (1990). It is perhaps unfair to ascribe the word 'failure' to the project, since it appears to have been relatively successful when judged by educational outcomes. Nevertheless, the project foundered, as did a number of other educational television initiatives during the 1970s. The venture was particularly remarkable because it was the largest and most ambitious of all such projects. Television was introduced in order to reform education in a newly independent country where conventional provision was perceived to be failing, where in 1960 only 30 per cent of the school-age population were in school, there was no university, and 90 per cent of adults were illiterate. Teaching was undertaken via television instead of face-to-face by live teachers. The schooling and literacy situations were significantly improved by the time the programme ceased in 1981, but the educational television programme closed in the face of considerable criticism. Koné ascribes its closure principally to a very high level of costs, combined with undue control exercised by parties outside the Côte d'Ivoire. Jenkins expresses an interest in the 'process of failure' (Koné and Jenkins 1990: 92), points out that there is little comment in the Koné report on educational methods and the quality of the teaching, and concludes that there is no evidence to show that in principle this kind of television teaching could not work. It is indicative of the continuing interest in this project and the issues arising from it that a new study is currently in preparation (Ba and Potashnik, in press).

Current practice in basic education

The most extensive examples of current practice in DE at basic education level are the institutions in Australia, Canada and New Zealand which provide formal education for school-age students and adults. Traditionally, these institutions, formerly known as correspondence schools, and now more usually designated distance learning centres, have provided printed materials, mediated in the case of very young students by parents, usually backed up with an infrequent but regular residential period, together with use of radio or telephone. These methods are still employed, but new technologies have also been embraced in order to provide the most effective possible service to students.

In Australia, for example, the Schools of Isolated and Distance Education (SIDE) of the Western Australia Ministry of Education operate three schools – Preparatory School (P–5), Middle School (6–10), and Post Compulsory School (11–12) – as well as five schools of the air. Adults are eligible to enrol, but are not offered the full range of services available to school-age students. Students are assigned individual subject teachers, are encouraged to telephone or visit teachers; will receive course materials produced by SIDE; can borrow from a large library of books and audio-visual materials; may attend camps and seminars held during the year; may visit Perth for specialised help from teachers for one or two weeks; will be visited at home by teachers; may be able to access one of a range of telematics courses; and may receive television programming broadcast or narrowcast from the Leederville Interactive Centre studio.

One of the Canadian institutions providing basic education at a distance, the Alberta Distance Learning Centre, founded in 1923, describes itself as 'a world leader in distance education' (http://www.adlc.ab.ca/home/500/interest.htm/). In addition to the types of traditional services described above, the centre has provided the opportunity for students to submit assignments over the Internet since 1995, and from 1996 has operated a virtual school. Courses are available to school-age and adult students. But the Alberta Distance Learning Centre also offers a proactive service to individual and institutional users; it provides the opportunity not only to take courses from the school curriculum, but also to supplement the curriculum with alternative courses, an option made more feasible by the new technologies.

In his foreword to a Commonwealth of Learning study of virtual education (Farrell 1999: ix), Professor Gajaraj Dhanarajan, President of COL, indicates that the study is 'but a snapshot of the state of virtual education at a given point in time'. The snapshot is useful because it provides an indication of the proportion of virtual education which is provided at kindergarten to year 12 levels, and at the same time provides regional surveys so that it is possible to compare the volume of provision from region to region. Not surprisingly, given the North American preoccupation with technology applications, examples are cited in both Canada and the United States of initiatives at basic education level (Farrell 1999: 15–16, 35–37).

The Canadian examples include the Alberta Distance Learning Centre and the Electronic Distributive Education Network Project, and in the United States the Star Schools Project, the Universal Service Fund, and the California Distant Learning Program, each of which is considered a leading-edge programme 'because of the infrastructure they are putting in place or the potential impact they will have on the way elementary and secondary education is offered in the 21st century' (Farrell 1999: 36). Respectively, the US programmes involve multimedia projects, which make outstanding teachers of specified subjects accessible to students who previously had no opportunity to study these subjects, through a variety of means, including live and interactive teleconferences; schools' heavily discounted access to telecommunications services, internal connections, and the Internet; and three online curricula – a holistic curriculum, a multi-sensory curriculum, and a traditional academic curriculum.

Only two projects are reported in Africa at basic education level. They comprise a schools Internet connectivity initiative in South Africa (where the figure is quoted of 1,000 schools out of 28,000 connected to the Internet) and a private school project, also in South Africa. The coverage of Asia and of other regions in the survey throws up few examples of specific projects at basic education level. The African example of a project involving the use of computers in schools is just one of many instances, most of which are to be found in wealthier countries, where computers are used in schools at basic education level. Most, though, are not used in DE.

Virtual education and the extensive use of information and communication technologies may not be a realistic option in developing countries at present, but there are examples of older technologies being used effectively. Robinson has written about the Gobi Women's Project (1992–6) in Mongolia, which aimed to provide opportunities to 16,000 nomadic women in functional literacy, health education, and income-generating skills, and its successor, the Surch Amidarya or Learning for Life project (1996–2000). The latter project, based upon printed materials and radio, with strong local support, is funded largely by Danish government aid and by the Mongolian government, and is implemented by UNESCO. The first phase concentrated on assisting unemployed and marginalised youth in urban centres. In connection with the Gobi Women's Project, Robinson identifies radio, with appropriate support, and in particular Interactive Radio Instruction (IRI), as 'at present the medium with the most potential for educational development in Mongolia' (1995: 11). A combination of printed materials and radio are also being used in the current project. Robinson also stresses the importance in the project of face-to-face support to both students and tutors (Berryman and Robinson 1999). In subsequent personal communications, she has described the extensive power cuts and general communications problems which affect Mongolian society and which seriously affect the functioning of technologies. The situation in Mongolia has parallels across the developing world.

An IRI programme was set up in 1992 in South Africa by the Open Learning Systems Educational Trust (OLSET), a non-governmental organisation, with funds from USAID and technical support from LearnTech. The programme's purpose is to provide programmes for teaching and for support for teachers in underresourced black primary schools. More than 500,000 grade 1, 2 and 3 black South African students in 3,300 schools currently study through IRI, and around 12,000 teachers also benefit (Edirisingha 1999). OLSET's work has been extensively evaluated from the early years, and is reckoned to have functioned effectively. It began life in a favourable socio-economic climate, but given its reliance on donor funds and its reported difficulty in maintaining sufficient access to broadcasting time, it remains to be seen whether this IRI programme can continue in the longer term.

By contrast, Matshazi (1999) describes the South African University of Fort Hare Adult Basic Education Project, which began in 1992 with funding from the European Commission through the Kagiso Trust, and has since become absorbed into the university as its extension programme. The project's approach was to research the community's basic educational needs and to develop and test a DE methodology for producing basic education courses for adults. Four study areas were identified – school equivalency education, trade and craft skills training, family and community education, and literacy and numeracy. The methodology relied heavily on printed materials and on group study directed by low-cost technologies comprising audio cassette programmes and flipchart illustrations.

All of the above examples have been extracted from the context in which they operate, and are in some instances only exemplars of much wider coverage within individual countries. This section concludes with an overview of past and current experiments in India using media and technologies for basic education.

Media have the potential to cover a large geographical area and to offer equality of opportunity in education. In India, the following experiments, where media and technology are used in basic education, are being successfully conducted. They are classified under two categories. First are media used for improving the quality of education for primary school children, and second, media used to upgrade the skills of primary school teachers.

For students

- Taleem Research Foundation has proposed to start an educational channel and integrate it into the conventional school system. The proposal is for Basic Education Support Television (BEST). The aim is to impart basic education at primary school level through television. The focus is on school-going children of classes 1 to 5 in the age group 5–10 years. The programmes will be based on the syllabi of classes 1 to 5, and the language will be Hindi. In the first phase there will be television programmes, which will be supported by BEST video series and BEST activity books. Compact discs (CDs) and interactive classrooms will be considered later. Ten thousand primary schools in selected districts in five Hindi-speaking states (Uttar Pradesh, Madhya Pradesh, Himachal Pradesh, Rajasthan and Bihar) will be covered (Agarwal 2000).

- Satellite Instructional Television (SITE) is a major experiment in the use of television for primary education, which began in 1975. Programmes were telecast for children in the age group 5–12 years studying in the grades 1–5 in the rural schools of Andhra Pradesh, Bihar, Karnataka, Madhya Pradesh, Orissa and Rajasthan. Research findings showed that children exposed to SITE programmes were more inquisitive during classroom teaching in general science.

Enrichment School Telecasts are telecasts for school children of 5–11 years of age. These programmes, which have educational content with specific learning objectives but are not linked with a specific syllabus, are received in all areas covered under satellite direct telecast by Indian National Satellite (INSAT) and are re-broadcast by a number of television transmitters. Exclusive School Telecasts are programmes which are transmitted for class-room instruction. They are telecast in the morning and are repeated in the afternoon in Mumbai, Delhi and Chennai. The lessons are based on textbook lessons and are meant for secondary school children (Agarwal *et al.* 1999).

- The Department of Women and Child Development, the National Centre for Educational Research and Training (NCERT) and All-India Radio launched the Children Enrichment Experiment Radio in 1992 for pre-school children to attempt to reduce the dropout rate and to enrich educational quality.

- The National Policy of Education 1986 and Programme of Action 1986 spelt out actions needed in the area of communication technology. The government introduced a centrally sponsored scheme, namely educational technology (ET), for qualitative improvement in elementary education. The scheme had two major dimensions: first, strengthening the two ET institutes, namely the Central Institute for Educational Technology (CIET) and the State Institutes for Educational Technology, and, second, the provision of colour television sets and radio/cassette players. Under this scheme, radio/cassette players and colour television sets have been given to primary schools. So far, 37,129 schools have been provided with television sets, and 256,566 schools have been provided with radio/cassette players. The problem in this scheme is in its implementation.

- The Indian government provided schools all over the country with BBC microcomputers under the Computer Literacy and Studies in Schools (CLASS) project. Through this project in 1984–5, 250 schools were provided with BBC microcomputers. In 1985–6, 500 schools were covered and another 500 schools were supplied in 1986–7. There are many arguments for and against the CLASS project, but at least a beginning was made to bring computer awareness to students, teachers and the parents.

- Radio has been recognised as a potential medium for language teaching. There was an experimental project on teaching first language (Hindi) with the help of radio undertaken by CIET and implemented in 480 primary schools located in rural areas of the district of Ajmer and Jaipur in Rajasthan. The experiment was conducted during 1976–80. It was designed to improve the listening skills and language development of young learners.

- The Central Institute of Indian Languages, Mysore, and the Central Institute of English and Foreign Languages have already produced language-teaching programmes for children and are experimenting with video.

- The Child Media Lab has existed at NCERT for almost a decade. It has evolved childrens' literature, educational toys and games. It has also made radio programmes for children, but has not entered into television production.
- The centrally sponsored scheme Operation Black Board was primarily an effort to standardise a minimum acceptable level of infrastructure – two all-weather rooms, two teachers, and certain instructional aids and materials in primary schools.
- In 1961, syllabus-based educational television programmes were started. A Television Branch was created by the Directorate of Education, Delhi. At present, lessons are telecast for classes 6–10 in maths, English and science. These programmes are telecast in Mumbai, Delhi and Chennai.

For teachers

- Indira Gandhi National Open University (IGNOU)'s Distance Education Programme–District Primary Education Programme focuses on total capacity building, teacher upgrading, instructional material, restructuring of pedagogy, etc. The programmes are delivered through interactive television.
  Primary school teachers were given training in science education during SITE. At present, a programme is telecast every Saturday for primary school teachers in all INSAT areas (Agarwal et al. 1999). Programmes are produced by CIET. The aim is to improve teachers' teaching ability. There are no studies to indicate the effectiveness of such programmes.
- UNICEF has introduced short duration 'spots' which are addressed to adults (parents), to protect their children from childhood disabilities through preventive means. There is, for example, a monthly programme known as *Palavi*, produced by Mumbai Doordarshan Kendra. Extensive research was conducted on the problems faced by children in schools (Agarwal et al. 1999).
- The Special Orientation Programme for Primary Teachers is a centrally sponsored scheme for in-service education of primary teachers. NCERT is responsible for its planning, programming, organisation, conduct and monitoring, and also academic output. Under this scheme, two specific experiments have been conducted using technology. In Karnataka, about 1,000 teachers were called into training centres established by the Department of Personnel and Administration; dish antennae were used for receiving signals for the Training and Development Communication channel. The lessons were delivered by experts in Kannada from the studios of IGNOU. This approach was repeated in July 1996 to train 1,500 primary school teachers in Madhya Pradesh.
- In the early 1990s, the Project on Radio Education for Adult Literacy was initiated under the Literacy Mission. Radio was used to supplement textbooks for rural adult women learners in Bihar, Madhya Pradesh, Rajasthan and Uttar Pradesh.
- The use of the radio broadcasting network All India Radio for basic education began in the mid-1960s with farmer training and functional literacy pro-

grammes in 144 districts. Separate farm and home units were constituted in forty-six broadcasting stations, which provided a specialised farm broadcasting service every day for forty to sixty minutes. On average, seven of these units conducted Farm Schools on the air.

Problems encountered in relation to technology

A broad issue which is particularly relevant to students at basic education level is that of gender inequalities in access to and use of information and communication technologies. In a paper discussing some of the current debates about the potential of the Internet as a liberatory tool for women, Kirkup concludes that 'For those of us concerned with women's education, we would be wise to begin with the premise that the new technologies are gendered, and gendered to the disadvantage of women' (1999: 17). Her illustrations of inequalities relate specifically to higher education students, but there seems to be every reason to believe that her conclusions are equally, if not more, applicable to women studying at basic education level, and also to other technologies in addition to information and communication technologies.

A range of technology-associated problems can be identified which affect distance education regardless of the level at which it is being offered, although programmes and projects operating at basic education level may be more susceptible or vulnerable than programmes and projects at other levels, for reasons which are enumerated below and which draw on Khan (1996).

Lack of access   One of the most frequently quoted advantages of DE is its ability to provide access to educational opportunities which would be unavailable via conventional means. There are a number of access problems, however, which militate against this potential advantage, and they may particularly affect students at basic education level. At a time when the benefits of information and communication technologies are being strongly promoted, the most obvious such problem is not having Internet access, or not possessing a computer. Similar problems, i.e., lack of access to television, radio, or other technologies – or the absence of power sources to operate them – have always affected a proportion of students or potential students. Access in a different sense may also present problems, particularly to students at basic education level; even if the student has access to the necessary hardware and communications links at home, at work, or at some public access point, he or she may lack the necessary skills to use them.

Sustainability   Khan (1996) points out that the capital cost of acquiring technology is only one component in the total costs. Production costs for television programmes, for computer software, and for other technologies, may be many times more expensive than the original capital cost of acquiring hardware, a factor which is often overlooked by donor agencies.

Scarce financial resources   Another frequently quoted advantage of DE is its relative cheapness in comparison to other means of providing education and training. This may well apply in many cases, but the fact remains that start-up costs of DE programmes and projects can be high, particularly if a form of technology is used for instructional purposes. Institutions with scarce financial resources need to be aware of this factor.

Attitude towards technology   Khan (1996: 44) describes the polarised attitudes towards DE which can hinder the acceptance of technology application in institutions. At the one extreme are those who are fanatically supportive of technologies and their universal application, and at the other extreme are those who regard media as simply a distraction from serious academic pursuits. Another facet of this problem is the perception that older technologies, regardless of their effectiveness in a given situation, are intrinsically less desirable than the latest technologies.

Lack of infrastructure   Inadequate infrastructure to support a DE system may be a national, an institutional, or an individual problem. The national radio or television services may, for example, only reach particular parts of the country, or the postal service may be very slow and inefficient.

Technology-centred approach   Many distance education institutions and programmes show evidence of technology-driven rather than learner-driven approaches. Too little care has been taken in acquiring technology which is appropriate for the task in hand, and the need for software to drive the technology is forgotten.

Lack of technological capability in an organisation   The introduction of a new technology into an institution will be seriously hampered until the institution's staff are very familiar with application of the technology. There will also be problems if a quick and effective troubleshooting and maintenance service is not in place.

Lack of trained human resources   Appropriately trained individuals are essential in an institution if technology is to be effectively introduced and used for teaching or for administrative purposes.

Dependence on donors   Institutions dependent on donors may find themselves in a weak position in a number of ways – for example, when it comes to specifying the technology they wish to introduce, and in relation to maintaining and upgrading equipment. Continuation of donor support is also inevitably a critical factor.

In the examples quoted above in previous sections, we have indicated that there are many instances where the use of one or more technologies can significantly enhance the quality of teaching at a distance. We have also described more than one example of unsuccessful use of technology. Authors are not much given to writing about the failures they have experienced and the difficulties they have encountered, so in this section we have identified a number of potential pitfalls in using technologies. Some of these relate to availability, in terms of both physical access and financial and infrastructural resources, to individual technologies or media, at national, insitutional and individual levels. Others have to do with the technology-related skills possessed by the teaching institution and the students. Yet others are linked with existing attitudes towards technologies. We hope that we have illustrated the point that pedagogical factors are by no means the only determinants of the application of particular technologies in particular contexts.

Implications of applications of technology and conclusions and pointers to the future

We have seen that information and communication technologies can already technically operate in any country in the world, although in practice in many countries only some, privileged, institutions will be equipped and resourced to use the new technologies extensively; most will not. There is frequently a yawning gap between the vision and the reality. Nevertheless, we have seen that in institutions in better resourced countries, such as Australia, Canada and New Zealand, new technologies are used widely in basic-education-level distance teaching. They have been adapted in a pragmatic way by established institutions to provide the best possible means of instruction and support for students.

We have also encountered a number of examples of successful basic education projects and programmes in which older technologies have been successfully employed. Several have, for example, used radio in one form or another for teaching. Radio as a medium has undergone a number of transformations on different dimensions, from the development of interactive radio instruction and digital radio to the invention of the clockwork radio. The use of radio obviously does not of itself guarantee success, as we have also seen, but the medium does seem to lend itself well to distance teaching at the basic level. It may be that a significant contributory factor to this success, in addition to its accessibility to individual students, has been the existence of a great deal of experience and expertise in the use of teaching by radio, which is not matched in relation to the newer technologies.

In several of the examples quoted above, the continuance or cessation of a project or programme has appeared to be dependent not just on successful exploitation of technologies, but also on factors such as the political and financial support received from the home institution or government or from the donor agency. The context in which the project is set up is critically important. Another potentially critical factor is the level of student support which is offered in addition to the teaching materials provided through print and other media. The influence of the tutor may be decisive in providing the motivation for the student to remain on the course.

It is inevitable that new technologies will continue to emerge in the coming years and will be sought after for use in DE. The experience of the last twenty years points to the likelihood that the fashion of the day will look upon older technologies as less desirable and less acceptable simply because they are older. The potential effectiveness of older technologies can easily be forgotten in the waves of publicity and advertising which new technologies receive. It is especially important in basic education that the technologies employed should be as accessible as possible and should match as closely as possible the needs of the student.

References

Agarwal, B. (2000) 'Proposal for basic education support television', Paper to be presented at the 30th Annual Conference on Educational Technology, All India Association for Educational Technology, 24–26 February, Coimbatore.

Agarwal, B., Kamik, K., Lal, C. and Vishwanath, K. (1999) *Children's Television in India: A Situational Analysis*, New Delhi: Concept Publishing Company.

Aguti, J. (1999) 'One year of Virtual University experience at Makerere University in Uganda: a case study', paper presented to the Commonwealth Pan-Commonwealth Forum on Open Learning, Brunei, March. Available HTTP: *http://www.col.org/forum/PCFpapers/aguti1.pdf/*

Ba, H. and Potashnik, M. (in press) *The Côte d'Ivoire Educational Television Project: Revisited 20 Years Later*, Draft report, World Bank.

Bates, A. (1995) *Technology, Open Learning and Distance Education*, London: Routledge.

Bates, A. (1999) Personal communication.

Berryman, L. and Robinson, B. (1999) 'Preparing unemployed youth for work in a market economy: The case of Mongolia', Paper presented at the Twentieth World Conference of the International Council for Distance Education, Vienna, Austria.

Butcher, N. (1999) 'A technology-enhanced learning decision making framework for South Africa', in *SAIDE Open Learning Through Distance Education*, 5: 6–8.

Donge, L. (1999) 'Distance education for rural community-based organizations: correspondence courses for rural co-operatives in Tanzania', Paper presented to the Commonwealth of Learning Pan-Commonwealth Forum on Open Learning, Brunei, March. Available HTTP: *http://www.col.org/forum/PCFpapers/donge.pdf/*

Edirisingha, P. (1999) Personal communication.

Farrell, G. (ed.) (1999) *The Development of Virtual Education: A Global Perspective: A Study of Current Trends in the Virtual Delivery of Education*, Vancouver: Commonwealth of Learning. Available HTTP: *http://www.col.org/virtualed/index.htm/*

Granites, R. and Holt, P. (1999) 'The Tanami Network: Placing the technology in the hands of the remote Central Australian desert communities', Paper presented to the Commonwealth of Learning Pan-Commonwealth Forum on Open Learning, Brunei, March. Available HTTP: *http://www.col.org/forum/PCFpapers/granites/pdf/*

Hall, B. and Dodds, T. (1974) *Voices for Development: The Tanzanian National Radio Study Campaigns*, Cambridge: International Extension College.

Kaye, A. and Harry, K. (eds) (1982) *Using the Media for Adult Basic Education*, London: Croom Helm.

Khan, A. (1996) 'Utilization of communication technologies for distance education', in K. Murali Manohar (ed.) *Distance Education Theory and Practice: Media and Communication Technology*, Hyderabad: Open Learning Society, Prof. G. Ram Reddy Memorial Endowment Committee, and Indian Distance Education Association.

Khan, A. and McWilliams, P. (1998) 'Application of interactive technologies in open and distance learning', in *Indian Journal of Open Learning*, 1: 7–22.

Kirkup, G. (1999) 'The potential of the Internet for women's education', in M. Hauff, G. Kirkup and C. von Prümmer (eds) *Frauen und neue Medien: Nutzen des Internets am Arbeitsplatz Hochschule und im Studium*, Hagen: FernUniversität.

Koné, H. and Jenkins, J. (1990) 'The Programme for Educational Television in the Ivory Coast', in *Educational Media International*, 27, 2: 86–93.

Matshazi, M. (1999) 'Open learning for adults with little or no formal education in Zimbabwe', Paper presented at the Commonwealth of Learning Pan-Commonwealth Forum on Open Learning, Brunei, March. Available HTTP: *http://www.col.org/forum/PCFpapers/matshazi.pdf/*

Nipper, S. (1989) 'Third generation distance learning and computer conferencing', in R. Mason and A. Kaye (eds) *Mindweave: Communication, Computers and Distance Education*, Oxford: Pergamon Press. Available HTTP: *http://www-icdl.open.ac.uk/mindweave/chap5.html/*

Robinson, B. (1995) 'Mongolia in transition: a role for distance education?' in *Open Learning*, 3, 3: 3–15.

Robinson, B. (1999) Personal communication.

TAD (1999) *Information Update 1*, October, Telematics for African Development Consortium.

Taylor, J. (1998) 'Flexible delivery: Globalization of lifelong learning', *Indian Journal of Lifelong Learning*, 7, 1: 55–65.

Chapter 8

Finance, costs and economics

François Orivel

It is sometimes argued that new information and communication technologies will become a powerful tool for eradicating illiteracy in the world more rapidly and more efficiently than would have been the case with traditional approaches. Such a view is highly disputable, because it ignores the fact that budgetary constraints in the financing of education are increasingly severe. Several authors have developed a theory according to which there exists a world system of education, meaning a converging trend of educational systems worldwide, and this trend is supposed to have a kind of autonomy with respect to economic development and economic disparities among countries. This theory is not supported by recent evidence, as shown by education indicators. The economic gap between rich and poor countries is increasing, as well as the gap in access to education. This new trend is closely linked to shortages of resources in the least advanced countries, and new technologies will not bring any easing in this resource constraint. Quite the opposite, for while the introduction of new technologies will have a limited impact on education budgets of developed countries (1 per cent to 5 per cent at the most), its impact on the education budgets of poor countries would be huge. For the first time in the history of education systems, the price of an educational input is determined not in accordance with the local purchasing power, but by world standards which apply in a similar way to rich and poor countries. As a consequence, the least advanced countries have a simple choice to make: either they introduce new technologies in their schools at the expense of expanding school opportunities to currently excluded children, or they concentrate their limited resources on educational expansion, and thus renounce the chance to develop new technologies in their school systems. As long as gross domestic product (GDP) per capita remains highly unequal from one country to another, the capacity of new technologies to reduce the education gap will not constitute a viable option.

The world system of education theory

Long before the introduction of 'economic globalisation', several authors developed the thesis of a world system of education. In particular, Meyer *et al.* (1977), or more recently Meyer (1999), have shown that the model of mass education initiated in developed countries is spreading in less developed countries significantly earlier than the achievement of the same level of economic development. This phenomenon was less true in the eighteenth and nineteenth centuries, when industry expanded in western Europe and north America. During this first phase of economic growth, education was led by economic expansion, both because the job market wanted more and more qualified workers, and because higher incomes eased the economic constraint, allowing the allocation of more resources for educational development. Of course, economic wealth was not the only cause of education expansion. For example, the Christian reform, namely the move from Roman Catholicism to Protestantism, was also a key element in spreading literacy quite early in some north European countries (believers were expected to be able to read the Bible). But, quite clearly, mass education followed rather than preceded economic expansion during this period.

After the Second World War, this sequence was reversed. Education started to develop in countries where economic development was still at a standstill. Education was promoted as a 'right', prescribed in the Declaration of Human Rights. UNESCO was created, becoming a world centre where international education authorities met in general assemblies, disseminating educational ideas and models. An international standard classification of education (ISCED) was adopted, facilitating the harmonisation of education systems across countries. In the late 1950s and early 1960s, a new economic theory, human capital theory, promoted the idea that education was a powerful factor of economic development. Contrary to previous economic orthodoxy, education should no longer be considered as consumption, but as an investment, generating flows of additional income and economic wealth during the whole life of educated individuals. As a consequence, in order to promote economic development, education was a desirable prerequisite, and many countries became convinced that education should expand at an accelerated rate for subsequent economic expansion.

In addition, several international conferences adopted common declarations for achieving the objective of universal access to education services as early as possible. The Addis Ababa conference held in the early 1960s fixed a precise agenda for attaining this objective by 1980. When 1980 passed, realisation of the objective was still far away in the future, and the Jomtien Conference in 1990 reiterated it with a new deadline, the year 2000. Now the new millennium has arrived, and universal access to basic education is still a remote objective in many poor countries. Today, the same group of international development agencies has set new deadlines, such as gender equality for the year 2005 and universal access to basic education for 2015, but, as some researchers have already claimed (see for instance Watkins 1999), such objectives remain unrealistic in a number of countries.

During the three decades that followed the Second World War, the general trend, with respect to educational development, could be characterised as a 'converging' trend. Less developed countries were progressively closing the gap with developed countries. Between 1960 and 1980, net schooling ratios for 6- to 11-year-old children, close to one hundred in the developed world, increased dramatically in the developing one, from 58 to 83 per cent in Latin America, from 54 to 70 per cent in Asia, and from 30 to 59 per cent in Africa – a near doubling of the ratio in the last case. Furthermore, access to secondary and tertiary education, which arrived several decades after the achievement of universal primary education in developed countries, started to grow at the same time. Unlike the dominant pattern seen in developed countries, there was no pause between the development of primary education and that of secondary. In France, for instance, primary education became general in the 1880s, while secondary education started to move towards mass education only in the 1950s, seventy years later.

At the same time, education budgets were expanding at an even faster rate. The share of GNP allocated to the sector from public sources increased from less than 2 per cent in 1950 to about 5 per cent in 1975. Here again, we observe a significant difference from the earlier Western model: during the first industrial revolution in Europe, education expenditure had a very low share of GNP, no more than about 1 per cent. In fact, public involvement in the early stages of education development was extremely limited. The bulk of education expenditure was born by families and churches. This is another important contrast with the current situation of the least developed countries, in which it is more difficult to generate private finance for educational development. There are two reasons for this change. First, least developed countries are poorer now, in absolute terms, than were the industrial countries in the nineteenth century, when universal access to primary schooling was achieved. Second, least developed countries have been exposed to new models of education provision, unlike their predecessors. The model of publicly financed education is predominant, and largely viewed as a better approach to educational finance than family- or church-based models.

Our purpose, in the following sections, is threefold: to show, first, that the world system theory for education has lost a great deal of its pertinence in the recent past, due to a serious tightening of economic constraints; second, that besides the budgetary constraint the major cause of the gap in educational opportunities among countries is linked to demographic structure; and third, that it is unlikely that new information and communication technologies (NICT) will provide a feasible and sustainable solution, in general, to this problem in least developed countries.

Why the world system theory is outdated

The world system theory is based firstly on the assumption that education systems worldwide are converging more rapidly than economies. Actually, the opposite trend is operating, for both education and economies. The gap between the developed and the least developed countries is growing, in spite of the fact that the group of developing countries, taken as a whole, is growing more rapidly than

Table 8.1 Average GNP per capita in developed and least developed countries

	Unit: current US $			
	1979	1983	1992	1995
Least developed countries[a]	240	200	370	290
Industrial market economies	9,440	11,060	22,160	24,930
Ratio developed:least developed	39	55	60	86

Sources: World Bank (1981, 1985, 1994, and 1997)

Note

a   Excluding India and China.

the group of developed countries. This is because within the developing world, certain countries are progressing rapidly while others are stagnating. And it is the gap between the richest and the poorest countries which is increasing.

As shown in table 8.1, the wealth gap between developed and least developed countries[1] has increased significantly over the past two decades, from a ratio of 1 to 39 to a ratio of 1 to 86. This is an enormous gap, and it is not without consequences for the supposed 'converging' process of educational systems.

In order to measure educational development, one needs education indicators which have the same kind of pertinence as GNP per capita has for measuring economic performance. The most common indicators are participation rates, calculated by level of education, gross or net. But rates of schooling have a drawback: one has to deal with a set of three (primary, secondary and tertiary), which makes comparative exercises more complex. A new synthetic indicator has recently been developed, which is quite convenient for the purpose of this chapter, namely the expected number of years of education a five-year-old child will receive. Table 8.2 presents values of this indicator for a number of geographical areas, including developed and least developed countries, and shows the evolution of the indicator for the last decade.

Two comments are suggested by these data. First, they show that the variability of the indicator between regions is quite large, a ratio of almost 1 to 3 when comparing developed and least developed countries (14.77 years in the case of developed countries, 4.93 years in the case of least developed ones). Second, they indicate that during the last decade, the gap between well-endowed countries and others has not narrowed, but widened. The largest gain has benefited the children of developed countries (plus 1.78 years of expected schooling), while least developed countries gained only 0.39 years. Transition countries, which before the collapse of the former Soviet Union used to be close to developed countries, have seen the value of the indicator declining by 0.66 years, creating a gap of almost two years if one adds the gains of the latter group. Apart from developed countries, there have been important gains for both Chinese and Indian children. Undoubtedly, the movement towards a unified world system of education has been significantly affected, to say the least, during the recent period.

Table 8.2 Expected number of years of education at age five

	1985	1995	Difference
Transition countries[a]	13.02	12.36	− 0.66
Developed countries	12.99	14.77	1.78
Least developed countries	4.54	4.93	0.39
Sub-Saharan Africa	5.41	5.54	0.12
Arab states	7.58	8.45	0.87
Latin America and Caribbean	9.40	10.17	0.77
East Asia and Oceania	9.01	10.39	1.38
of which China	9.06	10.79	1.73
South Asia	6.85	8.09	1.24
of which India	7.68	8.68	1.00

Source: Author's estimates, from UNESCO data

Note

a   Transition countries refers to a group of countries that used to have centrally planned economies until the breakdown of the former Soviet Union (FSU). It is a group that includes 15 republics previously belonging to the FSU, and 12 central and eastern European countries associated with the FSU.

On the other hand, there is an indicator which can be characterised by a converging pattern, and that is precisely the budgetary constraint. The most widespread indicator by which economists assess the level of resources allocated to education in a country is the percentage of GNP dedicated to the sector. Ideally, this indicator should include both public and private resources, but for lack of appropriate information, it is usually limited to public resources. This limitation does not raise a major issue, insofar as the bulk of education expenditure, about 85 per cent, is borne by public authorities, and ultimately by taxpayers. We saw above that from 1950 to 1975 this indicator significantly increased, from 2 to 5 per cent, allowing a rapid development of educational systems worldwide. But after 1975, this trend stabilised, and the only changes were precisely a movement towards a greater convergence: countries significantly below the 5-per-cent threshold tended to become closer, while those which went beyond the threshold tended to come back to a lower level of public expenditure (see table 8.3).[2]

Transition countries have reduced their share from 7.5 per cent in 1990 to 5.2 per cent in 1995. It is probably even lower currently, because the economic crisis has continued since 1995. Arab states have also reduced their share from 5.8 per cent to 5.2 per cent, because oil revenues have similarly declined. Developed countries have stabilised their share at about 5 per cent, and the other regions below the threshold have made slight increases, with the noticeable exception of the least developed countries, which are on a declining trend but below the threshold. It is also worth mentioning that China is on the same slope, but for different reasons, insofar as table 8.2 shows a significant improvement of education opportunities in this country.

It is difficult to explain this converging trend. It does not result from any international conference or organisation having recommended such a target, nor from an economic analysis showing that it was desirable for enhancing the rate of

Table 8.3   Public expenditure on education as a percentage of GNP

	1980	1985	1990	1995
Transition countries	6.4	6.3	7.5	5.2
Sub-Saharan Africa	5.1	4.8	5.1	5.6
Arab states	4.1	5.8	5.2	5.2
Latin America and Caribbean	3.8	3.9	4.1	4.5
East Asia and Oceania	2.8	3.1	3.0	3.0
of which China	2.5	2.5	2.3	2.3
South Asia	4.1	3.3	3.9	4.3
of which India	2.8	3.4	3.9	3.5
Least developed countries	2.9	3.0	2.7	2.5
All developing countries	3.8	3.9	3.9	4.1
Developed countries	5.2	5.0	5.0	5.1
World	4.9	4.9	4.9	4.9

Source: UNESCO (1998)

growth of GNP. The atypical case of least developed countries can be explained by the wave of structural adjustment plans which have affected a significant proportion of the group's members, and have more or less obliged them to reduce public expenditure in general, and consequently, very often, education expenditure, in order to eliminate permanent public deficits.

But there is no such thing as an implicit 'law' forbidding the allocation of more than 5 per cent of the GNP to public education expenditure. One might have anticipated quite the opposite, because education needs do not slow down with time, and it is a sector in which productivity improvement is not as high as in the rest of the economy. There are two possible types of explanation. First, education ministries are not powerful lobbies in governments, and they fail to attract a bigger share of the cake. Second, it has been widely argued, during the 1980s and 1990s, that education resources are badly managed, and not efficiently used.[3] Before any increase in the resources allocated to the sector, a full range of incentives should be introduced to enhance efficiency measures. If these arguments are correct, the 5-per-cent threshold could be seen as only temporary, one which could be removed if they are appropriately addressed.

Why the same amount of resources does not lead to similar education outcomes across countries

The converging trend in resource allocation for education has *de facto* increased the gap in educational opportunities between countries. Here the measure of educational outcomes is a purely quantitative indicator, the expected number of years of education at the age of five, and therefore does not deal with the qualitative dimension of educational systems. But this limitation does not raise a particular problem in the framework of the present analysis, because quality issues are relevant for children already in schools, and not so much for those who are still excluded.

Our analytical focus concerns access to education, which is a prerequisite for addressing the qualitative aspect of education supply.

If the budgetary constraint (5 per cent of GNP) is observed, the expected number of years of education is determined by two additional variables: the unit cost of providing one year of education to a child, and the dependency ratio, which indicates the relative size of the school-age population across countries. Others things being equal, a country with higher unit costs provides fewer years of education than a country with lower unit costs, and a country with a higher dependency ratio does not give as many years of education to its school-age population as a country with a lower dependency ratio.

Unit cost variability

Unit cost comparisons at the international level are based on indicators using total education expenditure for a given ISCED level (or two ISCED levels combined if that improves the comparability of data), for instance primary, secondary or tertiary. This total is divided by the number of pupils enrolled at the corresponding level. This gives a preliminary result expressed in the national currency, which does not allow direct comparisons. To make interpretable comparisons, it is necessary to transform these data into a common measurement unit. Two options are available. The first is based on using a dominant currency, such as the US dollar. This method has two flaws: a problem of excessive exchange fluctuations over time, and a problem of large price differences for similar inputs. The second method avoids these shortcomings, and is increasingly used in the literature. It estimates unit costs as a percentage of GNP per capita. This approach is based on the observation that most education inputs, from teachers' pay to furniture, from textbooks to school buildings, have their prices closely correlated with per capita GNP in the country.

Concerning the unit cost of the primary level, which is the key level addressed in this chapter, two patterns are observable (see table 8.4): a group of regions in which unit cost represents more or less 20 per cent of GNP per capita, and another group where it is closer to 10 per cent. In the first case, one can supply five students with a year of education by allocating the equivalent of one GNP per capita to the sector. This also means that with 5 per cent of GNP, 25 per cent of the population can be in school. In the second case, one can supply ten years of education for each GNP per capita. The first group includes developed countries, transition countries, sub-Saharan Africa and the Arab states. The second group includes all other developing regions. For secondary education, the 'expensive' group is limited to sub-Saharan Africa, where unit cost is three times the world average. For tertiary education, sub-Saharan Africa is once again the most expensive region (eight times the world average), and least developed countries are also quite costly (four times the developed countries ratio). Whatever the level, sub-Saharan Africa is either as expensive as the high cost group, or the most expensive of all regions. As the share of GNP allocated to education by sub-

Table 8.4 Unit cost as a percentage of the GNP per capita

	Primary		Secondary		Tertiary	
	1985	1995	1985	1995	1985	1995
Developed countries	17.3	19.9	17.3[a]	19.9[a]	30.5	25.5
Transition countries	18.8	17.9	18.8[a]	17.9[a]	26.5	21.7
Least developed countries	9.7	9.2	26.0	29.2	153.9	125.6
Sub-Saharan Africa	16.4	17.0	57.5	57.6	481.5	433.9
Arab states	24.9	20.5	24.9[a]	20.5[a]	115.6	73.5
Latin America and Caribbean	5.9	9.1	14.8	13.1	30.4	27.2
East Asia and Oceania	7.2	8.8	18.1	18.1	93.1	70.3
South Asia	10.7	10.2	17.7	21.3	77.6	89.1
World	17.5	18.2	17.5[a]	18.2[a]	66.1	58.2

Source: UNESCO (1998)

Note

a   For these regions, primary and secondary levels have been merged, due to data availability.

Saharan African countries is close to the world threshold of 5 per cent, the current cost structure implies that fewer children can have access to education than in the rest of the world.

Dependency ratio variability

The purpose of a dependency ratio is to measure the relative size of the school-age population with respect to the potentially active population, namely people who are generating the GNP. It is quite easy to understand that countries with a high dependency ratio (many school-age children per active adult) will find it more difficult to provide them with education than countries where this ratio is significantly lower. Table 8.5 shows clearly how the situation in the main world regions varies in this respect. Developed countries, transition countries and China share a common characteristic, namely a low and declining dependency ratio. At the other end of the spectrum, sub-Saharan Africa is characterised by a high dependency ratio, which is not declining. In 2005, it will still be three times higher than in the developed world. Most other developing regions of the world also have relatively high dependency ratios, in particular the Arab states and the group of least developed countries, although following a declining trend.

The role of the dependency ratio in explaining interregional differences in the provision of education is central. If cost were the same everywhere, sub-Saharan Africa would need to allocate about 15 per cent of its GNP to education in order to provide the same number of expected years of education to its school-age population as developed countries. It is an extraordinarily difficult challenge, because in many countries belonging to this group, total public resources (fiscal revenues) are not very much higher than 15 per cent. Least developed countries are characterised by a large informal sector, with a low level of monetarisation

Table 8.5 Dependency ratios (% 6–15 year-olds/16–65 year-olds)

	Dependency ratio (%)			Dependency ratio (Index = 100 for developed countries)		
	1985	1995	2005	1985	1995	2005
Transition countries	22.2	23.0	16.7	116	133	104
Sub-Saharan Africa	46.0	46.5	44.9	241	269	281
Arab states	43.3	41.2	35.0	227	238	219
Latin America and Caribbean	37.8	32.5	26.8	198	188	168
East Asia and Oceania	31.9	25.8	21.6	167	149	135
of which China	29.6	23.5	19.3	155	136	121
South Asia	38.0	36.9	30.2	199	213	189
of which India	35.8	34.0	28.0	187	197	175
Least developed countries	45.6	46.1	40.8	239	266	255
Developing countries	36.2	32.8	28.3	190	190	177
Developed countries	19.1	17.3	16.0	100	100	100
World	31.9	29.6	25.8	167	171	161

Source: UNESCO (1998) plus author's estimates

(households tend to consume their own production, not to exchange it), and consequently a low level of taxable income.

Which of these two factors, unit cost differences and dependency ratio variability, is responsible for the largest part of the unequal access to education between rich and poor countries? In Asia and Latin America, the higher dependency ratio tends to be balanced by lower unit costs, especially at the primary level. China is a special case, where the dependency ratio has fallen dramatically, and where unit costs are also very low. This unusual combination of factors allows China to allocate a lower percentage of GNP to education without sacrificing the objective of expanding education opportunities. In addition, having a relatively low level of social expenditure, China is able to allocate more resources to physical investment. Such a mix of resource allocation favours economic growth, which has reached a highly enviable level during the past decade.

As far as sub-Saharan Africa is concerned, the unit cost factor is not negligible, although for basic education it is not so different from that of several regions, such as developed countries, transition countries and the Arab states. Nevertheless, if these unit costs were as low as in Asia or Latin America, the expected number of years of education could be multiplied by two. But if the dependency ratio were the same as in developed countries, this number could be multiplied by three. In a sense, the disadvantage of having a high dependency ratio is more damaging than the fact of having an inadequate cost structure. Such a conclusion may have some policy relevance in terms of priorities, but it has to be remembered that both factors are difficult to manipulate, and furthermore that it is easier to manipulate unit costs than fertility rates.

Can NICT help least developed countries to expand basic education?

There have been numerous studies on the potential of technology for education in the context of developing countries (e.g. Perraton 1984, Orivel 1985). The major conclusions of these studies are as follows: first, the use of radio in schools can be a cost-effective instrument due to very low cost per student hour, while television is less likely to be cost-effective, due to significantly higher costs. Second, distance education can also be a powerful means of improving access and cost-effectiveness, but is more likely to be successful in the context of upper secondary and tertiary education than in basic education for school-age children. And third, some successful attempts have also been made to provide basic literacy to adults at a distance, through radio, television and printed material. But no convincing cost-effectiveness studies exist about the utilisation of technologies in which computers are the key input. When we refer today to new information and communication technologies (NICT), it is technologies based on multimedia systems which are meant, and no longer radio and television. These are technologies based on numerical systems, not on analogue systems, as was the case with the first generation of education technologies.

That does not necessarily mean that previous technologies are outdated. Radio can still be used in a cost-effective way, as recently shown by Nekatibeb (1998), in his study of primary education radio support programmes in Ethiopia. But the purpose of this chapter is different: it tries to assess whether NICT today constitute a promising way of solving education problems in developing countries, especially basic education in the group of least developed countries, where the greatest proportion of school-age children excluded from primary education are concentrated.

Education economists expect from NICT an impact on the productivity of education services. One can learn from different inputs, such as teachers, peers, parents, books or NICT. If some of the learning process shifts from the teacher to NICT, and the cost of a learning hour is cheaper with NICT as compared with one hour of face-to-face teaching, then the productivity of education services may increase. This productivity increase will be real if knowledge acquired is similar in both cases. There are some instances in which this assumption is verified. Let us look at learning activities for which NICT are as effective as face-to-face contact.

Information on the cost of learning through NICT is, as yet, limited. For instance, in the ERIC database,[4] there are 3,200 references for which the two research keywords are 'education' and 'Internet', but zero when 'cost' is introduced as a third keyword. One can only regret that such limited attention is given to this topic, but on the other hand, the rapid evolution of prices in this domain constitutes a highly discouraging factor, because the data are obsolete after a very short period.

The costs of NICT have an interesting feature when compared with other educational inputs: they are not linked to a national price structure, but quite the opposite, they tend to be similar worldwide for equipment, software, spare parts and consumables. The cost of the electricity used to operate this kind of equipment may vary from one country to another, but electricity represents a modest share of the cost of NICT. The only exception is for covering the cost of specialised staff in charge of operating the equipment, if any. In many cases, this is done by existing teaching staff, whose cost is the same, per hour, as for traditional teaching. It is therefore not a differentiating factor between face-to-face and NICT. As a consequence, cost information generated in the context of a given country may have some relevance for others. It entails a certain margin of error, but this cause of error is probably smaller than the obsolescence of data over time.

A handful of recent cost studies of NICT in schools has been identified, one for the USA, one for France, and two in Latin America (Chile and Costa Rica). The American study, carried out by Coley *et al.* (1999), is based on a representative sample of American schools, which allows comparisons, national averages and national extrapolations. It shows that in the US there is on average one computer per ten pupils and one multimedia computer (the latest generation of computers) per twenty-four pupils. The total annual expenditure generated by this equipment (investment, maintenance and operating costs, including peripheral devices such as printers and the like, software etc.) is about $3 billion, or $70 per student. This represents 1.3 per cent of the total education expenditure of American schools. One observes a significant variability from one state to another, with a minimum of six pupils per computer in Florida to a maximum of sixteen in Louisiana. Schools which seem to have the best equipment allocate about $300 instead of the average of $70. The best equipped schools have replaced the school computer laboratory, where each individual class goes once or twice a week, with classroom-based computers, with a ratio of five pupils per computer (even less in the best cases). If all schools were equipped like the best ones, it would cost about $13 billion per year, or 5.3 per cent of the consolidated education budget.

The study does not provide data on the average number of hours which pupils spend learning with computers. The intensity of use is reported from a 1994 survey, which is unfortunately probably outdated, but constitutes apparently the only available source of information in the US. Based on this survey, the average time spent on computers per pupil is 40 hours a year. As the annual cost is $70, the cost per hour/per pupil is therefore $1.75.

The French study (Talpin 1999) was carried out in the Burgundy region. In France, the availability of computers is lower than in the US: one computer for seventeen pupils in junior high schools, and one for thirty in primary schools, which makes an average of about one computer for twenty-four pupils, 2.4 times less than in the US. But as in the US, schools are unevenly equipped, and the study concentrates on schools having regular computer practice (on average one session of 1.5 hours a week or about 50 hours a year). The annual cost per pupil is about FF1,000, which is FF20 per pupil per hour. This is slightly more than in the US, because some schools do not rely on the class teacher for computer practice, but use a recently created body of young school assistants,[5] recruited by the MOE in 1997–8. In schools where there are no assistants, the unit cost per student/

hour is half as high, namely about FF10 or $1.67, close to the American cost. The monograph on which this estimate is based used a sound economic methodology, amortising equipment on the basis of the observed life expectancy of material in schools, and including maintenance and software costs, as well as electricity consumption.

The two Latin American case studies are quoted in Perraton and Creed (2000). They show slightly lower costs (from $22 to $83 per pupil, according to the size of the school), but are not strictly comparable with the two previous case studies. First, they are projected costs rather than actual, and second, they do not relate per-pupil yearly cost to an observed number of learning hours with computers. It is assumed, in the Chilean case, that pupils are exposed to a 'maximum of two hours per week', which says nothing about the actual average. They also show that in these middle income countries, technology represents a significantly higher share of the unit cost than in developed countries, namely 10 to 37 per cent in Chile, 13 per cent in Costa Rica, compared with the less than 5 per cent (actually closer to 1 to 2 per cent), observed in developed countries. Given these uncertainties, it is reasonable to conclude that the Latin American case studies do not contradict the results obtained from the North American and French cases.

Let us assume that in a school environment, the hourly cost of using a computer is about $1.7. This $1.7 covers the amortisation cost of the computer (without charging a discount rate), maintenance, software and electricity. It also includes additional equipment such as printers, networking equipment, and some specific furniture. As far as the Internet connection is concerned, it includes the subscription to a provider, which is a fixed cost, plus a lump sum for using a telephone line (half an hour a day at local call rates). These costs, which are observed in the context of developed countries, cannot be lower in the context of developing ones, where the technological environment is poorer. Is this competitive with face-to-face learning? It is clearly competitive in developed countries, where a learning hour with a teacher costs between $4 and $12. But this is rarely the case in developing countries.

If we go back to the data presented earlier, we can recall that the unit cost for basic education is between 10 and 20 per cent of the value of GNP per capita. The average GNP per capita in the group of forty-seven countries called least developed countries is $350. So the annual unit cost is between $35 and $70. For such a range of costs, a pupil has access to about 800 hours of face-to-face time with a teacher. The per hour/per pupil cost is therefore below $0.1, a very small amount if compared with the $1.7 implied by the use of NICT. NICT need to present very attractive comparative advantages in order to justify such a gap in relative costs. NICT have a highly different cost-effectiveness ratio in rich and poor countries.

Of course, it is possible to identify specific activities, linked with the running of basic education systems, which require more expensive training through face-to-face techniques, and for which potentially cost-effective utilisation of NICT may be justified. Such opportunities may be found in fields like the training of high-level specialists for national functions, the training of supervisors, counsellors, headmasters etc. Here the hourly cost should be compared with the cost of teaching not grade one or two pupils, but graduate or postgraduate students, which can be very different. But it has to be assessed on a case-by-case basis, and no general *a priori* rule can be provided.

Finally, NICT can be utilised for basic education in developing countries which have already covered part of the road towards development. If we assume a cost of $1.7 per hour for NICT, such a cost is equivalent to face-to-face learning when the unit cost per pupil approaches this level. Based on a unit cost equivalent to 20 per cent of GNP, and on a school year of 800 hours, the break-even point is reached with a unit cost of $(800 × 1.7) = $1,460, corresponding to a GNP of $7,300 per capita. Several Latin American countries, such as Argentina, Uruguay and Chile, or transition countries, such as the Czech Republic, Slovenia, Hungary and Croatia, will soon enter this break-even zone.

Conclusion

In spite of the rapid introduction of NICT in educational systems internationally, the great majority of learning hours are still based on face-to-face techniques. This method is characterised by very different costs among countries, from less than $0.1 per pupil/hour in some least developed countries to about $10 in developed ones. This makes a variability range of 1 to 100. The variability of the cost of learning for one hour with a computer is much smaller, because the technology is indeed a 'world' technology, with similar costs everywhere, whatever the local labour costs. This unit cost can be estimated at $1.7 per pupil. The issue of the effectiveness of learning through a teacher compared with a computer is still highly disputed, and the best assumption one can make is that one hour of learning in both cases generates on average the same educational outcome.

In this context, it is easy to understand that the substitution of teachers by computers is more likely to succeed, from an economic point of view, in places where the cost of face-to-face is above $1.7 per pupil/hour, than in places where the cost of face-to-face learning is significantly below this threshold. If computers are used in a country where face-to-face teaching costs $0.85, this implies that learning with a computer has to be twice as efficient as learning with a teacher. The lower the cost per pupil/hour with face-to-face teaching, the less likely it is that NICT can be a cost-effective alternative to traditional teaching.

Notes

1   The definition of developed and least developed countries is drawn from World Bank categories, as presented in the annual *World Development Report*. Developed countries refer to a group of industrialised market economies that is almost identical to the OECD membership. Least developed countries are the group of countries in which the GDP per capita is below a threshold that is adjusted every year in order to take inflation into account.

2   Data on private expenditure are collected by OECD for its members, and the 85 per cent mentioned above for the share of public expenditure is drawn from this database (OECD 1998). For developing countries, one has only partial evidence from country-specific case studies that indicates a greater

variability between countries than is the case with OECD ones. Private finance in this group does not differ significantly from the developed world model, but is probably slightly above (15–20 per cent instead of 15 per cent, Orivel 1995). For these countries, there is also a third source of funding, which is foreign assistance to education. But the volume of foreign assistance does not significantly affect the level of domestic resources, as it represents only about 2–3 per cent of total education expenditure. There is some speculation concerning the impact of recent moves towards debt cancellation in providing additional resources to education systems in least developed countries. Here again, one should not overestimate the impact of this measure. It is not fresh money, but mostly a reduction of budget deficits. A large proportion of this forgiven debt was not actually paid by debtor countries, and the amount of resources represented by this policy will be far below the present flow of external assistance to education.

3 The most common argument in support of this thesis can be found in Hanushek (1994), which shows a great variability of resources spent per student for a given level of education outcomes, other things being equal. Expensive educational institutions have no incentive to reduce costs, and they don't.

4 Educational Resources Information Centre of the United States Department of Education.

5 These school assistants are recruited in the framework of an employment scheme designed for increasing job opportunities for young French graduates who are unemployed. They have a five-year contract, in principle not renewable, and are paid close to the minimum salary.

References

Coley, R., Cradler J. and Engel, P. (1999) *Computers and Classrooms: The Status of Technology in US Schools*, Princeton, NJ: Educational Testing Service.

Hanushek, E. (1994) *Making Schools Work: Improving Performance and Controlling Costs*, Washington, DC: Brookings Institution.

Meyer, J. (1999) *Education, World Society, and Globalization*, Paper presented to the International Symposium of the Department of Psychology and Educational Science of the University of Lisbon, Portugal, 21 and 22 November.

Meyer, J., Ramirez, F., Robinson, R. and Boli-Bennett, J. (1977) 'The world education revolution, 1950–1970', *Sociology of Education*, 50, October: 242–58.

Nekatibeb, T. (1998) *Media Utilization and School Improvement*, Studies in Comparative and International Education 45, Stockholm: Institute of International Education, Stockholm University.

OECD (1998) *Education at a Glance*, Paris: OECD.

Orivel, F. (1985) 'Economics of educational technology', in T. Hüsen and T. Postlethwaite (eds) *International Encyclopaedia of Education* 3, Oxford: Pergamon Press.

Orivel, F. (1995), 'Problèmes et perspectives des systèmes éducatifs', in M. Vernières (ed.) *Ajustement, Éducation, Emploi*, Paris: Economica.

Perraton, H. (ed.) (1984) *Alternative Routes to Formal Education: Distance Teaching for School Equivalency*, Baltimore: Johns Hopkins University Press.

Perraton, H. and Creed C. (2000) *Applying New Technologies and Cost-Effective Delivery Systems in Basic Education*, Thematic study for Dakar conference on Education for All, draft.

Talpin, E. (1999) *Les Coûts de l'Informatique à l'École: Étude de Cas en Bourgogne*, Mémoire de DEA, Dijon: Iredu, Université de Bourgogne.

UNESCO (1998) *World Education Report*, Paris: UNESCO.

Watkins, K. (1999) *Education Now*, London: OXFAM.

World Bank (1981, 1985, 1994, 1997), *World Development Report*, Washington, DC: World Bank.

Part 3

Applications

Chapter 9

Literacy and adult education through distance and open learning

Usha Reddi and Anita Dighe[1]

As we enter the new millennium, illiteracy remains a worldwide problem. Official statistics claim that there are today more than one billion adults who are non-literate, vast numbers of whom are women. The world map of illiteracy is also the world map of poverty. By and large, the non-literate are poor, hungry, sick, powerless, exploited. Development planners claim that illiteracy is a bottleneck to development. Most national governments have therefore recognised the importance of dealing with the problem of adult illiteracy in order to accelerate the process of development.

Despite concerted efforts around the world, it is becoming increasingly clear that the existing programmes are ill equipped to deal with the challenges which lie ahead. New solutions to the old problems clearly have to be found. Distance and open learning systems present an alternative to the traditional modes of offering programmes for the education of adults. Opportunities are also emerging for making better use of technologies which have been previously underused in supporting learning processes (e.g. radio, television, print materials, audio and video cassettes). The emergence of powerful new information and communication technologies (NICT) has dramatically expanded our options for increasing access, promoting equity and ensuring interactivity, for the enhancement of learning.

This chapter starts with the current debate in the field of literacy and adult education and provides an analysis of experiences in the use of distance and open learning for literacy and adult education. While underscoring the importance of understanding the uniqueness of literacy and adult education programmes which use open and distance learning systems, an attempt is made to highlight issues for policy and system design.

Literacy and adult education: the current debate

The debate surrounding definitions of literacy and adult education is inconclusive. Are these two terms synonymous? Is adult education a more comprehensive term than literacy? While it would be hazardous to attempt answers to these questions, it might be useful to understand the broad contours of the two terms and to examine the current debate surrounding them.

According to Bhola (1984), it was the World Conference on Adult Education held in Montreal in 1960 which put adult illiteracy on the world educational agenda. Starting with the traditional emphasis on acquisition of the 3 Rs, by the mid-1960s the focus had shifted to 'functional literacy', which focused on economic betterment and productivity.

The 1970s witnessed other developments in the field of literacy and adult education. The exclusive focus on economic skills was broadened and even transformed. Literacy was now seen as a strategy for liberation. The aim was to teach adults not only how to read the word, but also how to read the world (Bataille 1976). Paulo Freire's (1970, 1973) emphasis on literacy to 'liberate' as opposed to literacy to 'domesticate' captured the imagination of those who started to understand the transformative potential of literacy.

During the 1980s, Street (1984) coined what he called the 'autonomous' model of literacy. According to him, literacy is generally conceptualised as a single thing which is the same everywhere, and it is assumed that without it people are in cognitive, social and cultural deficit. The argument for the autonomous model suggests that the acquisition of literacy has consequences for social progress, cognitive development, and economic take-off (Street 1999). Since Street's experience, as well as that of academics, researchers and practitioners around the world working in literacy, indicated that the autonomous model did not work, an alternative model was proposed. This was called the ideological model of literacy. This model starts from a different premise – that literacy is a social practice, not simply a technical and neutral skill, and that it is always rooted in cultural practices and cultural processes. Furthermore, literacy practices are inextricably linked to cultural and power structures in society (Street 1993).

Today there is a growing awareness of literacy as social practice, rather than a set of skills which a person has or does not have. Studies in the socio-cultural approach to literacy reveal that non-literate persons engage in literacy practices in their own communities, just as persons with advanced literacy skills engage in non-literate practices (Education for Development 1998). Thus, rather than categorising people as 'literate' and 'illiterate', there is a growing acceptance of the view that we are all in different respects both literate and illiterate.

These new approaches to literacy suggest that literacy is always contextualised, or situated within a particular socio-cultural setting. There is thus no one universally applicable form of literacy. Rather, there are different literacies and literacy practices for different occupational groups, for different kinds of activities and for different social and institutional contexts (Education for Development 1998). An important implication of seeing literacy as social practice, and literacy teaching programmes as assisting people with their current literacy practices, is that such programmes then have to be built on careful localised research. The literacy practices of the participants and literacy teaching programmes must be situated in real contexts rather than being generalised. According to Torres (2000), the focus now is clearly on acknowledging diversity and the need for context-specific and culture-sensitive responses to literacy practices.

It is apparent from the above discussion that there are no clear-cut boundaries – rather, there are different approaches and elements which constitute this fast-growing field. In countries where poverty and illiteracy levels are still high, adult education is either perceived narrowly as a literacy programme which focuses on providing reading and writing skills to adults, or it is linked with functional literacy in the overall context of development. This is the 'autonomous' model of literacy. It is also the 'universal literacy for all' model, which is generally advocated by international agencies. In some countries, the terminology used is 'non-formal education'. This encompasses a wide range of activities, such as health education, agricultural education and training of farmers, adult literacy programmes, women's group activities, work-based training, and vocational and skills training programmes. On the other hand, for the proponents of the new multiple literacies approach (the ideological model), illiteracy is not a problem which is endemic only in the less developed world. Rather, they believe that every one of us has an illiteracy or two (whether it is HTML, Front Page, tax forms or financial reports). What is then important is to see which literacies need addressing, for what kind of people and with what priority.

Literacy and adult education through distance and open learning: an analysis of experiences

Today's information and communication technologies offer an unparalleled opportunity for reaching out to the hitherto unreached groups. This implies that distance education, which has hitherto largely confined itself to the tertiary sector, has to be harnessed for expanding access to education. Presently, education remains a 'scarce' commodity, particularly in the countries of the south Asian region. Smaller numbers have access to education, while the vast majority, who need it, have neither the access nor the opportunity to take advantage of it. There is thus an in-built inequality of distribution of education and existing knowledge. Efforts to minimise or reduce the inequalities resulting from current educational realities have to be made, and the new media successfully exploited for this purpose.

Literature on adult basic education at a distance, however, is hard to find, diverse and dispersed across countries and cultures like the proverbial needle in a haystack. Edirisingha (1999) points out that one major drawback is that we are short of information about the effectiveness of, and the critical conditions which are necessary for, the successful implementation of open and distance learning (ODL) for basic education, for a variety of reasons. Thus, the use of ODL for basic education in developing countries is an under-researched and under-reported area (Perraton 1997). Most international attention is focused on open universities providing higher education. Also, most attention has been given to documenting the experiences of ODL in developed countries, rather than that of developing countries. This lack of reporting is probably partly due to the very nature of non-formal education – with no recognisable boundaries and approaches – much less a 'system' (Dodds 1996). Another reason is that, where there is some reporting on basic education programmes, it focuses on the practice, rather than on research (Perraton 1997). According to Edirisingha (1999), where documentation and research exists, it tends to be institution-based, reflecting practice in a single country, with only rare attempts at drawing generalisable conclusions. A research study, presently being undertaken by the International Research Foundation for Open Learning, will therefore attempt, through six in-depth studies, to develop policy guidelines on the use of ODL to extend the range and raise the quality of ODL in basic education.

An earlier attempt was made by the Commonwealth of Learning, when a project was commissioned in 1995. The purpose was to undertake an environmental scan of active non-formal education projects/activities, which were employing distance education methodologies. The survey (Dodds 1996) highlighted a wide variety of such projects being undertaken in different Commonwealth countries. Due to poor documentation of such initiatives, however, there is very limited opportunity for practitioners in one programme to learn from the experiences of other relevant and related programmes. But a more disturbing finding of the survey was that, while such projects were launched with great enthusiasm by those who believed in their educational potential, they were rarely taken seriously by governments, especially by ministries of education.

Despite this serious constraint, some projects had survived and had continued to operate over significant periods of time. They had developed approaches and media combinations which worked. But, more importantly, they had demonstrated that a variety of techniques and strategies need to be used for providing practical and life-related education to adults in most developing countries. Dodds (1996) therefore concluded that there was a need for much more detailed, carefully researched and analytical information on what was going on in non-formal education at a distance.

In 1993, a major impetus for distance education (DE) was provided when the leaders of the nine high-population countries identified DE as an important modality through which significant advances could be made in reaching EFA (Education for All) goals. Subsequently, on the basis of experience of each of the countries in the use of DE methodologies, the potential and requirements of DE were spelt out. Against the background of existing tendencies to think of DE in the first place as an option for tertiary education, this focus constitutes an interesting challenge, requiring careful thought about what kind of adjustments might be necessary in order to address the needs of audiences which are different from those traditionally using DE programmes. A listing of the potential and requirements of DE might be useful in understanding how the nine high population countries perceived the use of DE in providing educational opportunities to marginalised groups.

- DE can reach people who would otherwise be deprived of opportunities to learn
- Two-way communication is essential for effective distance learning of disadvantaged groups

- Besides print, radio has been found to be an effective means of communication
- Use of a media mix is normally more effective than DE that relies only on a single medium
- Face-to-face tutoring, and the inclusion in the organisational structure of the DE system of learning resource centres, can be an important contribution to delivering DE more effectively
- Good instructional design, involving sound planning and adequate formative evaluation, based on learner feedback, is key to quality DE
- Economies of scale often make DE more economical than traditional ways of delivering education
- Community participation and strengthening of local communication networks are key elements in successful approaches in DE
- Planning for sustainability is a key requirement for successful DE

Despite regional proclamations about the use of DE for providing basic education for all, most governments were reluctant to allocate resources to initiate such programmes. As a result, Edirisingha (1999) found that there were only a handful of initiatives, most of them still at the pilot stage, to use alternative ways to provide basic education. He is therefore of the view that it is time to examine how we could use distance learning, both on its own and in combination with conventional methods, to reach the so far unreached in developing countries.

By and large, experience seems to indicate that basically open and distance education (ODE) does not work for literacy *per se*. Our own experience in India has shown that attempts to promote literacy through the use of television (a series of programmes called *Khilti Kaliyan*) and radio (a series of broadcasts forming part of the Project in Radio Education for Adult Literacy) floundered for a variety of reasons (Dighe and Reddi 1999). On the other hand, ODE has been used to good effect for training large numbers of adult basic education staff or for training of trainers – as UNISA has demonstrated effectively in South Africa. The manner in which open and distance learning methodologies have been used for varied educational programmes of adults can be seen from some of the case study experiences given below.

The Sudan Open Learning Organisation (SOLO) was established in 1984 to provide education to the increasing number of refugees from Ethiopia and other countries who arrived in Sudan and who are not able to receive formal schooling (Edirisingha 1999). Courses include literacy, numeracy and life skills, and are open to refugees, both young and adult, and to displaced Sudanese citizens. Courses are provided through printed text, group study, and tutorial support and study kits. During 1994–5, 35,000 students were enrolled in a variety of non-formal courses.

Brazil's Telecurso 2000 was launched in 1994 by a consortium of agencies. Learners are employed youths and adults, who lack education. The project seeks to provide basic education, and thereby to improve the working conditions and the standard of living of learners. Instructional media and methods include television, print materials and study groups, which are run with the help of trained facilitators. The programme operates at the primary, secondary and tertiary levels in addition to having a vocational element (Edirisingha 1999).

The University of Fort Hare Adult Basic Education Project (UFH-ABEP), as reported by Matshazi (1999), was started in 1992 as a research project, with the prime objective of researching basic needs in the community, and developing and testing a DE methodology which would make suitable courses available to adults with little or no formal education. The project is intended to reach young adults who have dropped out of the school system, unemployed and self-employed adults, and employed adults seeking further education and training. The materials developed for the project include a combination of cassettes, flip charts and group discussions.

The Gobi Women's Project in Mongolia was started in 1991 (UNESCO 1999) to provide life skills to nomads, particularly women. Print and radio were identified as suitable media, as the combination allowed for overcoming the problems of distance in Mongolia. Income generation served as motivation for the literacy and numeracy content of the broadcasts. The visiting teacher reduced the nomadic women's isolation and supported their learning process. Small information centres, which were set up for the project, also served as meeting points for women.

Given the situation in Afghanistan and the collapse of several infrastructures, radio has to fill in on many fronts. *New Home, New Life* is a radio soap opera designed and produced for broadcast in Afghanistan by the BBC (UNESCO 1999). Dynamic contact with the listeners has been one of the hallmarks of the project since it was first aired in 1994. It has shown how everyday issues, of concern to people living in harsh conditions, can be incorporated into the programmes and solutions suggested. The soap opera is entirely Afghan in context and content and draws from the rich history of community action and customs to achieve its high degree of relevance.

In recent years, multipurpose community telecentres have been established on a pilot basis in a large number of countries. In 1997, the Canadian International Development Research Council (IDRC) launched ACACIA, an international initiative aimed at putting new information and communication technologies (NICT) to work on behalf of social and economic development for local communities in sub-Saharan Africa. The initiative has three objectives: to show that NICT can contribute to community development, to study and assess local experience with the use of NICT, and to promote the use of NICT internationally in support of community development. In Egypt, a pilot project has been initiated to provide rural and remote communities with public access to information technology, especially the Internet, and with the training to use it effectively. The ultimate goal of this project is the empowerment of community members and the use of such technologies for a variety of applications benefiting sustainable human development. The Commonwealth of Learning has now initiated a literacy project using technology-based community learning centres in India, Zambia and Bangladesh. The purpose of this pilot project is to enable communities to access new communications technologies and to use them for their development needs.

Multipurpose community telecentres are now in vogue everywhere and international organisations are actively initiating pilot projects in a number of countries around the world. On the basis of his experience in Africa, Fuchs (1997) has attempted a distillation of what is known about the development of telecentres, as the multipurpose telecentre pilot projects in Africa have moved through the early cycles of proposal, planning and implementation. The telecentre projects, however, are still in the pilot phase and while they appear to be promising, it is still somewhat premature to comment on their impact on adult learning, as evaluation reports are still awaited.

The uniqueness of literacy and adult education programmes which use open and distance learning systems

Unlike programmes offered at college and university levels, where the students tend to form a homogeneous group in terms of their age and educational background, in literacy and adult education programmes, the diversity of the learners with regard to their literacy levels, their socio-economic backgrounds, as well as varying motivation levels, pose challenges to distance educators. Adults have different learning styles. With regard to women learners, much has been written on the collaborative nature of their learning. In the case of many adult learning contexts, the interactive, participatory involvement of learners appears to contribute to success. Some of the principles of adult learning which have been distilled from adult education practitioners and theorists include the following:

- Adults learn best when free from undue stress, boredom, overload of information and when they are not trying to second guess the teacher's objectives
- Adults decide for themselves what is important to be learned
- Adults do not approach any additional learning with a 'clean slate', and thus, learning without a concrete link to life has little value. Adults draw upon past experience as a benchmark against which they measure any new information. They may already have fixed viewpoints on a given subject
- Adults have learning needs closely related to their lives and their work. They tend to define a useful learning experience as one in which they can link the new knowledge to their experience, in order to solve problems. They thus expect information given to them to be immediately useful
- They expect the process of learning to be easy, convenient and interesting, and the 'why' of learning is as important as the 'how'
- Adults need to experience a sense of achievement as an impetus to further learning. This helps in building their self-esteem and a confidence in their ability to learn
- More than anything else, adults have a significant ability to serve as a knowledgeable resource to the trainer as well as to fellow learners.

The immediate implication here is that learning strategies in non-formal DE programmes must match the processes of learning and must include a significant element of interactivity, enabling a 'partnership' in the process of learning. If materials are produced and transmitted in a one-way mode of communication, without taking into account the principles of adult learning (say in a television programme), interactivity will be lost and the partnership with the learner may be replaced by a didactic one-way mode of delivery of content.

Many literacy programmes and projects using DE methodologies fail, because they rely on notions of adult literacy which do not take into account the pedagogy of adult learning. Our observation of the literacy project undertaken by the Jhabua Development Communication Project, for example, showed that there was a mismatch between the expectations of the programme planners and the learning styles of the tribal people for whom the literacy programmes were intended. Sometimes literacy programmes rely on a concept of literacy which is isolated from social contexts and cultural practices. People must feel motivated to acquire literacy and to participate, not only in determining the context of learning, but in the shaping of their own development (UIE 1997b: 3).

The production of non-formal DE materials, suitable for use with illiterate adults or adults with low levels of literacy, also calls for new approaches and new strategies. Successful education at the basic level (perhaps more than at any higher levels) depends on the course producers knowing and being able to empathise with their learners. Field research therefore plays a central role in the production of course materials. Warr (1992) describes how the Basic Functional Education Programme was developed at the Allama Iqbal Open University in Pakistan based on the following principles:

- The courses should be learner centred (as opposed to subject centred), which means that the information should be relevant to village learners and should be presented from their perspective and in a way which they will find interesting, and of practical value; this calls for an interdisciplinary approach
- The courses should not be dependent on the written word (due to low literacy levels) but should use a multiple media approach with a strong audiovisual element
- The lecturing style, commonly used in academic courses at the tertiary level, should be avoided, as this is unsuitable for learners with little formal education
- The materials should incorporate a variety of presentation techniques to make the courses stimulating and easy to learn from
- The materials should enable learners to relate new ideas and information to their own circumstances, to learn from one another by sharing relevant knowledge and experience, and to apply what has been learnt through practical follow-up activities
- The courses should create a dialogue between learners and producers of media materials, by providing feedback from the learners and enabling the latter to modify and improve upon the materials

Most non-formal education programmes which use media enhance their impact and effectiveness by using them in a study or learning group context. Such groups give learners an opportunity to discuss the relevance of what they have been listening to or viewing, to share ideas and experiences, and to undertake group-based learning activities which allow them to apply knowledge, practise skills and explore attitudes and values (Spronk 1999). In other words, the kinds of self-instructional materials which form the cornerstone of most tertiary level courses would be inappropriate for adult learners with limited literacy skills. Also, the facilitator/co-ordinator needs to play a very important role in motivating, encouraging and facilitating the learning process. For the adult learner is not an autonomous learner to begin with, and will need to interact with the facilitator/co-ordinator in order to develop self-confidence and feel motivated to learn. This is particularly true of women learners. Support mechanisms of various kinds also need to be provided, to ensure that the adult is not daunted by the learning process, but is encouraged and offered the necessary support to continue learning.

Considerations for policy and system design

If technology lies at the heart of non-formal distance learning, the immense potential of these technologies, if effectively harnessed, can contribute substantially to providing such learning (Khan 1999). NICT are the link between the educator and the learner. They are a means to achieve an end, not ends in themselves. Today's NICT have special strengths, i.e. speed, reach, audiovisual richness and an ability to overcome barriers of time and space. Their effective use, however, depends on a large number of factors, any of which can determine the success or failure of a project. It is for this reason that we examine what we know about adult learning, DE methodologies, and NICT, in a search for the synergy which can bring concrete results.

Often discourses concerning technology construct the 'realities' of practice. We tend to start by assuming the availability of communication technology and try to fit our projects into this 'techno-utopian' discourse. Almost all of India's experiments in using satellite technology for education have been based on this premise, whether the Countrywide Classroom, School Television, the Kheda Communication Project, or the Jhabua Development Communication Project. Added to this is the glamour surrounding NICT; their promotion by international aid agencies; and the simplistic way in which political leaders and high-level decision makers are easily persuaded that today's NICT can single-handedly bring about transformation in areas where conventional systems and technologies have failed. This is particularly so in developing countries, hard pressed to maintain existing infrastructures for traditional forms of education. The desire to produce exponential change, in situations where change is slow, makes us turn to the fastest, widest means of delivering information. Technological innovation, the costs of technology and the introduction of technology into literacy and adult education are not the main problems. The real concern is the human factor – how to ensure that literacy and adult education providers have the capacity, the understanding of the processes and the political will to apply the technologies appropriately (UIE 1997b: 3). For this reason, in our discussion, we shall shift our attention from the technology to the beneficiaries, and to the context in which technology is being used, while suggesting parameters for design and implementation of projects which seek to use NICT for literacy and adult education.

To do this, we divide our discussion into six broad areas: issues in project planning and management; financing; media access and media choices; content; community involvement and participation; and monitoring and evaluation, drawing lessons from many cases. We also keep in mind that DE is acknowledged worldwide as a methodology for providing learner-centred, learner-paced, and user-friendly learning, flexible in time and space. DE is probably one of the few options left before us.

The authors may be forgiven for sounding prescriptive; it is certainly not our intention. We are merely placing a mirror before the reader and highlighting what is sometimes left unsaid.

Project planning and management

There is a tendency worldwide to start, not with the beneficiary, but with an agency which is planning a project or with the availability of NICT. To have any impact, the introduction of communication facilities and services must be done as an integral part of a cross-sectional, multidisciplinary effort of community building (Enberg 1998: 1). It is necessary to situate learning within the socio-political context – because it is these factors which can make the critical difference in providing a 'learning environment'. Literacy and learning practices are strongly embedded in social relations of power and inequity in any social system (Street 1999: 1).

One must start with the community for whose benefit the project is being launched. Well before a project is designed, critical information is required. Demographic and other details of infrastructure and facilities are no doubt essential – but it is more critical to undertake an ethnographic mapping of the community, to determine socio-economic, cultural and political realities which promote or inhibit learning. We need to read between the lines, and then to humanise the data, to translate from mere numbers and percentages to qualitative insights which will guide us in project planning and design.

The point we are trying to make is that no project can be designed without intensive field work to study the community which the project is supposed to serve. And this study of the beneficiary community is a precondition on which there can be no compromise, because the entire project design hinges upon the findings of the field study (Street 1999: 64).

Emerging from the field study will be the articulation of the goals of the project. All of us know from field experience that the desire to learn and to educate their families exists even among the most deprived communities. Despite this knowledge, we need to establish clear-cut project goals. Is basic education going to be related to the community's felt and expressed needs or determined by government/ funding agencies? Are we embarking on a project to test the technical feasibility of a given technology, simply because the technology is available? Or do we have concrete goals which emerged from the formative research undertaken? It is important to remember that empowering people with the right information and content often requires a dramatic shift in approach and attitudes.

Meticulous planning is a key ingredient for effective selection and deployment of NICT, especially in non-formal and community education, where we are not working with people who have had the benefit of formal training. Planning must begin long before a project is launched and it must bring together all the partners in the process, with equal individual and institutional support and commitment. Teams which develop programmes in this area are, by definition, interdisciplinary and interinstitutional in nature. Since commitment and participation have to be continuous and dedicated, it is critical that all partners share a common vision about goals and methodologies of implementation.

Very often, partners and stakeholders in projects evince only initial interest. Politicians, technocrats, and bureaucrats are generous in providing lip-service support to project proposals, but rarely is this translated into political will or action (Enberg 1998: 7). One way to draw in continuous involvement in a project is to develop interinstitutional project planning and monitoring boards, and to ensure that these boards meet regularly. A common vision, action plan and monitoring of a project can result from such an ongoing interaction between project partners.

Sponsorship and control of a project can make the difference between success and failure. At present, three existing kinds of sponsorship and control are discernible for projects engaged in literacy and adult education: government; quasi government, such as through autonomous distance education institutions; and non-governmental agencies. These are not cut-and-dried categories – there may be partnerships between different institutions and agencies involved in the field. Patterns of international aid support for projects, especially in developing countries, generally involve governments as partners; other bilateral or multilateral aid agencies also work alongside non-governmental agencies. Aid agencies sometimes do determine the project agendas, priorities, technologies to be used, and also content.

Within countries, patterns of sponsorship and control also influence effectiveness. Control over policy and implementation by a distant government office makes local flexibility and decision making difficult; while total decentralisation may not provide economies of scale and may prove to be difficult to sustain.

Project duration is another policy issue which is of concern, and policies concerning the duration of programmes must be inferred from practice, since the diversity of programmes suggests that norms do not exist. Project duration varies from short-term training programmes to several years and becomes important for two reasons – patterns of funding and effectiveness. Unit costs for programmes have an inverse relationship with duration – the longer the duration of a project, the lower the unit cost. On the other hand, short-term programmes have a limited effectiveness, in short-term learning as well as in long-term effectiveness. Short-term projects in literacy and adult education, if not followed up by a progression of programmes, can lead to situations of *status quo ante*. Long duration programmes have a better chance of being successful, if only because of the pedagogy of learning from communication technologies. There is also likely to be better planning and use of fixed inputs in a longer-term programme.

A review of case studies would show that limited success is not because of the absence of strategic long- or short-term planning, but is associated with the translation of planning to implementation. Most developmental projects in the developing world can be accused of this weakness. The problem is often well defined by policy makers, and missions and projects are drawn up to address it, funds identified and set aside and organisations created to deal with the issue. Implementation gets tied up in knots of administrative politics, bureaucracy, construction of huge buildings, purchase of equipment, 'secure' government jobs, unionisation and other social issues, so that goals, targets and time frames for implementation are lost in the process (Reddi and Sinvhal 1987). The authors have found this to be the case in most of the projects which they have evaluated.

Non-formal education programmes often lack organisational support because of their very nature. In the implementation process, such support is an important consideration. Unless it happens, survival and sustenance of the programme become difficult. Likewise, identification of personnel to run the programme is a necessary precondition. The roles and responsibilities of personnel at various levels need to be clearly defined. Training of these personnel is a *sine qua non* as an implementation consideration. Rather than only pre-service training, ongoing process-oriented training which is participatory in nature has been found to be effective. Resource support for training and materials – print and non-print – have to be planned for. Rather than centralised structures, the long-term vision should be of decentralised and local-level structures. Likewise, linkages have to be established with other agencies and departments to ensure availability of services in a smooth co-ordinated manner.

Financing of projects

It is both interesting and discouraging that the observation made by Coombs and Ahmed (1974), that the economics of non-formal education was a virtually nonexistent subject, remains valid even today. In order for an assessment of real costs to be made, we need to account for:

- 'hidden costs' such as volunteer labour, 'free air time', borrowed facilities and opportunity costs for trainees
- the problem of unscrambling joint costs for joint products – because the combined costs and activities of all the different partners and functional components produce the ultimate impact
- the parallel problem of isolating the influence of non-educational factors on the productivity of educational inputs and vice versa
- the fact that non-formal programmes function in a seamless web of interacting development factors which cannot easily be disentangled for statistical measurement

Mayo and Hornik (1983: 333) echoed these concerns when they stated that straightforward enquiries such as 'How much did the project cost?' are limited in the same way as the 'Did the project succeed?' kind of questions. This is especially so since overall cost figures are of little use in planning for projects in new environments, and also because the data available are imprecise, serving more as indicators of expenditure and commitment by an organisation. Further, policy and decision makers are generally concerned with the outcomes of projects. They measure success or failure on the basis of cost estimates and expenditure vis-à-vis visible benefits, whereas literacy and adult education projects are generally working toward improving the quality of life of people. The effectiveness of a project can rarely be measured in terms of cost per unit against the benefit derived, even though DE has been established as a potentially cost-effective way of providing learning content.

Cost elements in a literacy or adult learning project using ODL, while not very different from the costing of other development projects, do have special requirements and greater variation. There are fixed costs, which include capital costs, such as buildings and communication hardware. These initial start-up costs are generally higher than for conventional systems – but can be used for more than a fiscal year. Then there are recurring costs, which include wages and salaries of project staff, production of content materials, operational costs of communication technology, maintenance and updating and upgrading of capital facilities. If the project makes use of existing physical facilities, some costs come down. A combination of delivery media can also reduce costs.

Cost-cutting measures, unless dictated by the appropriate selection of media, can reduce the effectiveness of a project. Delays in project implementation can create cost and time overruns which negate the effective use of communication technologies for delivering content (Enberg 1998: 8).

The unfortunate reality in many literacy and adult learning projects using open and distance learning is that they are dependent on grants-in-aid and are forced to close down as soon as funds are exhausted and just when they are beginning to show results. In the present scenario of resource constraints, education is among the low-priority sectors and among the first where funds are cut. Those projects which have moved toward developing alternate sources of funding – either by revenue generation or through other means – are the ones which survive. The Internet Radio project in Sri Lanka (1999) is one example of an attempt at revenue generation for survival.

Issues relating to media access and media choices

There is still an inadequate understanding of the nature of various NICT and the conditions for their optimum use. It is not the media which are glamorous, trendy or the most modern which prove to be the most successful. Media which are readily accessible, familiar, user friendly, rugged, and inexpensive may prove more useful. When choice of media is given to the user, invariably what is chosen is cheap, easy to access and use, convenient and fun. Field experience shows that media accessible in a comfortable familiar setting, such as the radio or television located in an unobtrusive corner, are more likely to be used than if an individual has to trudge two kilometers after work to watch developmental programmes.

In many social settings there is a politics of media access. When community radio or television sets are placed in a sheltered government building or school, only those with social power may have access to the medium and the content. When men take the radio out to the fields, women lose out on access.

In addition to the appropriate selection of media, control over the medium must remain in the hands of the learner (not with village workers or custodians). Control over the medium demystifies it; it gives a sense of ownership, enabling the learner to use it more effectively.

In addition to the common parameters of access, reach, and ease of use by the learner, criteria for the selection and use of communication technologies in literacy and adult learning should include a flexible perspective which departs from conventional understanding of media technologies and structures. There is no need to build up extensive infrastructure facilities for content development and delivery – instead readily available media infrastructure, such as local printing presses, should be used. Scope for departing from existing strategies and structures and evolving project- and location-specific delivery mechanisms must be built in. One should focus on affordability of initial investment, avoiding systems with high start-up, operational, upgrading and maintenance costs. A training programme on the use of the medium chosen is necessary. Whatever its cost, such training could prove to be crucial to successful implementation of technology. Preliminary findings from the Information Village Project of the M.S. Swaminathan Research Foundation, Chennai, show the critical difference which training has provided (Balaji et al. 1999: 1–15).

For communication technologies to play an optimum role, they must be made accessible to those who have been deprived of them, avoiding the creation of new zones of power created for some, through access and ownership of technology. Choice of media should be such that the technology enables the expression of people's aspirations and provides answers to their questions. Overall, one has to remember that media remain delivery systems, capable of creating motivation and sustaining interest.

Content

Assuming that media choices have been made, the most important element in the implementation process is the development of content. Content must emerge from the learners and must be location- and culture-specific as well as culture-sensitive. Both the Mongolian Gobi Women's Project and the BBC Afghan Education Project used a judicious mix of common and local content in a simple format to relate to learners (UNESCO 1999). Content cannot be relevant to needs unless it emerges from the real-life experiences of learners and from their immediate field of experience, values, indigenous and vernacular knowledge, intermixed with exogenous knowledge (UIE 1997a: 6). If a problem is posed in a programme, learners must be encouraged to explore their own solutions. A 'talk down' approach is common when well-meaning government agencies are involved, because it is easy to bring an expert with a 'piece to the camera'. He or she may approach the issue prescriptively and thus transform content which should ideally engage the learner into a presentation of government policy. The issue is not merely whether materials are learner generated or specially prepared for learners. Content should provide the spark which will make the learner think, so that the solution arrived at is the learner's own. Content must emphasise how the learning can be applied, and must relate the content to learners' goals, past experiences and situational realities. Content must allow debate and challenge ideas, using and respecting the opinions of learners; and must encourage the learner to be a resource for content development and creation.

The communication of content must take precedence over production styles. It must be presented in a simple, yet realistic, manner with culturally relevant linkages. It should also be lively and interesting, without unnecessarily resorting to cinematic techniques. The abundance of entertainment media to which people are today exposed implies that the choice of exposure rests not with the producer of content, but with the learner. Under these circumstances, an indigestible dose of dull education will result in a mental rebellion, unless entertaining and interesting programmes are used to offset the difficult content.

Community involvement and participation

Equally important to appropriate selection of media, and the 'appropriation of control over the medium by learners', are active community involvement and participation in all phases of planning, implementation and evaluation. Participation has a catalytic effect, creating a sense of ownership and partnership. Basic education projects have succeeded wherever such a partnership has been created, whether in the Deccan Development Society's use of video (Dighe and Reddi 1999: 8) or in Guyana (O'Toole and O'Toole 1997).

One of the most important ways in which programmes or projects can be sustained is if the community is involved in the planning and implementation phases. The success of the Kheda project in the 1980s in Gujarat (Agrawal and Aghi 1987) was a result of community involvement in content definition and production of programmes. Such involvement also enables project managers to build on indigenous knowledge and skills, local resources and technologies, as well as empowering communities through capacity building among beneficiaries and local support staff. The result is that a project can be sustained and, in the long run, handed over to the local community to manage, as the critical task of capacity building takes place.

Issues relating to monitoring, evaluation and research

Proper monitoring and timely evaluation are the most neglected aspects of basic education projects using DE methodologies, and are often noticeable by their absence. Governments and funding agencies want visible results such as 'meeting of targets specified'. The absence of such evidence makes 'funding cuts' easy. Unfortunately, when evaluation is carried out, the emphasis tends to be on generating quantitative data, on a one-off basis or in a one-time survey in a situation where longitudinal analysis is essential. Rarely are process-oriented insights provided. In a field as eclectic as literacy and adult education, critical insights, which will help to modify design, content, media selection and access, or levels of community and worker involvement in the programme, can come only from qualitative micro and macro analyses of the situation on the ground. This is an ongoing process, one which combines the rigour of scientific research with speedy reporting of results, so that necessary mid-course modifications and corrections can take place.

Unless monitoring and evaluation take place, we know neither what succeeds nor why a project has failed. Nor can we build up a body of knowledge which can be shared cross-culturally. And each time a new project or programme is launched, we end up 'reinventing the wheel'.

In conclusion

As we researched and wrote this chapter, we found the range and the depth of the issues as challenging as we found reading the case studies. Our field work during the last few months has supported the conclusions of the many case studies which we examined.

We hope that we have drawn your attention to the complexity and the challenges, to the diversity and uniqueness of literacy and adult learning, and to the use of information and communication technologies coupled with the rigour of DE methodologies.

To our mind, the important issues are not distance education or the NICT. The issues are the learners and their specific literacy needs, contexts and content, economic realities, and the power relations which any discussion of literacy and adult education raises. We have to look beyond merely literacy and basic education to the provision of equitable access to learning opportunities. It is here that the significance of all our efforts and the effective use of today's information technologies assume importance.

Note

1 The views expressed in this chapter are those of the authors and do not necessarily represent the views of the organisations to which they belong.

References

Agrawal, B. and Aghi, M. (1987) *Television and the Indian Child: A Handbook*, New Delhi: Concept Publishers.

Balaji, V., Rajamohan, K., Rajasekara Pandy, R. and Senthilkumaran, S. (1999) *Impact of Information Technology in Rural Areas: India: A Report* Prepared by the M.S. Swaminathan Research Foundation, Chennai, unpublished.

Bataille, L. (ed.) (1976) *A Turning Point for Literacy*, Proceedings of the International Symposium for Literacy, Persepolis, Iran, Paris: UNESCO.

Bhola, H. (1984) *Campaigning for Literacy*, Paris: UNESCO.

Coombs, P. and Ahmed, M. (1974) *Attacking Rural Poverty: How Non Formal Education can Help*, Baltimore: Johns Hopkins University Press.

Dighe, A. and Reddi, U. (1999) *Use of Communication Technologies in Open Learning: Non Formal Adult and Community Education*, Plenary paper presented at the Pan-Commonwealth Forum on Open Learning, Bandar Seri Begawan, Brunei Darussalam, 1–5 March.

Dodds, T. (1996) *The Use of Distance Learning in Non-Formal Education*, Vancouver: Commonwealth of Learning and Cambridge: International Extension College.

Education for Development (1998) *Changing Post Literacy in a Changing World*, Report submitted to DFID.

Edirisingha, P. (1999) *Open and Distance Learning for Basic and Non Formal Education in Developing Countries*, Paper presented at the Pan-Commonwealth Forum on Open Learning, Bandar Seri Begawan, Brunei Darussalam, 1–5 March.

Enberg, J. (1998) *Toward a Framework for Evaluation of Multipurpose Community Telecentre Pilot Projects Implemented by ITU and its Partners*, Paper presented at a conference on Partnerships and Participation in Telecommunications for Rural Development: What Works and Why, University of Guelph, Guelph, Ontario, 26–7 October. Available HTTP: *http://www.itu.int/ITU-D-UniversalAccess/johan/papers/guelph.htm*

Freire, P. (1970) *The Pedagogy of the Oppressed*, New York: Herder and Herder.

Freire, P. (1973) *Education for Critical Consciousness*, New York: Seabury Press.

Fuchs, R. (1997) *If You Have a Lemon, Make Lemonade: A Guide to the Start Up of the African Multipurpose Community Telecentre Pilot Projects*, available from the author by email: *rfuchs@fastfwd.com*

Internet Radio in Sri Lanka (1999) from personal visit. Also available HTTP: *http://www.unesco.org/webworld/highlights/internet_radio 130599.html*

Khan, A. (1999) *Application of New Technologies for Non Formal Distance Learning*, Paper presented at the ICDE Conference, Vienna, June.

Matshazi, M. (1999) *Open Learning for Adults with Little or no Formal Education in Zimbabwe*, Paper presented at the Pan-Commonwealth Forum on Open Learning, Bandar Seri Begawan, Brunei Darussalam, 1–5 March.

Mayo, J. and Hornik, R. (1983) 'Evaluation's role in the planning, development and support of non-formal education', in J. Bock and G. Papagiannis (eds) *Non Formal Education and National Development*, New York: Praeger.

O'Toole, P. and O'Toole, B. (1997) 'Literacy as a means of empowerment and transformation', in J. Lynch, C. Modgil and S. Modgil (eds) *Education and Development: Tradition and Innovation*, 3, London: Cassell.

Perraton, H. (1997) *International Research in Open and Distance Learning: Report of a Feasibility Study*, Cambridge: International Research Foundation for Open Learning.

Reddi, U. and Sinvhal, H. (1987) 'Television in higher education: The Indian experience', in *Media in Education and Development* December: 128–33.

Spronk, B. (1999) *Non Formal Education at a Distance: A Framework for Discussion,* Reports on sectoral developments and issues, paper presented at the Pan-Commonwealth Forum on Open Learning, Bandar Seri Begawan, Brunei Darussalam, 1–5 March.

Street, B. (1984) *Literacy in Theory and Practice,* Cambridge: Cambridge University Press.

Street, B. (ed.) (1993) *Cross Cultural Approaches to Literacy,* Cambridge: Cambridge University Press.

Street, B. (1999) 'Meanings of culture and development', in F. Leach and A. Little (eds) *Education, Culture and Economics: Dilemmas for Development,* London: Palmer Press.

Torres, R. (2000) *One Decade of Education for All: The Challenge Ahead,* Background paper for the Second Uppingham Seminar on the Implications of Increasing Diversity in Education in Developing Countries, 24–26 February.

UIE (1997a) *Literacy, Education, and Social Development,* Paper from a series of 29 booklets documenting workshops held at the Fifth International Conference on Adult Education, CONFINTEA, Hamburg: UNESCO Institute for Education.

UIE (1997b) *Literacy and Technology,* Paper from a series of 29 booklets documenting workshops held at the Fifth International Conference on Adult Education, CONFINTEA, Hamburg: UNESCO Institute for Education.

UNESCO (1999) *Technology and Learning: Cases,* Learning without Frontiers document.

Warr, D. (1992) *Distance Teaching in the Village,* Cambridge: International Extension College.

Chapter 10

Basic education for refugees and nomads

Jason Pennells and Chimah Ezeomah

> The Fulani do not hate Western education, but the system which does not
> favour them ...
>
> (Baraya 1979)

An examination of basic education for people who are marginalised and excluded
from formal education systems necessitates considering the cases of refugees and
nomads, groups who fall outside the mainstream of society and thus often outside
the mainstream provision of education.

Firstly, we need to consider what we mean by 'nomads', 'refugees' and other
related labels; and to distinguish nomads (travellers, migrants) from refugees and
thus nomadic education from refugee education. Having made these distinctions,
and briefly considered refugee education and the place of open and distance learning within that field, this chapter will focus primarily on nomadic education.
The focus will also be mainly, but not exclusively, on Africa, and particularly will
draw on examples from Nigeria.

By looking at examples of basic education programmes for nomads, we can
begin to identify some common issues in nomadic education. Several questions
need to be explored:

- What are the goals and purposes of nomadic education and policies?
- What delivery methods have been used to provide nomads with access to
  education?
- How far have open learning and distance education approaches been used
  and found effective?
- What levels of education have been addressed and for what audiences?
- What can we learn from the evidence on nomadic education initiatives?
- What key issues arise in connection with nomadic education which are
  relevant to policy and planning?

Definitions

In general usage, refugees are groups or nationalities who have been abruptly
uprooted from their traditional homes by man-made crises such as wars, conflicts

or political unrest, or by natural disasters such as epidemics, floods, cyclones, drought, famine or earthquakes. The consistent occurrence and enormity of these man-made and natural disasters has, over the years, resulted in the mass movement and displacement of many people from their homes to new locations or countries. The United Nations High Commission for Refugees (UNHCR) classifies those whose displacement is contained within the boundaries of a recognised state as 'displaced people' rather than as refugees. This distinction can have more than technical significance, as it impacts both on the legal status and provision of services to the people concerned and also possibly on the educational, linguistic and cultural relationship between these people and their host environment.

Although the initial movement of refugees may be sudden, and the assumption is that where possible they will return home once the current crisis has passed, their stay in the new environment they move to may be short or long term, and may lead to permanent settlement in the new location (Egwu 1987).

Nomads are variously defined. Broadly, discussion of nomads is of ethnic or socio-economic groups who constantly travel and migrate, in large or small groups, in search of means of livelihood, within a community or country or across international boundaries. These groups contrast with the settled or sedentary population, living in villages, towns and cities, and tied to fixed locations by agriculture, employment, housing and social and cultural factors. This bipolar picture is complicated, however, by differences of usage and implications of several related terms.

Pastoralism, sometimes used as a term interchangeably with nomadism, reflects a lifestyle based on maintenance of herds of animals which depend mainly on natural vegetation for their food; this dependence, along with migration to water, away from disease and in response to other pressures, determines the seasonal and daily movements of pastoralists (Awogbade 1991: 2).

Although the pastoral nomad is the classic example and the predominating one in discussion of nomadic education in Africa, there are many other occupations and socio-cultural groups which are based on a mobile lifestyle. Examples include the migrant fishermen of Nigeria (Ezewu and Tahir 1997), the Romany gypsies of Europe, circus and fairground people (Danaher 1998, 1999), hunter/gatherers such as the Hadzabe in Tanzania (Bugeke 1997: 71), migrant agricultural workers and new age travellers.

For the purposes of the present discussion, the main distinction is between refugees (and displaced persons) on the one hand, and nomads (including pastoralists, itinerant and migrant workers and travellers) on the other.

Contrasts between nomads and refugees

Nomads and refugees both represent groups identifiably separate from the society which surrounds them. Both refugees and nomads fall outside the standard frameworks of sedentary communities. However, in very many ways the situation of nomads and that of refugees differ from each other. Table 10.1 lays out some

Table 10.1 Comparisons between situations of nomads and refugees

Aspect	Nomads, in relation to surrounding context	Refugees, in relation to surrounding context
Cultural distinction from sedentary context	• May be very distinct • May share much common ground, e.g. religion, national allegiance	• May be very distinct or similar • From foreign country
Homogeneity	• Highly homogeneous within group • Internal differentiation	• May be homogeneous or very mixed, in representing all strata and groups of displaced society
Language	• Different or the same	• Different or the same
Social status in surrounding society	• Often excluded • Often inferior status • Mutual mistrust and antagonism common	• Typically tolerated or • resented (occasionally welcomed) • Often 'invisible' • May seek to pass/assimilate into host society, or to retain distinctive identity
Location	• Mobile • Familiar routes and locations • May cross internal administrative and international borders • Predominantly rural (especially pastoralists) • On the fringes of settled communities • Groups may be dispersed	• Concentrated in large camps or scattered • May be rural camp near international borders, or camp on periphery of conurbation (where may hope to become assimilated into the urban population) • May be dispersed into host country society
Age group and gender	• All ages, male and female	• All ages, male and female
Legal rights	• National and citizen's rights • Often abused due to ignorance, prejudice, conflict with landowners lack of influence, etc.	• Rights accorded to refugees by host country and international charter • Often difficult to enact these rights • Internally displaced people not accorded refugee rights
Access to education and other services	• Limited by necessities of mobile/working lifestyle • Temporary access to schools and services of sedentary community	• Severely disrupted by dislocation • Programmes set up within refugee communities or provided by relief agencies • May share in host society's mainstream provision

continued ...

Table 10.1 Comparisons between situations of nomads and refugees (continued)

Aspect	Nomads, in relation to surrounding context	Refugees, in relation to surrounding context
Integration	• Typically maintaining own cultural and social identity over generations • May resist administrative and political pressures to assimilate into mainstream	• May seek to integrate and participate, and to be absorbed into the new host context • May seek to preserve and pass on own culture
Economic status	• Traditional bases of wealth (e.g. cattle) • Community base of wealth (e.g. within clan)	• Often destitute, even if prosperous before becoming refugees • May be dependent on external support • May be able to become self-supporting through employment
Facilities	• Tents, huts, no electricity • Schools may be under trees, tents, grass shelters, or in permanent buildings	• Range from basic tent or shanty camps to those available in the mainstream domestic context of a settled house
Agencies and structures to respond to needs	• National government and NGO agencies	• International dedicated agencies • NGOs • Host country bodies
Own motivation for learning	• Protect selves from exploitation • Income generation • Life skills (livestock, health, literacy, numeracy) • Access professional career (to exit from nomadic life, or to serve the nomadic community)	• Return to normality and future orientation after trauma of refugee experience • Preservation of own culture • Personal development and prospects • Preparation for repatriation or resettlement • Integration into host society[a]
Policy motivations for providing education	• Nation-building • Settlement • Social development • Economic development • Conflict reductions • Promote citizenship	• International responsibility • Moral and humanitarian necessity • Political support to refugees • Avoid social and economic disruption of hosting uneducated refugees

continued ...

Table 10.1 Comparisons between situations of nomads and refugees (continued)

Aspect	Nomads, in relation to surrounding context	Refugees, in relation to surrounding context
Future goals	• Maintenance of community/clan interests and culture • Economic betterment	• Repatriation, resettlement or assimilation
Educational background	• Limited to traditional/religious school • Possibly attendance at mainstream primary school	• Very diverse, from no schooling to postgraduate doctorates and professional qualifications
Learning needs	• Basic functional literacy and numeracy • Income generation and marketing • Savings and credit • Livestock management • National education curriculum to access mainstream society and education	• Mainstream education of host country for assimilation *or* • Education for return to country of origin *or* • Education for onward movement to third country of settlement • Basic survival skills, income generation • General education at all levels from primary to adult, from basic literacy to postgraduate study
Obstacles to learning	• Mobility • Lifestyle • Remote locations • Ambivalence towards education • Lack of money	• Living conditions • Struggle to survive and support family in refugee situation • Disrupted life and psychology
Curriculum	• Typically, national curriculum adjusted to nomads' culture • Custom-designed functional curricula	• According to learning needs, future goals accreditation and agency support
Delivery methods	• Face-to-face teaching • Mobile or drop-in schools • Facilitated study groups • Radio broadcasts • Internet[b]	• Face-to-face teaching • Distance education packages (audio tapes, printed study material, correspondence tuition, etc.)

continued ...

Table 10.1 Comparisons between situations of nomads and refugees (continued)

Aspect	Nomads, in relation to surrounding context	Refugees, in relation to surrounding context
Accreditation	• Mainstream for formal education • Providing for non-formal courses	• Mainstream system of host country *or* • System of country of origin *or* • Third party course provider/examiner *or* • NGO or agency (internal certification)

Notes
a   Dodds 1988: 42–3.
b   For example, the TOPILOT project in UK, which was designed to use the world wide web as a means for British travellers to maintain contact with a centralised education service (Mykytyn 1997).

contrasts and some similarities between the characteristic situations of nomads and of refugees and the implications their respective situations have for their education.

From the point of view of providing educational opportunities, the range of variables attributable to refugees and to nomads indicates there is no single model or characterisation which would allow a universal 'blueprint' for the use of open learning or distance education (DE) approaches for these audiences. What is true of a Fulbe (Fulani) pastoral nomad in Nigeria will have little relation to what is true of a travelling show person in Australia or a traveller in Britain. The situation of a refugee in an emergency and temporary camp just over the border from a conflict, such as for many Rwandese refugees in Goma in Zaire in the 1990s, is very different from that of a Palestinian living in a long-established camp or that of a South African living and working in one of the front-line states during the apartheid era, but hoping one day to return home.

Refugee education

Providing refugees with access to education is a necessity for various reasons, although in general priority attention is paid to satisfying the survival needs of security, shelter, food, water and health care, and education is treated as of secondary importance (Thomas 1996: 4). Reasons for striving to provide education in refugee situations may be summarised as (Thomas 1996: 3–5):

- To fulfil a legal and moral duty, according to international conventions and declarations
- To alleviate post-traumatic stress and establish elements of normality and a sense of purpose by setting up primary schools

- To provide purposeful activity to adolescents
- To develop survival and self-reliance skills in adult refugees to cope with their refugee situation
- To maintain the cultural and educational link with the refugees' own country and thus to facilitate repatriation when possible
- To equip refugees for return and reconstruction, for coexistence in the host country or possible assimilation or transfer to a third country for settlement

The mixed educational levels of refugees may be turned to advantage in arranging access to education, in that, in some cases, teachers and other resource people may be recruited from within the refugee community to run education programmes. This diversity also means, however, that there is likely to be a demand for a wide range of courses at different levels. Among large numbers of peasant families creating the need for mass basic education programmes, there may be smaller but nevertheless substantial numbers needing secondary and higher education or completion of interrupted professional training (Dodds 1983: 3–5).

Problems with refugee education may arise if the host country's education facilities are already stretched to the limit and unable to accommodate refugees (Dodds 1983: 5) or if relief agencies 'cream off' the best-qualified refugees and provide them with 'escape' scholarships to other countries, leaving behind the masses with diminished expertise resources in their midst (Inquai 1983: 2).

Although there are various NGOs and educational institutions which pursue refugee education as part of their core mandate (Thomas 1996: 149–68) and others which implement or support individual projects, for example the GTZ-BEFARe Afghan refugee education project (GTZ-BEFARe 1999), the field is not substantially served or resourced, given the scale of the need. Education appears to be a relatively low priority of UNHCR, and is not one of the agency's activities listed on the current UNHCR website (http://www.unhcr.ch).

Open and distance education for refugees

DE can be appropriate for refugees because conventional provision is unlikely to be readily available to them; because it can in some instances provide high-quality education and training swiftly, to large numbers at low cost; and because it can enable refugees to access education and training without having to leave their families and other commitments (Thomas 1996: 5).

Examples of the use of open learning and DE approaches for refugee learners include:

- the Refugee Adult Education (RAE) Programme in Somalia, set up to deliver adult literacy and basic education, using facilitated study group methods such as audio cassettes, flipcharts and posters, group facilitation materials and study group learning (Thomas 1996: 69)
- the Institute of In-service Teacher Training (IITT), also in Somalia, which provided basic and more advanced teacher training programmes to refugees,

using printed DE materials, audio cassettes, self-help study groups and face-to-face tutorials (Thomas 1996: 9)

- the South African Extension Unit (SAEU), based in Tanzania, established to provide basic education and secondary education courses to South African exiles in the 'frontline states' during the apartheid era; the basic education programme used printed and audio materials developed inhouse, in conjunction with study groups, while the secondary programme used bought-in Wolsey Hall materials from Britain (Thomas 1996: 30–1)

- the Sudan Open Learning Unit, originally set up to provide a wide range of education and training courses to Ethiopian and Eritrean refugees in eastern Sudan, and latterly, as the Sudan Open Learning Organisation, catering for displaced southern Sudanese who have fled the civil war in the south and congregated around the three cities of the capital; courses include primary health care (using flipcharts, radio/audio programmes and facilitated group meetings) and a teacher assistance course (using printed self-study booklets and group meetings) (Thomas 1996: 17, 74)

Nomadic education

The education of nomads is an area of some debate, with differing positions held regarding its underlying rationale and its technical means of delivery. The predominant conviction among educators and politicians over several decades has been, and continues to be, that the welfare and development of nomads requires that they become settled and cease living their mobile lifestyle (Obanya 1997: viii). How far this can be achieved without the nomads losing their distinct cultural identity, or creating new social or environmental problems as a result, is a moot point (UNICEF 1978: 122).

In Kenya, as elsewhere, the government has often sought to engineer the settlement of nomads, since their mobile lifestyle has been seen as an impediment to their education, to their integration into national society and to improvement in their standard of living (Akaranga 1997: 38). At the start of the twenty-first century, settlement is seen as an inevitability, as in many places the pressure on land increases drastically and it becomes ever more difficult to maintain a nomadic lifestyle without coming into conflict with sedentary farmers and land owners. However reluctantly, settlement is seen as a necessary survival strategy (Dyer and Choksi 1998: 101–2, Ezeomah 1987b).

Education is seen to go hand in hand with sedentarisation, both as a contributing cause and as a result of the process (Dyer and Choksi 1998: 94 ff., Ezeomah 1987a: 5). The reluctance to settle in some instances is not merely sentimentality or conservatism: in the case of the Rubari in India, it is feared settlement may lead to economic pressure, loss of cultural identity, decay of community and unemployment (Dyer and Choksi 1998: 102).

In Nigeria, the introduction of successive laws and decrees regarding land use and grazing rights has contributed directly to shaping the movement patterns and the pressure on nomads for settlement, as free-ranging pastoralism has become increasingly difficult and conflict-ridden as a way of life (Ezeomah 1987b: 29, Aminu 1991: 50). Comparable issues apply in Britain, where trespass and vagrancy laws have made it increasingly difficult for travellers to stop overnight without prosecution (Rafferty 1998: 4, Klein 1997: 39).

There is frequently mistrust of education among nomads, the nomadic parents and elders fearing that education will spoil their children and lead them away from their traditional values and lifestyle (Dyer and Choksi 1998: 100). Non-formal and DE approaches can help to avoid the feared influence of attending a full-time day school or a boarding institution, by taking education to the children without necessitating that they leave their community or abandon their daily duties, such as herding.

By contrast to these misgivings about the social effects of education, there is also a strong body of thought and energy devoted to using education as a means to empower nomads, to counteract their marginalisation and disenfranchisement and to enable them to achieve self-realisation. This is seen as a process and shift in consciousness which must also include the non-nomadic policy makers and implementers of programmes. Ezeomah advocates 'redemptive egalitarianism' in determinedly providing relevant education for nomads (Ezeomah 1998b: 111), while Anyanwu invokes 'transformative research' to enlighten policy makers and educators as a way forward (Anyanwu 1998: 44).

As one might anticipate from the norms of participatory practice in any field, a broad consensus is evolving on the importance of involving nomads in the determination of their educational aims, systems and curricula, rather than imposing policies and designs by a 'top-down' approach. This has emerged with conviction in, for example, Nigeria (Ezeomah 1987a: 6, Ezeomah 1998b: 115ff, Abba and Bakari 1999: 8-9), Kenya (Adano 1998: 3) and India (Dyer and Choksi 1998: 101).

The aims and objectives of nomadic education have typically been identified in Nigeria as falling into two groups: 'citizenship' aims, on the one hand, and aims to do with improving nomads' quality of life, on the other. Literacy is seen as vital to both kinds of aims (Ezeomah 1993: 50–1). In one manifestation of this framework, the 1986 policy guidelines for education of nomads, developed from the Nigeria national education policy of 1981, identified 'integrative objectives' ('inculcation of the right type of values and attitudes') and 'distinctive objectives' (objectives tailored to the learning needs of nomads as distinct from other members of society) (Ezeomah 1997: 22–3).

The content and audiences of nomadic education include general primary education for children, for example those of Australian show and circus people (Danaher 1999: 25, Haughey 1999: 113) and many African countries (UNICEF 1978); pastoralist skills for youth in Tanzania (Bugeke 1997: 75); and a range of skills including income generation, business skills, family care, literacy support and livestock management for women, in the Gobi Women's Project in Mongolia (Robinson 1999: 188).

Curriculum and language issues

One central way in which the aims of integration and of fulfilling distinctively nomadic needs are manifested is through the curriculum. To take the example of Nigeria again, national primary school curricula were adapted for nomadic schools in 1990, to be culturally relevant to the nomadic child but 'on a par with' non-nomadic schools and to satisfy the national policy of integration and equity (Ezeomah 1993: 1). The use of the nomads' mother tongue or of the national language in schools is also an issue bearing directly on identity (Muhammad 1991: 109–17).

When Nigeria developed the nomadic primary school curriculum, each school subject was developed so that its content should be relevant to the life and environment of the nomads. However, the English curriculum specifies additionally that its purpose is to facilitate progress to higher education and to promote a national language (Nwoke 1993: 82).

In an as yet unpublished paper written for a curriculum conference in Lagos (Abba and Bakari 1999), the argument is reinforced that nomads should be closely involved in the process of planning their own curriculum, to turn the tide on a long history of ineffective education since the 1920s based on irrelevant curricula.

Issues of programme focus and delivery

Regarding the technical delivery of primary education, in Nigeria the debate has focused on whether to provide mobile schools and programmes which travel around with the nomads, or to provide stationary schools and to contrive for the nomads to settle to attend these schools (Aminu 1991: 49). Mobile schools have been used, with specially constructed tents or temporary shades under trees or thatches, staffed by teachers who move with the nomads during the migrations. 'On-site' schools, which are in fixed locations in the nomads' wet season and dry season areas, have also been used. The mobile schools have encountered problems with the design of the collapsible classrooms, lack of finance to supply and maintain adequate numbers of the tents, and the reluctance of non-nomadic teachers to travel and live a nomadic lifestyle (Tahir 1997: 56–7, Ardo 1991: 82–3). There are also administrative problems of resources and staff management when nomadic movements cross state borders.

The address by the then Executive Secretary of the National Commission for Nomadic Education (NCNE) to the workshop which produced the *Handbook for Teachers in Nomadic Schools* (Ezeomah 1993) sets out concerns about who should teach nomads; whom they should teach; and where, when and what they should teach. In the handbook, the movement patterns of nomads are analysed in terms of the logistical implications they have for organising mobile classes. For the system to function, it is stressed that the teacher/organiser has to be familiar with the nomads' movements, and that the nomads in their turn need to organise their family or group movements in such a co-ordinated way as to make for viably sized classes. The primary teacher should also serve as an adult literacy instructor to the nomadic group (Adepetu 1993: 179–83).

Open and distance education for nomads: theory

Open education approaches tend toward offering opportunities for nomads to access education in the course of their normal migratory movement, rather than demanding that they settle in one place or attend a rigid institutional programme such as a boarding school. To the extent that ODE strategies achieve this flexibility, they could be seen as supporting the preservation of the learners' nomadic lifestyle and culture, in contrast to conventional school attendance, which would tend to break down traditional behaviour patterns such as migration, herding and clan-based cultural intercourse.

As has been indicated, ODE also allows for alternative, culturally tailored curricula to be used, in contrast to the homogenising effect on nomadic children of attending mainstream schools and studying the standard national curriculum material. ODE need not be a force for conservatism, however: the content can have a modernising agenda as readily as a traditional one. An example would be teaching modern animal husbandry techniques (NCNE 1999), or raising awareness of the importance of education (Umar and Tahir 1998: 31–9).

A workshop was held in 1994 from which the edited papers were later published as *Readings on Distance Education for the Pastoral Nomads of Nigeria* (Tahir and Muhammad 1998). The range and content of papers included indicates the stage thinking had reached about DE for nomads in Nigeria at that time. Most significantly, there are detailed underpinnings for the planning of DE programmes based on detailed knowledge of the patterns and conditions of nomadic life and the characteristics of nomadic Fulbe (Ezeomah 1998a: 3–9), an analysis of the problems of developing DE for nomads (Egede 1998) and reviews of the national policy background (Kaliel 1998, Agwu 1998). Agwu cites Ezeomah (1993), pointing out that national policy implies that nomadic education is for children, without explicit reference to adult education.

Ezeomah's paper analyses the communications networks used by Fulbe nomads, based on meetings at markets, in the clan leader's camp and by sending out scouts ahead of the cattle movements. He argues that these should be used as the basis of communication in DE programmes, along with transistor radios, which are commonly accessible to the nomads. Complementary factors to these in maintaining contact with Fulbe nomads for the purposes of open or distance education are the patterns of long-distance migrations and shorter dispersions which the nomads undertake, and the need for programme providers and nomads to discuss and agree in advance the convenient movement patterns and study schedules.

There are also several general papers rehearsing the characteristics of DE and speculating about the possible application of such methods. These papers are written from the perspectives of materials development and production (print and audio), management, administration, record keeping and broadcasting. The workshop was to prepare a blueprint for DE for nomadic children, including both curriculum and delivery model (Ukachi 1998).

Open and distance education for nomads: experience

Among a majority of papers from this 1994 workshop which propose what should be done by way of DE for nomads, some describe what has been done. One such paper (Umar and Tahir 1998, updated in the interim between the workshop and publication of the book) describes a nomadic radio series, *Don Makiyaya a Ruga* ('For Nomadic Pastoralists in the Homestead'). The radio series was a general magazine-format, open broadcast without extension support services. It was transmitted over thirteen weeks in 1996, its purpose being to raise awareness among nomads about the importance of education.

In June 1999, NCNE held a workshop to develop 'radio curricula for a distance learning scheme for adult pastoralists'. The new basic education curricula developed were for animal husbandry, health education, political education and income-generating skills (NCNE 1999). NCNE expressed commitment to developing its DE activities; how far these will extend beyond unsupported open broadcast radio programmes remains as a challenge.

Radio broadcasting has been a medium used repeatedly in nomadic education in Nigeria. An earlier example was the Nomadic Fulani Educational Radio Programme broadcast by Radio Plateau in 1981. The purpose of the programme was to popularise the nomadic education project among the nomads and 'to affect their minds towards social change' (Ezeomah 1983: 44). The programme was weakened by lacking field support and by the target audience not knowing when to listen. In retrospect, it was felt it would have been more effective to organise the listeners into listening groups (Ezeomah 1997: 16–17).

Other Nigerian experiments have included a mobile cinema in Bauchi State to mobilise the nomadic population and persuade them of the value of education (Ezeomah 1983: 30), and single teacher mobile schools (which largely failed, for a combination of reasons, including lack of government policy, using non-nomadic teachers, an irrelevant curriculum and lack of effective administration) (Ezeomah 1997: 19).

It might be noted at this point that in areas other than basic education for nomads, Nigeria has had considerable experience in DE. Notably, the National Teachers' Institute has trained large numbers of teachers to Grade II Certificate by Distance Education and to Nigeria Certificate in Education, reportedly more than 185,000 between 1984 and 1989 (Ezeomah 1990: Annex).

Proposals for DE for nomads in Nigeria include a 'multimedia distance learning system' for school education and adult education (NCNE 1998: 11). As in many countries (Ezeomah 1997), such plans have had a tendency to be easier to propose than to bring to concrete reality (Ezeomah 1990: 10, 16, Tahir 1998: 16–21).

Other African experience of ODE for nomadic education includes a basic literacy and numeracy project to help Lesotho herd boys, whose lifestyle was very fragmented into blocks of time away herding, then back in the village, then off to work in the mines at a later age. The Lesotho Distance Teaching Centre organised courses and produced printed study materials; the village community leaders held the materials, organised regular study meetings and supported the young boys, who, it was felt, would not have settled to study otherwise. Despite the communities' commitment, the learning gains were reportedly disappointing (Murphy 1978: 36–40).

In Sudan, the UNICEF Nomadic Education Project in Darfur state used collapsible classroom tents, and attempted to provide skills development in animal husbandry as well as basic education, through a modified version of the national curriculum. The results were mixed: few male adults participated in the adult education classes, and there was high drop-out. The intended mobility did not work out. When the nomads dispersed into small family groups during the wet season, it did not prove possible to continue classes by the (face-to-face) model used. The tents were found to be inappropriate and were not used, but they were felt to be a status symbol for the communities which held them. Essentially, regular classes were taught during the dry season, when the nomads reassembled (Gore *et al.* 1998: 7–9, 44).

Zanzibar has a Fishery Zone for which the Adult Education Department developed non-formal courses to train migrant fishermen in modern fishing, fish-processing techniques and literacy. Literacy animators were trained and were given teaching materials. The fishermen studied from printed primers and classes using a special curriculum for the three months they were away at a fishing camp, then enrolled in their village literacy classes on returning home at the end of the season of absence. Plans were also made to develop DE courses for migrant women farmers. Limited funding curtailed the full implementation of the planned courses on a large scale (Juma 1997: 83–7).

In Britain, children of fairground, circus and bargee families also suffer discontinuity of schooling due to their mobile lifestyles. A European Union funded project has linked up traveller children with one another, and with a tutor and learning resources, by using the world wide web, accessed by each pupil through an individual workstation with wireless modem and interactive multimedia compact disks (CDi). There is a central tutor workstation, to control the interactions and the distribution of learning activities to the learners. Partner colleges based near the winter quarters of the fairground families co-operate in developing and providing the multimedia materials (Mykytyn 1997).

In Australia, teachers from Brisbane School of Distance Education travel for part of the year to provide education to circus and show people (the former following an erratic and *ad hoc* schedule of movement, according to the contingencies of business and competition, the latter following relatively regular and predictable itineraries, as they follow scheduled agricultural shows). During the remainder of the year, the school sends out printed DE packages to the children, who may be mentored locally by their mothers or by a hired tutor (Danaher 1998).

In Mongolia, DE was used to reach a very thinly scattered population of nomads, over a vast area in the Gobi Women's Project. Radio broadcasts, centrally produced booklets with locally developed supplements, 'travelling boxes' of materials and face-to-face contact with voluntary tutors were combined for the course. The course dealt with livestock, family care, literacy, income generation and business skills. Extensive preparation was carried out, which was vital since the environ-ment was extremely difficult, in terms of the absence of communication infra-structure, and the geographical scale was very large. Due to slowness in print production, coupled with the distances involved, the printed materials and the radio broadcasts did not coincide as planned. However, the project established DE in Mongolia as a means of delivering basic education on a mass scale (Robinson 1999).

Conclusions concerning nomadic education

Although there is some common ground between the uses of open and distance learning for nomadic education and for refugee education, the specific demands, constraints and possibilities of each are distinct. As such, the lessons to be learned and the solutions to be found differ.

Ezeomah summarises eight major lessons learnt about nomadic education in Africa, as identified in the proceedings of the 1995 Kaduna conference (Ezeomah 1997: 28–9):

- Recognition of nomadic culture is necessary for programmes to be successful
- Research is needed into nomadic culture
- Nomads dislike Western delivery systems, not education as such
- Education should be taken to nomads on the move, by various means
- Education needs to be developed to suit nomadic lifestyles in order to succeed
- Nomads should be involved in planning, implementing and evaluating their education programmes
- Development of suitable skills and knowledge will improve the lives of individual nomads, their societies and their nations
- Nomadic education is an international responsibility, as nomads spread across national borders

The political dimension of curriculum and course design

Nomadic education can serve directly political purposes; the question of whose political purpose is implicit in every decision, from the initial decision to plan to implement a nomadic education programme, through designing the curriculum and delivery model, to funding, recruiting learners and staff and evaluating the programme. Goals of nomadic education (whether implicit or explicit, imposed from above or identified by the nomads) may include integration, settlement, nation-building, improving economic prosperity, strengthening government control, development or protection and preservation of one's own nomadic culture and society, developing life skills, or shifting towards empowerment and self-determination.

The inevitability and benefit of the settlement of nomads is an assumption underpinning the great majority of nomadic development and education projects. Sometimes this may concur with the nomads' own wishes, such as when their access to grazing land has come under pressure (Ezeomah 1987b: 26–30); very often, it is a top-down policy. The extent to which the nomads affected buy in to the idea, as opposed to being manipulated by it, is central to the validity and strength of settlement-oriented projects in which they take part.

As is a truism in any educational endeavour, the suitability of the design of ODE programmes to the culture and lifestyle of the intended participants is a basic concern. The appropriateness of the curriculum, delivery methods and timetabling must all be considered. In most cases, balances will need to be struck between the 'integrative' and the 'distinctive' qualities of any programme for nomads. This applies not only to the content of the course materials but also to the delivery and support systems. It applies also to the language or languages used on courses.

Costs and resources

Economies of scale, the standard triumphal flag-waver of DE programmes, may not readily be achievable with small, remote nomadic groups and intensive support systems. Unlike refugee education, where for some education and training levels, materials and whole courses may be accessed ready-made from elsewhere, at the basic education level where the bulk of nomadic education courses are likely to be, course content and materials generally have to be developed locally to fit the characteristics of the learners closely, while tuition, mentoring and other forms of learner support are likely to be relatively labour-intensive and thus costly.

Resources are everywhere limited, reflecting political priorities. This perhaps unsurprising constraint, allied with underestimating the resources required to develop and implement ODE programmes, helps to explain why less has been achieved in using these approaches for the education of nomads than was seen as the potential. In the future, the possibilities remain for ODE, in one form or another, to serve the needs of nomads.

Open and distance education for nomadic basic education: achievements so far

Diverse delivery models and technologies have been used for ODE for nomadic learners, including printed materials, radio broadcasts, facilitated and self-help study group meetings, fixed-location schools, mobile schools, mobile cinema, audio cassettes and the Internet. Using the channels and structures of nomads' communities may compensate for the lack of facilities and systems more easily available in non-nomadic life, on which many ODE programmes rely, such as transport, mail, study centres, electricity, administrative offices, formal information channels and counselling contacts.

According to the nature of the environment and the requirements of a specific situation, an open or DE system for nomads may feature more or less decentralisation. Centralised co-ordination is likely to be important (funding, other resources, course development and accreditation, learners and staff may cross administrative boundaries in maintaining the continuity of a project or programme for nomads). Yet communication within a large centralised system is likely to be tortuous, and the differences in conceptualisation among project participants (learners, staff and other stakeholders) are likely to be substantial. The greatest gap may be between the nomad learner and the co-ordinator in a project office. Rather than have a project-binding bureaucracy, positive results are more likely to be yielded by subsidiarity and flexibility applied within clear and consistent frameworks.

ODE approaches have so far had limited impact on basic education for nomadic populations. Despite general recognition and exhortation that DE has great potential for nomadic education, the majority of what has been implemented has been unsupported open broadcasting or face-to-face teaching; and the majority of the learning environments have been fixed schools.

Not surprisingly, in view of the marginalisation which is implicit in nomadism, there has been, with some notable exceptions, a lack of experience, research and commitment associated with developing open and distance learning for nomadic education.

In the span of time from the 1970s and earlier, through the 1980s and 1990s, despite changes and developments, by and large the same issues have continued to emerge: these include the interface between nomads and the state, how far the state can or should support and protect nomads' traditional way of life, and how far the nomads wish to become assimilated into the state, as opposed to maintaining their traditional clan loyalties above all else. How education contributes to this set of balances, and how ODE in particular may be used to fulfil the aims of whoever is setting the agenda, look set to remain topical for some considerable time to come.

References

Abba, M. and Bakari, S. (1999) 'Empowering the socially deprived through the curriculum: The case of Fulbe nomads in Nigeria', Mimeo, paper prepared for postponed conference Re-thinking the Curricula for Schools Effectiveness in the Next Millennium, the Nigeria Chapter of the World Council for the Curriculum and Instruction, scheduled for September 1999, Lagos State University.

Adano, U. (1998) 'Education and development for nomadic pastoralists in Kenya: A pastoralist's perspective', Mimeo, unpublished.

Adepetu, A. (1993) 'School and community relationship in mobile setting', in C. Ezeomah (ed.) Handbook for Teachers in Nomadic Schools, Kaduna: National Commission for Nomadic Education.

Agwu, S. (1998) 'Education curriculum for nomads', in G. Tahir and N. Muhammad (eds) *Readings on Distance Education for the Pastoral Nomads of Nigeria*, Zaria: Ahmadu Bello University Press.

Akaranga, J. (1997) 'Nomadic education in Kenya', in C. Ezeomah (ed.) *The Education of Nomadic Populations in Africa: Papers Presented at the UNESCO (Breda) Regional Seminar on the Education of Nomadic Populations in Africa, 11–15 December 1995, Kaduna, Nigeria*, Dakar: UNESCO.

Aminu, J. (1991) 'The evolution of nomadic education policy in Nigeria', in G. Tahir (ed.) *Education and Pastoralism in Nigeria*, Zaria: Ahmadu Bello University Press.

Anyanwu, C. (1998) 'Transformative research for the promotion of nomadic education in Nigeria', in *Journal of Nomadic Studies* 1, 1: 44–51.

Ardo, G. (1991) 'Planning for minority education with particular reference to pastoralists of Nigeria', in G. Tahir (ed.) *Education and Pastoralism in Nigeria*, Zaria: Ahmadu Bello University Press.

Awogbade, M. (1991) 'Nomadism and pastoralism: A conceptual framework', in G. Tahir (ed.) *Education and Pastoralism in Nigeria*, Zaria: Ahmadu Bello University Press.

Baraya, A. (1979) *Report on Nomadic Education in Ningi Local Government Area*, cited in C. Ezeomah (1983) *The Education of Nomadic People*, Driffield: Nafferton Books.

Bugeke, C.J. (1997) 'Nomadic education in Tanzania', in C. Ezeomah (ed.) *The Education of Nomadic Populations in Africa: Papers Presented at the UNESCO (Breda) Regional Seminar on the Education of Nomadic Populations in Africa, 11–15 December 1995, Kaduna, Nigeria*, Dakar: UNESCO.

Danaher, P. (ed.) (1998) *Beyond the Ferris Wheel: Educating Queensland Show Children. Studies in Open and Distance Learning Number 1*, Rockhampton: Central Queensland University Press.

Danaher, P. (1999) 'Learning under ferris wheels and big tops: comparing the education of Australian show and circus people', in *Journal of Nomadic Studies*, 2: 24–31.

Dodds, T. (1983) 'The International Extension College launches a new refugee education service', in *About Distance Education*, 18: 3–5.

Dodds, T. (1988) 'The education of refugees in Africa: the role of distance education and open learning', in *Media in Education and Development*, 21, 2: 39–43.

Dyer, C. and Choksi A. (1998) 'Education for Indian pastoralists: strategies for provision', in *Journal of Nomadic Studies*, 1, 1: 94–103.

Egede, F. (1998) 'Problems with developing distance education', in G. Tahir and N.D. Muhammad (eds) *Readings on Distance Education for the Pastoral Nomads of Nigeria*, Zaria: Ahmadu Bello University Press.

Egwu, E. (1987) 'Educating refugees: problems and prospects', in *International Journal of Nomadic and Minority Education*, 1, 2: 39–46.

Ezeomah, C. (1983) *The Education of Nomadic People*, Driffield: Nafferton Books.

Ezeomah, C. (1987a) 'Incorporating education with integrated rural development scheme in nomadic Fulbe community', in *International Journal of Nomadic and Minority Education*, 1, 2: 1–11.

Ezeomah, C. (1987b) *The Settlement Patterns of Nomadic Fulbe in Nigeria: Implications for Educational Development*, Betley: Deanhouse.

Ezeomah, C. (1990) 'Distance education for nomads in Nigeria', Mimeo, paper presented at Priority Africa distance education seminar, Arusha, Tanzania, 24–28 September.

Ezeomah, C. (1993) 'The aims and objectives of nomadic education', in C. Ezeomah (ed.) *Handbook for Teachers in Nomadic Schools*, Kaduna: National Commission for Nomadic Education.

Ezeomah, C. (1997) 'Basic issues on nomadic education in Africa', in C. Ezeomah (ed.) *The Education of Nomadic Populations in Africa: Papers Presented at the UNESCO (Breda) Regional Seminar on the Education of Nomadic Populations in Africa, 11–15 December 1995, Kaduna, Nigeria,* Dakar: UNESCO.

Ezeomah, C. (1998a) 'Distance education for nomads', in G. Tahir and N.D. Muhammad (eds) *Readings on Distance Education for the Pastoral Nomads of Nigeria,* Zaria: Ahmadu Bello University Press.

Ezeomah, C. (1998b) 'Redemptive egalitarianism as a strategy for equalising educational opportunities: The case of the nomads of Nigeria', in *Journal of Nomadic Studies* 1, 1: 111–21.

Ezewu, E. and Tahir, G. (eds) (1997) *Ecology and Education in Nigeria: Studies on the Education of Migrant Fishermen,* Onitsha: Tabansi Publishers.

Gore, P., Eissa, S. and Rahma, A. (1998) *A Comprehensive Evaluation of the Nomadic Education Project in Darfur State,* Khartoum: UNICEF.

GTZ-BEFARe (1999) 'Brief on the project Basic Education for Afghan Refugees (BEFARe)', Peshawar: Gesellschaft für Technische Zusammenarbeit – Basic Education for Afghan Refugees project.

Haughey, M. (1999) 'Review of Danaher (1998)', in *Journal of Distance Education* 14, 1: 112–14.

Inquai, S. (1983) 'Refugee education: problems and prospects', in *About Distance Education,* 18: 1–3.

Juma, R. (1997) 'Nomadic education in Zanzibar', in C. Ezeomah (ed.) *The Education of Nomadic Populations in Africa: Papers Presented at the UNESCO (Breda) Regional Seminar on the Education of Nomadic Populations in Africa, 11–15 December 1995, Kaduna, Nigeria,* Dakar: UNESCO.

Kaliel, M. (1998) 'Chairman's opening remarks', in G. Tahir and N. Muhammad (eds) *Readings on Distance Education for the Pastoral Nomads of Nigeria,* Zaria: Ahmadu Bello University Press.

Klein, R. (1997) 'Upwardly mobile', in *Times Educational Supplement,* 23 May 1997: 4–5, London: Times Newspapers.

Muhammad, N. (1991) 'The viability and justifications for the use of Fulfulde in primary schools', in G. Tahir (ed.) *Education and Pastoralism in Nigeria,* Zaria: Ahmadu Bello University Press.

Murphy, P. (1978) *The Lesotho Distance Teaching Centre: Five Years' Learning,* Cambridge: International Extension College.

Mykytyn, I. (1997) 'Continuity for travellers', in *Open Learning Systems News,* 61: 4.

NCNE (1998) *Annual Report 1998,* Kaduna: National Commission for Nomadic Education.

NCNE (1999) 'Radio curriculum for the distance learning scheme for adult pastoralists in Nigeria', Mimeo, Kaduna: National Commission for Nomadic Education.

Nwoke, A. (1993) 'The English language curriculum for nomadic schools', in C. Ezeomah (ed.) *Handbook for Teachers in Nomadic Schools,* Kaduna: National Commission for Nomadic Education.

Obanya, P. (1997) 'Preface', in C. Ezeomah (ed.) *The Education of Nomadic Populations in Africa: Papers Presented at the UNESCO (Breda) Regional Seminar on the Education of Nomadic Populations in Africa, 11–15 December 1995, Kaduna, Nigeria,* Dakar: UNESCO.

Rafferty, J. (1998) 'Road to nowhere', in *Guardian Weekend*, 28 November 1998: 39–44, London: Guardian Group Newspapers.

Robinson, B. (1999) 'Open and distance learning in the Gobi Desert: non-formal education for nomadic women', in *Distance Education*, 20, 2: 180–204.

Tahir, G. (1997) 'Nomadic education in Nigeria', in C. Ezeomah (ed.) *The Education of Nomadic Populations in Africa: Papers Presented at the UNESCO (Breda) Regional Seminar on the Education of Nomadic Populations in Africa, 11–15 December 1995, Kaduna, Nigeria*, Dakar: UNESCO.

Tahir, G. (1998) 'Nomadic education in Nigeria: Issues, problems and prospects', in *Journal of Nomadic Studies*, 1, 1: 10–26.

Tahir, G. and Muhammad, N. (ed.) (1998) *Readings on Distance Education for the Pastoral Nomads of Nigeria*, Zaria: Ahmadu Bello University Press.

Thomas, J. (1996) *Distance Education for Refugees: The Experience of Using Distance and Open Learning with Refugees in Africa, 1980–1995, with Guidelines for Action and a Directory of Information*, Cambridge: International Extension College.

Ukachi, L. (1998) 'Distance education for nomadic children', in G. Tahir and N. Muhammad (eds) *Readings on Distance Education for the Pastoral Nomads of Nigeria*, Zaria: Ahmadu Bello University Press.

Umar, A. and Tahir, G. (1998) 'Open broadcasting for nomadic pastoralists', in G. Tahir and N. Muhammad (eds) *Readings on Distance Education for the Pastoral Nomads of Nigeria*, Zaria: Ahmadu Bello University Press.

UNICEF (1978) *Basic Education for Nomads: Report of a Seminar Held in Mogadishu, Somalia, 1–9 April 1978*, Nairobi: UNICEF.

Chapter 11

The power of open and distance learning in basic education for health and the environment

Pat Pridmore and Stephanie Nduba

When open and distance learning (ODL) is used as a vehicle for basic education in health it can build on the synergism between education, health and the environment to yield increased benefits. Education, especially of women and girls, has been shown to increase child survival and improve family health and productivity (Cochrane, Leslie and O'Hara 1982, Blaug 1985, Psacharopoulos 1985). This happens by enhancing women's ability to manage children's health problems, by improving family nutrition and by ensuring more effective diagnosis and timely treatment (Caldwell 1994, 1996). Improving health can also improve educational achievement by increasing school attendance and reducing the micronutrient deficiencies, such as lack of iron or iodine, which decrease children's ability to learn (Pollitt 1990, Nokes, van den Bosch and Bundy 1998, World Bank 1993, Heward 1999). Better family health can also mean that girls are not taken out of school so often to care for sick relatives (Watkins 1999).

Despite its potential, using ODL for health poses many challenges. To be effective, programmes need to be sensitively adapted to local contexts and cultures and do more than just deliver health messages. They must avoid promoting behaviours which people cannot adopt (even if they want to) and build essential life skills such as self-confidence, communication skills and the ability to resist peer-group pressure. Programmes also need to do more than just deliver successful learning gains. They must take account of the structural, managerial, financial and political factors which influence sustainability.

In this chapter we shall review experience of using ODL for health in different countries, including that of AMREF (the African Medical and Research Foundation), and assess its potential to meet these challenges. We shall then draw out the lessons learned to guide future policy development and make recommendations for change. This assessment comes at a time when governments are striving to achieve the twin goals of 'Health for All' (WHO 1978) and 'Education for All' (WCEFA 1990). With structural adjustment policies eroding their ability to reach these goals and with the current emphasis on cost recovery, low-cost ways of delivering health care and training such as ODL may appear increasingly attractive. This is also a time of intense and rapid social change, when increasing numbers of people have access to some form of mass media. Innovative approaches such as interactive radio instruction (IRI) and social marketing have brought mass media back into fashion as an effective means of improving health. At the start of this new millennium a small window of opportunity has opened for mass media communication to prove itself in this field.

How have open and distance learning been used in basic education for health?

A typology of ODL in health includes both in-school and out-of-school programmes for adults and children, through formal, non-formal and informal delivery at the mass media and experimental levels. Programme goals have included:

- *Expanding access to education, especially for remote or marginalised groups*, as in the School of the Air in Australia, the radio schools in Latin America, and AMREF's basic training for health workers.
- *Enriching the quality of schooling and thereby child survival and family health*, as in the schools broadcasting services in England and interactive radio instruction projects in Asia, Africa and Latin America.
- *Raising public consciousness and stimulating popular action in support of national, regional and local health initiatives*, as in mass campaigns and social mobilisation, family planning and rural health in China, Cuba and Tanzania.
- *Disseminating information and persuading people to avoid, alter, adopt or discontinue health-related habits*. For example, social marketing campaigns have promoted the use of condoms to help prevent the spread of HIV infection in African, southeast Asian and Caribbean countries. In the Philippines, Nigeria and Mexico, radio and television – often known as 'info-tainment' and 'edu-tainment' initiatives – have incorporated family planning messages within popular songs and soap operas

The examples cited above also illustrate how health has been carried through the primary curriculum by a variety of ODL delivery structures. Early efforts include the radio schools movement of the 1960s and 1970s and the educational television (ETV) projects and mass campaigns of the 1970s and 1980s. The 1990s have seen an expansion of the open schools movement, interactive radio instruction, social marketing campaigns and radio and television dramas.

Radio schools

Many of the early radio education projects, drawing inspiration from (Christian) liberation theology or neo-Marxist socialism (see Freire 1972), aimed to raise critical awareness of poor people about their situation. A number of innovative experiments conducted in central and south America showed promising results in terms of student achievement, but were short-lived for a variety of reasons. For example, students on Mexico's Radioprimaria performed better than those in non-radio schools, but the project lacked resources to maintain the radios and receivers (Jamison and McAnany 1978: 47). The Tarahumara Indian Project failed because the programme designers did not adapt the curriculum to the needs of the children and few of these children were enrolled (Schmelkes, cited in Jamison and McAnany 1978). Programmes have also failed because of reception difficulties due to faulty transmission and erratic power supplies, scheduling conflicts, insufficient feedback and lack of support structures within schools or other community institutions to reinforce the broadcast lessons (Mayo 1999).

Educational television

Early ETV programmes also experienced mixed fortunes. The Côte d'Ivoire Television Scheme, aimed at improving the quality of education in primary schools, ran for ten years and carried health to most primary school children. However, according to Koné and Jenkins (1988), it suffered from cultural imperialism (expressed by excessive influence of the French culture, economy and language) and became so expensive that the government could not sustain it as donor funds dried up.

Mass campaigns

ODL has been widely used in large public health campaigns with diverse goals, audiences, channels and effectiveness (see Jenkins 1983). Immunisation campaigns have a good record of success. The 1981 campaign for polio immunisation in Nicaragua resulted in 75 per cent (750,000) of the country's under-five-year-olds being vaccinated in one day (Jenkins 1983). The 1990 USAID Healthcom project in the Philippines also achieved a substantial increase in vaccination coverage and timeliness of vaccination. Success was attributed to a high level of access to the media, sufficient expertise and funds available to develop and produce high-quality radio and television advertisements, full support from the Ministry of Health (MOH) and a health system able to meet the increased demand for vaccination (Zimicki et al. 1994). By contrast, efforts to improve nutrition have a relatively poor record of success. In the mid 1970s the nutrition education programme in the Philippines used radio broadcasts alone and achieved little change in weaning practices (Jenkins 1983). Hornik (1988) laments the lack of good evaluations of ODL nutrition projects. He notes that the little evidence available suggests media-based projects complemented by specific face-to-face and other support activities are most likely to bring about change in practices.

Open schools

Open schools are now rapidly expanding in less developed countries and some carry health messages. For example, the National Open School (NOS) in India has a community health course in its life enrichment programme (Dewal 1994: 35) and the Indonesian Open Junior High School also runs a middle school programme with biology, physical education and health as subjects (Sadiman 1994:

9). Experience has shown that open school institutions can become large scale, and make a significant difference to access at the basic level. For example, the open school in Zambia now reaches 7.9 per cent of the total national grade 7 enrolment. There is also some evidence that open schools can be cost-effective (Mukhopadhyay and Phillips 1994). The NOS in India is largely self-funded through uptake of its very low-cost units. Dewal (1994) notes that its change in status in becoming the NOS provided the mandate needed to expand throughout the country. This strategy could prove attractive to other high population countries.

Interactive Radio Instruction

IRI promotes active learning by requiring the students to interact with the radio instructors and by providing time within the broadcast lessons for them to make oral, written and physical responses. It frequently involves group work and longer activities may be included after the broadcast has finished. Broadcasts are linked to other pedagogic innovations, including restructured curricula, teachers' guides, and student worksheets. These features of IRI greatly enhance its potential as a vehicle for improving health, by helping children develop the understanding and skills they need to avoid, adopt, alter or discontinue health practices. Since 1974 IRI systems have continually adapted to a succession of educational environments, learning objectives and audiences. Evaluations consistently show that IRI projects can address systemic problems, such as equity, access, internal efficiency and cost-effectiveness (Leigh and Cash 1999). IRI projects have been launched in more than twenty countries over a period of twenty-five years and new models are still being developed in Asia, Africa and Latin America with support from an increasing number of governments and agencies (see Dock and Helwig 1999). For example, the Radio-Assisted Community Basic Education Project (RADECO), broadcast in the Dominican Republic since 1983, has been shown to be a cost-effective way of delivering high-quality instruction to 140,000 rural children. Success is attributed to effective dialogue between the project and the Ministry of Education (MOE) to ensure goals are agreed and that ownership of the project and responsibility for recurrent costs rests with the MOE (USAID 1990). The Preventive Health programme (PARI) in Bolivia, started in 1992, has achieved highly significant gains in children's knowledge, attitudes and behaviours (Fryer 1991). Broadcasts now reach approximately 125,000 students in sixty-nine schools and success is attributed to extensive pre-programme research (McGuire-Teas and Tilson 1989). A controlled study of IRI early childhood development projects launched in Bolivia in 1994 and 1995 found they had reached approximately 40,000 teachers, caregivers and parents and over 250,000 children and made a significant impact on child development, especially of high-risk children (Suxo 1997).

Despite their success, programmes such as RADECO and PARI are now criticised because their methodology is viewed as being out of line with the current national educational reforms based on constructivist learning theory. The Bolivian early childhood development projects have avoided this criticism by responding to current pedagogical trends. They have also adapted to government policies by decentralising implementation, creating partnerships across formal and non-formal boundaries, adapting the programmes for two local languages and marketing the programme to local municipalities, health and education programmes, kinder-garten programmes and indigenous social programmes. Adaptations of this model have now begun in South Africa, Nepal and Ecuador and the Bolivian programmes themselves are being used in Colombia and Ecuador (Helwig, Bosch and Dock 1999).

Radio and television dramas

During the late 1980s and 1990s radio and television dramas have become increasingly popular for entertaining and educating the public about health issues in the developing world. Sexual and reproductive health projects focusing on family planning and HIV/AIDS have been launched in Zimbabwe, Nigeria and the Gambia. This is another difficult area for ODL because change in knowledge rarely leads to change in practice (as women lack decision making power in many societies), and because it is very difficult to develop effective evaluation designs which enable programme effects to be realistically isolated. However, experience has shown that using a multichannel approach with support from health workers and family-planning providers increases the success of ODL in this area (Piotrow *et al.* 1990). The Zambia programme, using humorous radio drama, motivational talks for men and pamphlets on family planning, reached more than half of the men of reproductive age in the country and achieved a significant impact on awareness, attitudes and increased condom use (Piotrow *et al.* 1990). The Gambian programme used radio drama and 30-second radio spots and also developed support materials to train field workers and clinical assistants in family planning. A comparison of men and women before and after the broadcasts showed that uneducated women who heard the drama were significantly more likely to have talked about family planning to their spouses than those who had not listened (Valente *et al.* 1994). This is an important finding because such discussion is strongly associated with contraceptive use.

Social marketing

Social marketing applies the principles and techniques of commercial marketing to plan public health campaigns and there is a fair body of evidence to support its effectiveness (Clift 1989, Tones *et al.* 1994, Hornik 1988). The strengths of social marketing are its extensive research into the local culture and context and the way it combines mass media and face-to-face communication methods with health service delivery. The limitations reflect the difficulties of trying to apply commer-cial marketing techniques to social problems. Health education programmes usually have smaller budgets than commercial enterprises and involve professionals who are concerned with helping people make informed decisions, rather than using techniques which manipulate and coerce. They are also likely to be selling a product such as 'stopping smoking', which is more intangible and offers less immediate gratification than a commercial product such as Coca-Cola. They frequently seek to change more deeply seated attitudes and influence the adoption of complex behaviours such as safer sexual practices.

Summary so far

The programme experiences reviewed above illustrate how health has been carried through the primary curriculum by a variety of ODL delivery structures in many different countries. Although achievements have been mixed, many programmes, especially immunisation campaigns, open schools and IRI projects, have success-fully reached a high percentage of the national population. Evaluations have recorded increased health knowledge, awareness and sometimes positive change in behaviour. The new generation of IRI programmes have shown how the model can be successfully adapted to changing educational theories. We shall now move on to look at a short case study of AMREF's experience of using ODL to provide education and training for health personnel and the general public.

AMREF's experience of using ODL for health

Getting started

In the late 1970s the Kenyan government was faced with insurmountable demands for education and training from health personnel and the general public. AMREF responded to this demand by conducting baseline surveys to identify training needs and developing a pilot distance education (DE) project. This pilot demon-strated that:

- Health workers are interested in learning through DE (300 people applied for 100 places on the course)
- Health workers can learn knowledge, skills and attitudes through DE (results compared pre- and post-test gains from an experimental group learning by DE and a control group learning by traditional face-to-face methods)
- Professional health bodies and Ministries of Health in the East African region will accept DE as a credible method of teaching health workers and the general public (by the end of the project phase the MOH had played a very supportive role)

The pilot also yielded useful information on how best to deliver materials to the learners, how to move the assignments between the learner and tutor, how long this took, and how to keep effective records.

From a pilot project to regional programme

There is an African proverb which says: 'Cows going to graze start around the homestead'. Thus AMREF started by building its own in-house capacity. Firstly, it sent its staff on a training course in DE at the London Institute of Education. Secondly, it requested local institutions involved in DE, including the University of Nairobi and the Kenya Institute of Education, to facilitate in-house training and to allow it to use facilities such as an audio studio at a reasonable fee.

Once the staff had been trained and the pilot project had demonstrated that DE was relevant, affordable and effective, AMREF started replicating it in other countries. It started by incorporating DE within its existing projects using the materials developed for the pilot. For example, during tutor training programmes in Ethiopia, Kenya, Tanzania, Uganda and Zambia, DE courses were offered to the trainees to help update their knowledge and skills. By the end of the eight-week programme the trainees were not only updated but also convinced that this was an effective method of teaching. At the same time AMREF used workshops and on-the-job experience to train middle-level health personnel on how to develop or adopt DE materials and run programmes. To ensure that the DE was responding to the training needs of each country, district health teams were trained to identify these needs, to develop some DE materials and to facilitate practical demonstrations (face-to-face) which could develop specific skills. Following the large response of the secondary audience to the health workers' radio programme, AMREF introduced Dr AMREF, both as a radio talk and as a column in the local papers, to respond to questions raised by the general public and specifically educate them on how to take care of their health. In addition to these training efforts, intensive lobbying was carried out with high-level health officials.

Problems faced

- It has been difficult to get good writers to develop the DE materials. Even after attending writers' workshops conducted for AMREF staff and staff of universities and medical institutions, few people can write courses
- The good intention of developing skills of middle-level health personnel from other ministries of health has sometimes been frustrated by people being nominated for writers' workshops because of their connections rather than their interest or capabilities.
- Writers, who are experts in a given field and commissioned to write materials, often take a very long time to deliver the work and then it may be of poor quality or need substantial editing
- Materials are frequently stolen during distribution and therefore have to be sent by registered post, which is costly
- There are no postal services to some remote areas. Postal services have sometimes broken down, for example in Uganda. In this case, public transport such as lorries or buses has to be used

- Health workers are frequently transferred and do not always leave a forwarding address. The importance of communicating changes of address has been highlighted, in the DE newsletter
- Poor record keeping has been a problem. At first it was done manually but with more than 2,000 persons enrolled, ten courses running concurrently, and with students enrolling at any time and working at their own pace, it was necessary to use a computer. After about four attempts at designing a good database system, the programmer finally modified one donated by the Commonwealth of Learning, which is still being used
- Untrained health workers are awarded a Certificate of Completion at the end of each course. This certificate does not entitle them to any promotion or salary increase and is a source of discontent. Discussions with various countries are currently ongoing on this issue
- Many African governments exert control over the information disseminated to their people. There is a general tendency to keep people ignorant in order to remain in power

Secrets of success

- AMREF works in partnership with governments who have a duty to provide basic education to the people. Its role has been that of a catalyst, creating an enabling environment. In this way the DE programmes established are government owned or co-owned
- The autonomy and flexibility of AMREF allows it to respond to priority health needs using different media and targeting different audiences
- Continuous monitoring and periodic review of course contents has enabled programmes to be adapted to increase relevance and acceptability
- Programme evaluation has enabled AMREF to show that DE is able to make a significant impact on meeting priority needs
- Sensitive scheduling of programmes ensures that messages are sent at the right time and without disrupting people's way of life or work schedules. For example, malaria programmes are transmitted when there are outbreaks of malaria on Saturday and Sunday evenings after the news, when people are ready to hear about it
- AMREF encourages continuous communication between learners and the centre and replies promptly to learners' letters and questions
- It is important to have relevant and up-to-date materials ready to meet training needs and mechanisms for face-to-face teaching to reinforce skills
- Addressing real issues with practical solutions ensures good impact

Towards a new policy framework for open and distance learning in health

From the foregoing review of programme experience we have seen that ODL has had successes and failures over the years. Out of this we can now draw a convergent set of lessons which need to be more widely disseminated, and make recommendations for policy development in the areas of political, financial, technical and management support.

Although programme quality still needs to be ensured, future policy development is most needed in the areas of programme leadership and sustainability. Experience from the successful programmes reviewed has shown that initiatives must be vigorously led by dynamic, local individuals who invest personal enthusiasm and status in the project. Such leaders are crucial to maintain the political and social support and long-term financial commitment needed to secure integration of the programme into the education system. (This includes keeping the programme methodology in line with current educational reforms.) When ODL is used as a vehicle for health, internal ownership needs to be built within both the MOE and MOH, with one ministry taking the lead role. If schools are involved this should normally be the MOE.

Political support

Information and education about health are a basic human right (WHO/UNICEF 2000). As we have noted, many ODL projects, especially in central and south America, have aimed to empower poor people by providing information and raising their critical awareness about their situation. However, many governments, aware that 'knowledge is power', control what information is given to their people, and resist efforts to use the national media to raise critical consciousness of poor people about their condition. It is therefore essential to constantly nurture political links and use strong advocacy, in order to gain the full commitment of national governments to the provision of basic education for the people, and enable free flow of health communications. Outside agencies must maintain credibility, good working relationships, open dialogue and advocacy not only with government ministries but also with groups who may be pushing for political change. Agencies need to pay attention to image building and to providing information which can be used by the MOE and MOH as political currency. We have noted, for example, the ability of some IRI programmes to demonstrate that they are an effective and an affordable means of tackling the systemic problems of equity and access, while making real progress in the quality of teaching and learning gains for health.

Projects also need to be commended widely to universities, medical and nursing schools, relevant non-government organisations, businesses, politicians, intellectual leaders and the media. Developing ownership of and commitment to ODL projects by teachers, parents, Parent–Teacher Associations (PTAs) and community groups has potential value in the political arena which needs to be more widely recognised.

Financial policy

We have seen that health education programmes usually have small budgets (compared to commercial enterprises). This is not surprising considering that health and education sectors receive less than 7 per cent of GDP in many countries and health education is given a low priority for funding within these sectors. Consequently, commitment from the MOE and MOH to provide adequate programme funding must be secured from the start and to facilitate such commitment it is important to avoid high-profile management by outside agencies. Externally funded projects need to ensure that policies are put in place to complete the integration of the project into government or local structures when external funding ceases. This means that the financial demands made by institution-alisation, including staff and broadcast costs, need to be anticipated and adequate provision made for them in the budget. Four major cost areas must be covered: first, transmission costs, including air time, which may initially be free as part of the start-up support package but need to be paid for later; second, costs of teacher guides, student materials, radio repairs or replacement; third, costs of programme management, supervision and training; and fourth, staff costs arising from making and transmitting the broadcasts and support materials, and in some cases paying people to facilitate learning groups.

All those involved in the implementation of financial strategies need to receive specific orientation and training.

Technical and management policy

Internal policy development needs to focus on three areas: improving the quality of research for programme planning; broadening the narrow focus on communication activities; and using more effective evaluation designs.

Experience, for example, from the current IRI and social marketing programmes reviewed, shows that extensive pre-programme research is needed to ensure lesson materials are relevant, appropriate, regularly updated and broadcast at the right time. Educational methodologies must match those currently being promoted by the national government. For example, in countries where constructivist theories have superseded behaviourist ones, ODL needs to use methodologies which are flexible enough to accommodate the different ways in which individuals learn and recognise that there are often multiple correct answers and ways of solving problems. This has implications for the professional development of teachers and their supervisors. It is important that ODL courses can be accredited and used for professional promotion. Initial training of new teachers needs to be followed up by regular in-service training and retraining of teachers already in the classroom. A regular newsletter for teachers, featuring articles written by teachers themselves, builds confidence and helps share experiences. Such contact nurtures teachers, maintains motivation, allows for fine-tuning of the programme and materials and builds ownership in the school to support sustainability. Ministry officers at the district, regional and national level and project staff will also need to be oriented to the programme. We have seen that where ODL is being developed within bilingual, multicultural education, language policies are needed to support the adaptation of programmes into local languages, including the development of educational media and newspapers.

One of the central issues this chapter brings out is that ODL in health is most successful when a broad comprehensive approach is used. Consequently, policies are needed to guide the development of multichannel communication systems and of structures to manage them. Such systems would use mass media supported by face-to-face communication to deliver health messages, linked to provision of the resources and incentives needed for people to be able to act on the messages. For example, efforts to teach children, teachers and parents about the importance of vaccination should be supported by the provision of an effective cold chain and availability of vaccines. Management structures need to be able to oversee the complex design and delivery of health communications linked to the demands, expectations and training needs of field workers delivering health services. A new policy framework could also include the re-deployment of teachers and health workers for data collection. These professionals are ideally situated to facilitate the generation of good-quality information for programme planning and evaluation, as well as for providing the direct support and follow-up needed to achieve sustainable change. However, strong advocacy would be needed to secure funds for retraining, and to overcome resistance from MOE, MOH and other relevant arms of the government and local institutions.

Another further critical issue we have highlighted is the need for policies to be framed to ensure ODL programmes are effectively monitored, evaluated and institutionalised. Plans need to be made during the development stage, and pre-production research should be followed up with pre-testing of messages, monitoring to track local reception patterns and measurement of programme impacts. Experience has clearly shown the need for more long-term evaluations and evaluations of cost-effectiveness and of the local political realities likely to affect project sustainability. We also need to assess the need for ODL to reach out to schools in remote and disadvantaged areas, as the national education system evolves and new schools are built in these areas. Where integrated multichannel systems are used, evaluation designs need to disaggregate the impact of ODL efforts from activities such as health service delivery. Ministries may need to be convinced that it makes sound political and economic sense to evaluate programmes to assess effectiveness and obtain feedback from all participants.

At the beginning of the new millennium, evidence is strengthening for the benefits of using ODL in health. ODL has proved to be a dynamic and evolving methodology which is flexible and adaptable to different political, economic and educational contexts. Consequently, increasing numbers of national governments and donor agencies are committed to investment in ODL systems and in the future many more countries are likely to be experimenting with multi-channel, integrated pilot programmes. It remains to be seen whether there is sufficient political will to allocate adequate resources to such projects, so that they can retain all the elements of a comprehensive approach. We can only hope that at least one example of large-scale implementation will be unequivocally effective and establish that worthwhile improvements can be made using ODL as a vehicle for health.

References

Blaug, M. (1985) 'Where are we now in the economics of education?', in *Economics of Education Review*, 4, 1: 17–28.

Caldwell, J. (1994) 'How is greater maternal education translated into lower child mortality?', in *Health Transition Review*, 4, 2: 224–9.

Caldwell, P. (1996) 'Child survival: physical vulnerability and resilience in adversity in the European past and the contemporary Third World', in *Social Science and Medicine*, 43, 5: 609–19.

Clift, E. (1989) 'Social marketing and communication: Changing health behaviour in the Third World', in *American Journal of Health Promotion*, 3, 4: 17–24.

Cochrane, S., Leslie, J. and O'Hara, D. (1982) *The Effects of Education on Health*, World Bank Staff Working Paper No. 405, Washington, DC: World Bank.

Dewal, O. (1994) 'Open learning in Indian school education', in M. Mukhopadhyay and S. Phillips (eds) *Open Schooling: Selected Experiences*, Vancouver: Commonwealth of Learning.

Dock, A. and Helwig, J. (1999) 'An overview of IRI experience to date', in A. Dock and J. Helwig (eds) *Interactive Radio Instruction: Impact, Sustainability, and Future Directions*, Education and Technology Notes Series 4, 1, Washington, DC: USAID/World Bank.

Freire, P. (1972) *Pedagogy of the Oppressed*, Harmondsworth: Penguin.

Fryer, M. (1991) 'Health education through interactive radio: A Child-to-Child project in Bolivia', in *Health Education Quarterly*, 18, 1: 65–77.

Helwig, J., Bosch, A. and Dock, A. (1999) 'Brief case studies of six IRI initiatives', in A. Dock and J. Helwig (ed.) *Interactive Radio Instruction: Impact, Sustainability, and Future Directions*, Education and Technology Notes Series 4, 1, Washington, DC: USAID/World Bank.

Heward, C. (1999) 'Introduction: The new discourses of gender, education and development', in C. Heward and S. Bunwaree (eds) *Gender, Education and Development: Beyond Access to Empowerment*, London: Zed Books.

Hornik, R. (1988) *Development Communication: Information, Agriculture, and Nutrition in the Third World*, London: University Press of America.

Koné, H. and Jenkins, J (1988) 'The programme for educational television in the Ivory Coast', in *Media in Education and Development 21*: 2.

Jamison, D. and McAnany, E. (1978) *Radio for Education and Development*, London: Sage.

Jenkins, J. (1983) *Mass Media for Health Education*, Cambridge: International Extension College.

Leigh, S. and Cash, F. (1999) 'Effectiveness and methodology of IRI', in A. Dock and J. Helwig (eds) *Interactive Radio Instruction: Impact, Sustainability, and Future Directions*, Education and Technology Notes Series 4, 1, Washington, DC: USAID/World Bank.

McGuire-Teas, M. and Tilson, T. (1989) 'Bolivia instruction through interactive radio', in *Mothers and Children Bulletin on Infant Feeding and Maternal Nutrition*, 8, 1: 4–5.

Mayo, J. (1999) 'Radio's role in education and development: Introduction and overview', in A. Dock and J. Helwig (eds) *Interactive Radio Instruction: Impact, Sustainability, and Future Directions*, Education and Technology Notes Series 4, 1, Washington, DC: USAID/World Bank.

Mukhopadhyay, M. and Phillips, S. (eds) (1994) *Open Schooling: Selected Experience*, Vancouver: Commonwealth of Learning.

Nokes, C., van den Bosch, C. and Bundy, D. (1998) *The Effects of Iron Deficiency and Anaemia on Mental and Motor Performance, Educational Achievement, and Behaviour in Children*, A report of the International Anaemia Consultative Group (INACG), Washington, DC: INACG, c/o ILSI Human Nutrition Institute.

Piotrow, P., Rimon, J., Winnard, K., Kincaid, D., Huntingdon, D. and Convisser, J. (1990) 'Mass media family planning promotion in three Nigerian cities', in *Studies in Family Planning*, 21, 5: 265–74.

Pollitt, E. (1990) *Malnutrition and Infection in the Classroom*, Paris: UNESCO.

Psacharopoulos, G. (1985) 'Returns to education: A further international update and implications', in *Journal of Human Resources*, XX: 583–604.

Sadiman, A. S. (1994) 'Open Junior Secondary Schools in Indonesia', in M. Mukhopadhyay and S. Phillips (eds) *Open Schooling: Selected Experiences*, Vancouver: Commonwealth of Learning.

Suxo, T. (1997) *Formative and Summative Evaluation of the IRI Package, Aprendamos Jugando*, Washington, DC: USAID.

Tones, K., Tilford, S. and Robinson, Y.K. (1994) 'The mass media in health promotion', in K. Tones and S. Tilford (eds) *Health Education: Effectiveness, Efficiency and Equity*, London: Chapman and Hall (second edition).

USAID (1990) *Interactive Radio Instruction: Confronting Crisis in Basic Education*, Science and Technology in Development Series, Newton, Massachusetts: United States Agency for International Development.

Valente, T., Kim, Y., Lettermaler, C., Glass, W. and Dibba, Y.(1994) 'Radio promotion of family planning in the Gambia', in *International Family Planning Perspectives*. 20, 3: 96–100.

Watkins, K. (1999) *Education Now: Break the Cycle of Poverty*, Oxford: Oxfam.

World Bank (1993) *World Development Report: Investing in Health*, Oxford: Oxford University Press.

WCEFA (1990) *World Declaration on Education for All and Framework for Action to Meet Basic Learning Needs*, New York: Inter-agency Commission.

WHO (1978) *Alma-Ata 1978 Primary Health Care* Health for All Series, 1, Geneva: WHO.

WHO/UNICEF (2000) *Facts for Life*, Geneva: WHO (second edition).

Zimicki, S., Hornik, R., Verzosa, C., Hernandez, J., de Guzman, E., Dayrit, M., Fausto, A., Lee, M. and Abad, M. (1994) 'Improving vaccination coverage in urban areas through a health communication campaign: The 1990 Philippine experience', in *Bulletin of the World Health Organisation*, 72, 3: 409–22.

Chapter 12

Open schooling at basic level

Janet Jenkins and Arief S. Sadiman

The concept of open schooling

This chapter presents a selective and critical world review of 'open schooling' – the use of the methods of distance education to provide basic education to adults or children.[1]

Open schooling extends formal education to learners outside traditional school environments. This may be achieved through special institutions – 'open schools' – or through the use of the techniques of distance education (DE) to extend opportunity for schooling to those otherwise excluded. The methods of DE are also used to enhance the range and quality of instruction which takes place in school. This may be through using distance teaching materials to take high-quality teaching to every child, through expanding subject choice, or through enabling educational communication outside the school. Such techniques are increasingly known as 'open classroom'.[2]

Open schools are autonomous institutions which use the methods of DE to provide schooling to out-of-school learners. They are usually established in order to increase access to schooling, and are generally designed to accommodate tens of thousands of pupils in one 'school'. The idea is particularly attractive to those responsible for education in countries with large populations and a need for considerable expansion of the school system (Visser 1994). Bangladesh, Brazil, India, Indonesia and Mexico, for example, all have open schools catering for large numbers of out-of-school pupils.

Like a formal school, an open school offers a complete, sequenced course of study between two points on the school curriculum. For example, Mexico's Telesecundaria offers the complete basic secondary cycle (Grades 7–9), while India's National Open School offers the entire secondary curriculum. The curriculum taught is normally similar to that of formal school, leading to the same or equivalent examinations as those taken by regular pupils. The quality of provision is expected to be equal to that of formal schools, although the methods of teaching and learning are different. But open schools differ from formal schools in several respects. They may be 'open' as to age of pupils, 'class' size, place, time and pace of study. Sometimes no prior qualifications are required for entry, and sometimes schooling is free or of minimal cost even to adult learners. Each open school has its own formula.

The idea is not new. Some open schools have been operating for several decades, proof of their value to the communities they serve. Others, established more recently, have grown rapidly, their student numbers rivalling those of open universities. Is this the way of the future? Will more open schools emerge? Or is open schooling a transitory phenomenon, a response to the demand for Education for All?

There is no simple answer to questions such as these. On the one hand most children (and their parents) would prefer to learn with their peers in class. On the other, the resource and infrastructure for universal high-quality basic education are not always available. Poor high-population countries are particularly challenged. Open schooling is one option for addressing the problem.

Open schools can be an efficient and potentially cost-effective means of expanding school coverage. They can open opportunity to those excluded from traditional schools, whether by age, place of residence, health, economic factors, or mobility. But, as with all DE, context and circumstance affect impact.

It is possible, too, to improve the quality of traditional schools by using the techniques of open and distance learning. But DE itself is in the process of transformation. Its rise has been in part a response to the triple challenge facing education: improved access, high-quality outcomes, reasonable cost (Ehrmann 1996). Technology has also driven its growth. Over the last few years new techniques using information technology and computer communications have spread rapidly. They have not replaced the old learning technologies, but rather offer new opportunities, notably greater potential for individualised learning and interpersonal interaction. These techniques form the basis of today's open classroom.

This chapter follows the story of open schooling from the original schools of the air through to the open classroom, reviews present status and identifies strengths, weaknesses and conditions for success. Some predict that, in the near future, the predominant mode of schooling will become 'open' and the virtual classroom will replace the physical one (see Tiffin and Rajasingham 1995). Others predict that open and traditional learning methodologies will be progressively integrated, enhancing traditional classroom learning. Our conclusions will address the issue of increasing convergence between traditional and open schooling.

Open schooling in the age of broadcasting

The idea of using distance teaching methods in an organised way to provide school education dates from early in the twentieth century, with the arrival of broadcasting.

Schools of the air

In the 1920s an exciting new communications technology – radio – presented an opportunity for education over distance. In countries such as Australia, New Zealand and Canada, radio was used in combination with correspondence courses to reach children on remote farms (Young *et al.* 1980: 16–17). These schools continue today. In western Australia, for example, around 1,000 children a year from isolated homes study with the Education Department's Schools of Distance Education.[3]

These schools of the air or correspondence schools were small compared with today's open schools, but are nonetheless significant as models. First and foremost, their longevity provides evidence that distance learning can work even for small children. Of necessity, they tackled the entire school curriculum, from infancy upward.

These schools addressed questions of quality through strategies which remain the basis of good DE today. The content of lessons was transmitted through correspondence texts, radio programmes and, later, television programmes. One issue was literacy. If the main medium of instruction was the printed word, how could it be effective with young children or even adults with limited reading skills? Radio – and later television – introduced exciting new possibilities. The idea of multiple media[4] was born.

Great attention was paid to the human element. Teacher-pupil ratios were kept low, so that each child had access to good learning support. This is still the case today. In Western Australia, for example, each student is allocated an individual teacher for each subject, and is supervised by a regional teacher. To support younger children, parents work in partnership with teachers. Social relationships amongst children are encouraged, through summer camps, for example. The annual calendar of the New Zealand Correspondence School contained a photo of every teacher and every child, with the children dressed in school uniform even though they studied at home. Measures such as these helped to create learning communities.

Such open schooling is not a cheap option. The multiple media learning packages and the high level of teacher support for each individual are inevitably costly. While the education provided is of the best quality possible, it does not aim to be a substitute for regular school. It is only offered to the minority of children who for some reason cannot attend such schools.

Television

To address problems of mass access to high-quality education different techniques were needed. In the 1960s television held out new promise. But in many parts of the world electricity, let alone television, was not then available in ordinary homes. This wonderful new tool was useless as a means of educating individuals at home. But could it be used in schools, to deliver the curriculum? This seemed an excellent strategy in countries where there was a shortage of teachers, or teachers were poorly qualified. Attention turned to improving schools through teaching by television, and a number of grand projects were launched in developing countries (Schramm 1967). Some survived, but most were short lived. Not for the last time, the experience underscored the danger of technology-driven approaches to distance education.

What were the principal causes of failure? First, the developing countries which took up the idea did not have the financial resource, technical capacity and know-how to produce the vast number of television programmes required. Large national projects – famously that of the Côte d'Ivoire – were unsustainable because of dependence on foreign aid. Second, schoolteachers did not buy the idea. In El Salvador, for example, teachers went on strike in protest at television usurping their role, while in one Pacific country they simply turned off the sets and went back to teaching by rote. It took several decades, and a lot of expensive failures, to work out how best to use broadcasts to extend school (Arnove 1976).

There were a few exceptions. Mexico's Telesecundaria, for example, was established in 1968 as a distance learning system to provide basic secondary education (grades 7–9) to young people in rural communities too small to support a full secondary school. Today, pupils attend daily at one of over 14,000 specially built schools where they watch special television lessons as a group and do class work under the supervision of a single teacher who deals with all sixteen subjects of the curriculum. Over 100 programmes are broadcast for each subject at each grade per annum, some 3,850 programmes in all.

Telesecundaria displays several features which are characteristic of successful open schooling. It is a self-contained system of education, designed to address the specific problem of schooling in small communities. It operates through what we might call mini-schools, although they differ from traditional schools in several ways. Every aspect of teaching and learning is centrally designed, and television, text and teacher support are all integrated, offering a 'complete package of support to teachers and students' (Calderoni 1998; data are also taken from de Moura Castro et al. 1999 and Ortiz 1999). The system operates through a partnership between state, community, schools and parents, as well as teachers and pupils. The result is a rounded education, 'integrating curriculum with community activity and constructivist pedagogy' (Calderoni 1998: 10).

There have been many difficulties, such as teacher recruitment and retention, and resistance to having only one teacher per grade. Most 'schools' operate from reasonable buildings but a significant minority of 15 per cent operate from inadequate premises. The reliance on broadcast television results in some inflexibility in curriculum delivery. Pupils have performed well in their final examinations, but few have continued to higher secondary education, probably because opportunities are not available. Even with the large scale of operation, costs of schooling are much the same as those of traditional alternatives. However the system is now robust, growing, and developing further, and continues to have government support:

> The Mexican Government views Telesecundaria as a social project, committed to ensuring that all children have an equal opportunity of high quality schooling ... [in] small villages and rural areas which could not otherwise provide comparable educational services.
>
> (Calderoni 1998: 8)

Interactive Radio Instruction

The search for a better-quality alternative led to revisiting simpler learning technologies. One was radio (see Mayo 1999).

In the late 1940s a priest in Colombia started Acción Cultural Popular (ACPO), the first radiophonic school (Bernal Alarcón 1978). The terrain in much of Colombia was mountainous, roads bad, and schools, even villages, many miles apart. Radio was an obvious means of communication with the millions of citizens living in isolated homesteads. Using full length radio lessons and special primers, he taught his parishioners in family groups to read and write, as well as providing them with skills for survival and community development. ACPO grew to reach 160–220,000 learners.[5]

By the 1970s there were radiophonic school systems throughout Latin America, catering for adults or rural families. As television spread, they inevitably lost some of their market, but not before they had attracted international attention. Could the techniques be applied to educate children? Gradually, a new idea was born – interactive radio.

The critical characteristic of Interactive Radio Instruction (IRI) is time on air. Full-length radio lessons provide a complete course of study in a subject. Programmes are for use in class, and include frequent gaps when children answer questions or perform activities.

The system quickly proved successful in enhancing learning, first with maths in Nicaragua, then with science and language studies in countries such as the Dominican Republic, Thailand and Kenya (McTigue Zirker 1990). By 1988 the World Bank, in its sector review of education in sub-Saharan Africa, wrote:

> Experience has shown that interactive radio can be used effectively by untrained classroom monitors as well as trained teachers, with little training or special support. Furthermore, once radio lessons are developed, the annual per pupil cost is modest, since few supplementary learning materials are required.
>
> (World Bank 1998: 43)

Here was a low-cost technological solution which could be applied to certain specific problems. It was suited to situations where teachers acknowledged that they needed support, for example with a new approach to a subject (maths) or teaching a language which was not their mother tongue (English). It resulted in better performance in the subject. But, as with television, there are barriers to wider use. All teachers need training to use the system, a substantial commitment even if the training is brief. Handouts have to be printed and distributed, even if they are short. Finally, although radio production is cheap, a large amount of transmission time is needed every year to broadcast the lessons.

These difficulties have not stood in the way. Interactive radio is now flourishing in many more countries, for example in South Africa, through the Open Learning

Systems Education Trust (OLSET) (Naidoo 1999). But – like television projects – in some countries IRI has been short lived. Will IRI survive the new challenge of computers? A recent analysis suggests it may have a lasting role:

> In an increasing number of countries, children are exposed to the rapid-fire approach of commercial radio and television, and the teacher is challenged to make the classroom learning environment just as lively, exciting and flexible through his/her own delivery methods. The classroom environment is being transformed from a teacher-centred information source to a mosaic of sources, each appropriate to a particular learning context. Carefully designed IRI programs can form an important part of this mosaic.
>
> (article in on-line journal *TechKnowLogia* November/December 1999, from Dock and Helwig 1999)

Multichannel learning

Good teaching and learning today goes further than exploring a 'mosaic of resources'; it also explores the increasing range of technological tools available to access those sources. The notion of 'multichannel learning' combines these two strands. The idea is to use different communication channels and strategies in a flexible way to 'connect all to learning' (Anzalone 1995).

Flexible multichannel approaches have been explored in a number of settings, both in and out of school. In the Philippines, for example, 'Project No Drops' improved primary school performance and reduced drop-out by 'knitting multiple channels of learning together', treating school as a joint endeavour of teachers, pupils, parents and community (Sutaria 1995). In Brazil, Telecurso – another survivor from the 1960s – has launched Telecurso 2000, a new programme of basic education for young adults. It provides 'drop in' open schooling using television and textbooks. The broadcasting strategy is unusual, with repeat showings, programmes rebroadcast on a number of channels, and video versions readily available. Learning support is provided through *telesalas* – meetings of learners arranged on a self-help or private basis. At present over 200,000 students attend such classes. At least a further 200,000 pupils in regular schools attend classes which rely on the Telecurso television programmes (de Moura Castro 1999).

Multichannel learning can thus narrow the gap between in- and out-of-school learning. In contrast to open schools, it is relatively unstructured, flexible, and relies on community-based support and creative commitment. Open schools, to which we now turn, are in the mainstream tradition of DE – a central organisation which teaches a large number of widely dispersed pupils in a carefully structured environment.

Open schools and their impact

Open schools are the flagships of open schooling. They are not new, but, like Telesecundaria, have evolved over the years, and attracted new attention in the search for solutions to the challenge of Education for All. Most open schools operate principally at secondary level and cater for very large numbers of students. The two examples which follow demonstrate their power and point to challenges which remain.

Open Junior Secondary School, Indonesia

One of the major players is Indonesia. Since 1979 the Ministry of Education has provided an Open Junior Secondary School (OJSS) for elementary school graduates without access to regular secondary schooling. OJSS was piloted in five provinces in Indonesia in 1979: Lampung, West Java, Central Java, East Java and West Nusa Tenggara. Currently (1998/9) there are 376,620 students in 3,773 locations throughout the country. By 2004 it is hoped that OJSS will accommodate 2.25 million students annually.

OJSS is run by the government, and is recognised as one of ten alternative pathways of universal basic education. The dissemination of the system was originally planned to help meet a shortfall in the school building programme. But in 1994 universal basic education of nine years' duration was made mandatory. Today, with just over 13 million young people of junior secondary age, there are school places for only 6.9 million. The government aims to accommodate about one third of these in OJSS. A solution has yet to be found for the remaining young people.

The OJSS uses the same curriculum, offers the same course of study, administers the same national examination and issues the same certificates as regular junior high schools. The only difference is in the way it delivers courses. It relies on individual learning from self-instructional materials – printed material, radio, audio cassettes and video programmes – supported by limited face-to-face tutorial sessions. The students can learn anytime and anywhere, but since learning independently is a problem for these youngsters, they are expected to attend a learning centre five days a week. Centres are located near to students' homes, usually in a primary school building, a parent's house, a village hall, mosque or other public building. Students gather there to learn in groups or to study individually. Once a week, usually at the weekend, students have to go to a 'base school' for tutorial sessions with subject teachers to discuss problems encountered during the week.

To join OJSS, students should be certificated graduates of primary school. They do not have to pay anything since this school is part of the universal basic education programme. In its efforts to accelerate the accomplishment of nine years' education for all, government saw OJSS as a viable means of providing educational opportunity not only to graduates of primary school, but also to graduates of Madrasah Ibtidaiyah, the Islamic primary school and to junior secondary school drop-outs.

Graduates of OJSS get the same certificate and rights as their peers in regular schools, the same right to continue education to a higher level, the same recognition from employers. Recognition is vital in persuading parents to send their children to OJSS. It took at least three years to convince them that this school was as good as the regular one. They were not familiar with a school where daily attendance was not compulsory and did not believe that it would work. But once the first OJSS students graduated, attitudes changed. Pressure is maintained through use of mass media to publicise OJSS. International recognition, by UNESCO and COL for example, has strengthened conviction.

Good learning material is essential, the foundation of delivery of the entire curriculum. There is no teacher standing in front of the class teaching. All the students have to learn from materials in their own time, place and pace. OJSS has a total of 771 printed modules covering ten subjects at grades 1 to 3. To facilitate understanding OJSS also provides radio/audio cassettes (409 programmes) and video programmes (455).

Support for learning comes from three types of 'teacher'. At the learning centres, students study their materials with the assistance of a *guru pamong* (teacher aide), usually a primary school teacher or school principal with no specialist subject expertise. The *guru pamong* may also counsel individual students when necessary. Students also learn practical skills from professionals or experts from the community, invited to be the special *guru pamong* in such matters. Facilities for fieldwork and physical education are also provided at the centres. At least once a week students meet subject matter teachers at their base school for tutorials. In some places they can meet more often, in others due to geographical constraints they can meet only once a fortnight or even once a month. All these personnel receive special training for these jobs.

Social learning is given high priority. As it is hard for youngsters to learn alone, OJSS expects students to attend their centres for group learning four to five times a week. Tutorials provide another opportunity for peer interaction and social learning. There are other ways, too, in which students communicate amongst themselves: a student magazine *Warta Siswa* is published every three months, and a radio magazine is broadcast every weekend. All these facilities give students the opportunity to interact, get to know each other, and feel that they are not alone but part of the big family of OJSS.

Community participation is another crucial element. There are various possibilities for parents and community to participate, such as lending their house as space for a learning centre, becoming a special *guru pamong* and sharing their expertise, letting the students use facilities for learning practical skills, and donating money.

System management has received much attention. OJSS has three levels of management: central/national, provincial, and school level. Central management operates through a combined technical team consisting of Pustekkom (Ministry of Education and Culture's Centre for Communication Technology), who designed the system, and the Directorate for General Secondary Education, each with a specific task force. The development task force is based at Pustekkom, while the implementation task force is at the Directorate for General Secondary Education. At the provincial level a team is responsible for distributing the centrally developed learning materials, equipment and facilities to base schools and their clusters of learning centres. The team is also responsible for management activities such as feasibility studies, monitoring local management, the teaching-learning activities, and paying the various staff. At the base school level a principal, assisted by a vice-principal and subject matter teachers, is responsible for cluster administration and management. The close and good working relationship between these three levels of management is significant to the success of OJSS. OJSS has a relatively high degree of sustainability since it involves both parents and community (local government) in managing the system.

Is OJSS really a good school? How does the quality of its graduates compare with those of regular schools? Which one is better? Can these young pupils manage to learn independently? These are some of the questions often raised by sceptics. But after more than twenty years in operation, OJSS has to be considered credible. The government supports it, it is inexpensive, operating at just over 50 per cent of the cost of regular schools,[6] and makes optimal use of existing resources such as teaching staff, learning facilities and space.

The mode of operation is typical of many open schools: centrally produced learning materials, operation through groups attached to affiliated schools, learning support provided by the regular teachers. Such a system has a number of strengths:

- the learning materials can be designed and developed to a common high standard
- operation through groups ensures that there is peer interaction and social learning amongst pupils
- pupils have access to regular contact with teachers
- the syllabus and examinations are fully recognised
- the system can easily be expanded by adding new groups

But OJSS faces many difficulties, unsurprising in a country of 17,000 islands and over 200 million people. Many problems derive from remoteness. The main target market is children from low-income families, which often have a poor educational background. Such families are hard to reach, often living in remote places, and generally with a low appreciation of schooling and education. Due to the fact that most of the OJSS students live in remote areas where transportation is a big constraint, timely distribution of the learning materials is still a problem. The co-ordination of such a large and complex system is challenging. There is inevitably a tension between the need to reach out to those who are still excluded from school and the requirement to maintain quality.

The centrally controlled curriculum and learning material is both a strength, since quality is assured, and a weakness, since it offers little flexibility in the face of different needs. Provision of feedback to learners on progress is another challenging job. Ultimately, these young people must learn to teach themselves. Does the system help them enough? Such issues are critical for all open schools which aim to combine education for large numbers of people with sensitivity to individual difference.

National Open School, India

The National Open School (NOS) in India operates on a similar scale, but there are several differences in its status, operation and remit. It was established as a semi-autonomous national organisation in 1989 with a remit to extend education to adults and children out of school using distance education methods.[7] Within the broad framework of the formal school curriculum, it creates its own syllabuses and conducts its own examinations. Its qualifications are widely recognised. It charges fees, and may set their level. It has grown fast – it now attracts over 100,000 new enrolments a year. It began operating at secondary level but its development strategy, in line with government priorities, covers the whole spectrum of primary and secondary education. It works closely with the national literacy programme, state level ministries of education, and more recently with the Ministry of Welfare to extend outreach to disadvantaged children.

NOS has a small staff, about 160 in all, with only thirty to forty in its academic section. It uses committees of experts to design its courses. Teams of writers are commissioned and trained on the recommendation of the committees, and production is dealt with in-house or on contract. Almost all professional activity, academic and technical, is out-sourced. Most NOS learning materials are printed texts, with some audio and video cassettes, and recently some television broadcasts. It has a national network of over 800 accredited institutions which enrol learners and provide tutorial and counselling support. NOS headquarters looks after central functions such as the delivery of materials, preparation of assignments, organisation of examinations and research. NOS is subsidised by central government but recovers about 75 per cent of its course running costs.

Like OJSS, NOS has as yet reached only a small proportion of those excluded from regular school. But its strategy for expansion is rather different. In India for many decades there have been state correspondence schools, very large in states like Orissa and Tamil Nadu, which operate in state languages. NOS has, under law, a co-ordinating role, with a remit to target improved quality in open schooling right across the country. It is only just beginning to tackle this role. But it is leading the way by introducing new kinds of flexibility, such as courses in employment-related subjects, and its own curricula and examinations. Semi-independent status gives it freedom to respond to the demands of the market, to support innovation and experiment with different technologies and new applications.

'Education for all – greater equity and justice in society – the evolution of a learning society': the mission statement of NOS encapsulates the challenge it faces. Open access is a paramount principle, so independent learning at home is the norm and attendance at centres is voluntary. The situation is further complicated by openness as to age – adults and children study the same courses. In such circumstances it is very difficult to provide adequate feedback and personal support. The linguistic complexity of India adds another dimension. The strategy of developing operational partnerships between national headquarters and each state should result in greater responsiveness to local difference and stronger support and feedback.

Towards principles for good practice

Policy makers turn to open schooling because they believe it will be a cost-effective means of extending access at the same time as maintaining quality. The experience of open schools which we have described suggests the following requirements:

- government or official recognition of certificates awarded
- clearly structured organisation of the teaching and learning process
- good learning material covering the entire curriculum
- regular and reliable learner support from teachers
- peer interaction and provision for social learning wherever possible
- building on partnership involving local community
- choice of media and technology appropriate to scale and cost of operation
- efficient central administration with regional/local representation
- flexibility sufficient to meet a variety of need and circumstance

The open schools which we have examined show widely different responses to demand, but the problems are similar. The relationship between costs, access and quality is always a complex one. An underlying issue is to what extent the quality of the learning experience of each individual in a mass learning system can match quality in regular schools. We have seen that open schools devise different ways to create learning environments which provide the interaction, support and responsiveness to the individual pupil which is part of good education. But there are two dimensions of perpetual tension: a greater amount of interaction amongst learners and teachers can improve learning, but at a higher cost; and group work tends to enhance learning but an expectation of attendance at class reduces access to learning.

Open schooling does not reduce the cost of school systems. Any distance learning system which is in addition to a traditional system will add to the total bill. Rather, as Ehrmann observes in relation to technology in education, it can help control costs per learner (Ehrmann 1996). The questions to be addressed are therefore about value added and returns on investment.

In Indonesia the OJSS has enabled expansion of the schools system to accommodate – so far – an extra 376,620 students. The Indonesian government started the system on the understanding that the operational cost should not exceed 60 per cent of the comparable JSS budget. In 1992 a comparative cost analysis of each system found the unit cost per OJSS student was about 52 per cent of that of regular students.

The cost components considered were: building facilities, which include classrooms, laboratories, libraries and office spaces; materials and equipment, which include laboratory equipment, demonstration objects for the social sciences, vocational instruments, audiocassettes, radio/audio programmes, learning packages, modules, batteries, television monitors and VCRs, and library materials/ books; salary and wages, which include honorariums for subject matter teachers, *guru pamong*, support staff and others; and the operational cost, which includes repair, maintenance and replacements.

The result of the study indicated that when costs for building, materials and equipment, salaries and wages and operational costs are taken together, the unit cost per student a year is Rp 152,910 for OJSS, compared to Rp 392,228 for regular junior secondary school; in which case the yearly OJSS budget is about 39 per cent of the regular JSS. When the last three components are calculated the yearly OJSS budget is about 52 per cent of the regular one. When only the operational cost is considered the cost per student of OJSS is Rp 152,910 compared to Rp 293,936 per year. (Currently, Rp 7,000 is equal to US $1.)

NOS recovers 75 per cent of its course running costs, largely from students' fees. But if it is to achieve greater economies and reduce the level of state subsidy, fees may have to rise to a level which makes the courses inaccessible to the most economically disadvantaged. Alternatively, quality of support services would be adversely affected. All too often quantity of learners is at the expense of quality of learning.

A recent study of the Mexican Telesecundaria reports that per-student costs are slightly greater – about 16 per cent – than those of urban secondary schools (de Moura Castro *et al.* 1999: 31). Some 75 per cent of the costs are recurrent. But the alternative, the cost of traditional secondary schools in rural areas, would be prohibitive. Given the quality of outputs, for example good exam pass rates, the Mexican government considers that Telesecundaria gives value for money. But, as the analysts point out, today's high quality is the result of many years' commitment to improvement.

Similarly, recent analysis of the costs of Telecurso 2000 suggests that, where students study alone and informally, the costs are lower than traditional school, but for study in supervised groups in *telesalas*, the costs are similar to those of regular schools (de Moura Castro 1999).

Unsurprisingly our examples all show that the more teacher input, the greater the cost. How does this affect quality? This question is hard to answer. Open schools can help make resources go further. They may be a cheaper way of increasing access to education providing that they grow large enough to reap economies of scale. But what of the quality of learning they provide? It is relatively simple to compute the numbers of those who pass or fail, take part or drop out. But do statistics tell us enough? Questions of quality run deeper, raising issues of the nature of the learning experience, its relevance and functionality. The analysts of Telecurso put it well:

> Are the results commensurate with the costs? No rigorous study allows us to give a precise and reliable answer. Costs are easy to compute. The delivery

and its organization are clear enough. But good measurements of outputs are lacking.

(de Moura Castro 1999)

Seven dilemmas about quality

A number of unanswered or debatable questions make it difficult to determine adequate qualitative measures.

I Wide recognition of learning versus curriculum flexibility

The easiest way to ensure recognition of learning is for the pupils of an open school to cover exactly the same curriculum and sit exactly the same examinations as regular school pupils. However, this is not a simple matter. Good practice requires flexibility in the following aspects:

- regulations for examinations: for example, standard practice may require examinations in several subjects to be completed at a single sitting, unsuitable for many out-of-school students
- choice of subjects: as we saw with NOS, students in open schools may benefit from a wider choice of subjects to increase their chances of employment
- content of learning: distance learners may need different content from regular learners

But national authorities or employers may be reluctant to recognise such variants.

Telesecundaria provides a good illustration of the final point. In 1993 Mexico introduced a new national curriculum, which laid emphasis on young people engaging with their communities. In consideration of the circumstances of its students, Telesecundaria organised this aspect of learning as follows, within the curriculum framework:

> Special days are set aside throughout the year to promote health, arts and culture, or productivity, particularly in areas of local economic interest, such as farming or animal care and production. Three times a year, students present to their communities specially-planned group projects intended to benefit the community. Students both promote the projects and are responsible for ensuring that their parents are involved in the projects.
>
> (Calderoni 1998)

2 Technology choice

Technology choice in distance learning is a well-rehearsed theme. Choice for successful open schools seems to have been based largely on accessibility, experience and tradition. The traditional triumvirate of distance education – print, radio and television – dominate, with the traditional technology of school – the printed text – usually in the lead position.

The experience of open schooling has made it clear that there is one element in the system which is indispensable – the teacher (although the teacher's role in the open and traditional classroom differs). It also suggests that, in general, open schooling for young people is best if there are opportunities for group learning.

The dilemma is therefore not simply which technologies to use, but also what combination, and in what relation to teachers. We habitually think of books for schools, but as paper and distribution costs rise, printed material may give way to other technologies. The Internet is a cheaper way to distribute words and pictures, as well as offering flexibility in content and immediacy in communications. But Internet connections are not yet widely available in schools. Broadcasts are a good way of reaching large numbers, but are time bound and need organised support to be effective. Technology choice is harder than ever.

There is little doubt that it is desirable to make information technology a part of open schooling, to ensure that learners acquire the skills they need for employability in the information age. The idea of 'multichannel learning' – a range of opportunity – may be a better platform for the future than the highly structured approach of traditional distance learning.

3 How much learner support? Quantity or quality?

Schools of the air provide a high level of teacher input for every pupil. In contrast, open schools offer regular support for learners, but it is left to individual learners to use these opportunities. Many do not. To what extent is performance affected?

One of the weakest points of large open schools is limited feedback on learning. In Indonesia, several measures have been devised to provide better feedback. One is the problem book where students at the learning centre list their problems. This book is then sent to the subject teacher at the base school for discussion during tutorials. But there was also demand for more immediate feedback. So since 1996 OJSS has been piloting two-way radio communications in ten provinces to facilitate more frequent interaction between students and teachers. The use of telephone, facsimile and computer (Internet) is not yet feasible. If better quality in open schooling requires more teacher input, how much is enough? Can the level of input decrease with the age of the learner? And how significant is peer support, through group learning? Research is necessary to determine whether such measures make a significant difference and to identify those measures which are most valuable. Too little is known in answer to such questions.

In university-level distance education, on-line tutorial support is now becoming popular. Open schools are at the starting line with new technologies. Can they offer means of enhancing communication without increasing the burden on teachers?

4 Teaching quality

Telesecundaria teachers 'usually like to leave these rural areas as soon as possible' (de Moura Castro 1999: 33). The issue of teacher commitment dogs open schooling everywhere. The main problem can be defined as follows. Open school central authorities aim to control quality by producing the best possible learning materials. Good teachers like to control the teaching and learning which takes place in their classes. But teaching and learning in DE is different. The individual student has to learn independently. So the teacher has to accept that the curriculum is delivered by a central source and the learning is under the control of the individual learner.

Teachers thus have to become facilitators of learning rather than transmitters of knowledge – as the catch phrase has it, 'guide on the side not sage on the stage'. Teachers need not only to acquire skills of facilitation and learning support, but also discover that this is a job to be proud of. It is often hard to recruit enough people with the insight and enthusiasm necessary. Then, training to transform teachers for the new role is costly and often logistically difficult, especially when open school targets are in remote regions.

5 Super-structure or infrastructure?

Faced with a target of 2.25 million learners, Indonesia's open school has to be tightly organised, with strong control from the centre. It now has mechanisms for local participation. But as the system expands, it may be more challenging to remain sensitive to local difference. Telecurso, in contrast, has a free market approach where learners and their communities set up their own support arrangements. Growing from the grassroots may ensure greater relevance and higher motivation among students but, equally, there are risks to quality. As open school systems expand further, it will be desirable to explore new modalities for creating a balance between central and local.

It is critical that children and their parents are able to identify with their school, and this requires a strong local presence, and permanent marketing. In Indonesia, radio and television broadcasts have a dual purpose, for instruction and also for influence, shaping positive attitudes toward OJSS and marketing the system as a whole. The student magazine is also used for marketing since it is displayed on the notice board at learning centres. As many of these are primary schools, their students can also read the magazine and gradually get a good perception of OJSS.

6 Partnership or competition?

Schools everywhere belong to their communities. Open schools make every effort to build links in communities where they operate. But they are different, and often managed by a different authority from that in charge of local schools. This can lead to competition. In New Zealand, for example, district education authorities recently came up with the idea of providing teaching over the Internet to small rural schools. An excellent idea – except that they did not have the resources to do it well, while the national correspondence college not only had the expertise but also the material. Rather than enter on a collision course of competition, the college began to work in partnership with the authorities to adapt their distance learning materials for the new technologies (Gamlin 1996). In time we may see increasing collaboration between central bodies and local schools. The result could be school networks linking open and traditional education.

7 Equity

Equity demands access to education for all, but at what cost? Some governments have set up open schooling systems, but then expected them to operate effectively with an unrealistically low budget. This has been particularly true of the African study centres. Unsurprisingly, results have been disappointing (see e.g. Siaciwena 1994, Jenkins 1989, Curran and Murphy 1989). An alternative strategy is to pass on costs to learners, or their parents. This may be unacceptable if those who are already disadvantaged are expected to pay for schooling which, for the privileged, is free.

The use of information and communications technologies raises further issues. At the 1995 European Information Technology Summit, EU Commissioner Bangemann warned of the danger of these new and emerging technologies further marginalising those who were already marginal. Some five years later, we still have little experience of how best to use these new tools in the often marginal environments inhabited by the students of open schools. What potential do these new tools offer to improve teaching and learning in open schools? What possibilities are emerging for using them to widen access still further?

Diversifying the strategy

Open school is a simple formula, using tried and tested technology, in a reasonably cost-effective manner. But it is not appropriate for every context. Before concluding the chapter, we need to consider other strategies which use DE for extending school, to school-age pupils or to adults who have missed out on school.

Young people

First, what problems are faced in countries with small populations? National statistics on schooling in poor countries with small populations are often dismal. Most children start school, very few complete basic education. Poverty is probably the major factor, but amongst the many other reasons for non-completion are those of geography and population distribution. In large but thinly populated countries, there are often too few children of an age in one place to make a class and too few teachers capable of taking them beyond the basics.

As long ago as the 1960s, some African countries turned to DE to address this problem. The correspondence schools of Australasia offered a model. But it would not work to transpose the model unchanged into Africa. Teacher shortage as well as poor communications infrastructure meant the strong individual pupil-teacher relationship was not an option. An alternative was devised, the idea of the open secondary study group.

This is how it works in Malawi. Students register with the Malawi College of Distance Education (MCDE) and study in special centres, reading distance learning texts and following radio programmes in class-groups, each supported by a teacher-supervisor. There are over 150,000 students in over 520 centres. The numbers are very high, because more pupils attend the MCDE centres than attend regular schools. Local communities raise funds to establish centres in places without a regular secondary school. Teacher-supervisors perform a similar role to the facilitators in Telesecundaria or *guru pamong* in Indonesia. But practice is different, conditioned by the limited level of financial support from government. Results of MCDE examination candidates have been deteriorating over the last five years. This is attributed to a combination of factors – lack of study materials, unprepared facilitators, poor learning conditions, and no system for selecting students (Laymaman 1999). There is little hope of improvement without commitment of more resources to revitalise and enhance the system.

Open secondary study groups have operated in several other African countries, including Zambia and Zimbabwe. They have had a chequered history, affected by fluctuations in national economies, at times drained of resources even to buy the paper to print the course books. As publicly funded operations, they have been subject to political whim, sometimes little more than teacherless schools.

Open secondary study groups were usually linked to traditional correspondence colleges, which also provided correspondence courses for adults. The linkage meant on the one hand advantages of scale and added value, on the other restricted flexibility. It was difficult to explore new possibilities, such as those offered by new communications technologies. The economic case for open secondary study groups is theoretically quite strong. Where governments do not have the resource to expand formal schools, as in Zambia, they 'appear to be a necessary alternative' (Siaciwena 1994). In reality there have been problems, such as low status, poor quality of learning materials and learning environment, sustainability and teaching resources. Most schemes have been as underresourced as the regular schools in the countries where they operate.

Some recent initiatives are exploiting new technological possibilities in association with delinking from government control. In Botswana, for example, the new Botswana College of Distance and Open Learning (BOCODOL) plans to plug in to the government datanet and operate through a network of learning centres in schools, vocational training centres and other community facilities, linked through five regional hubs.[8] This new system, built on an old one, aims to be customer-centred and in the long run self-funding.

Adults

Many of BOCODOL's students will be adults. It would be hard to identify a country where every adult had acquired a level of basic education adequate for lifelong employability. As long as there have been correspondence schools for children, there have also been courses open to adults. In France, for example, in 1939 the government established a correspondence school for children displaced by war. This national centre for distance education (CNED) still operates, now one of the world's largest distance learning institutions. However the majority of its students learning at school-level today are adults.

But even though most open schools, large and small, cater for large numbers of adults as well as school-age pupils, the impact on society of adult open schooling is not great. The debate about participation in adult basic education is covered elsewhere in this book. Here we address some pedagogic problems facing open schooling for adults.

First, many adults seeking to re-enter education have poor literacy skills, often accompanied by anxiety about their capacity to learn, and low self-esteem. Such people are not ready for open learning. Some strategies have been developed to assist such people to benefit from open learning opportunities, but most depend on a high level of individual support for learning, and are costly to implement.

Post-literacy, there are few primary-level distance programmes for adults. One notable exception is Teleprimaria in Brazil, a television-based primary programme for adults which, with Telecurso, provides a complete school-equivalence programme (Ortiz 1999).

But often adults demand an education which is more directly functional than the school curriculum. For example, a distance learning programme for uneducated nomadic Mongolian women, the Gobi Women's Project, focuses on income generation and health topics to complement literacy and numeracy (report, 1999, on web pages of UNESCO Learning Without Frontiers initiative *www.unesco.org/education/educprog/lwf/* see also chapter 6).

Adults come to learning with a set of experiences which can form a foundation for rapid progress – for example, handling money regularly is a good starting point for numeracy development. Content needs to be relevant if learning is to be transferable from one context to another. This may make it desirable to devise an alternative school curriculum for adults. The Telecurso 2000 curriculum has for example been developed around four guiding principles: job-oriented education; development of basic skills; citizenship education; contextualisation. The selection of content for each discipline is determined by these principles (de Moura Castro 1999: 2).

So perhaps for adults we need a different kind of open school. Rather than reproducing the school curriculum, it might offer packages of learning which on the one hand meet specific and immediate needs and on the other can be put together to form a learning pathway suited to the individual. The 'pick and mix' approach of multichannel learning is attractive.

Young children

As we have seen, there are few opportunities for organised open schooling for young children. Indeed, it is the majority view that 'young children need some type of formal institution like school if they are to learn an orthodox basic curriculum effectively' (Perraton 1982: 10). But there are ways in which open schooling can support young children. There is untold and as yet unmeasured value in an informal learning infrastructure for young children. In the USA some years ago a major problem was identified – the poor performance at school of disadvantaged children. The television programme *Sesame Street* began as one of a slate of interventions, known as Project Headstart, to prepare very young children from poor communities for school. Over the years these pre-school interventions have proved effective in improving later school performance. In the USA Project Headstart survives today, and *Sesame Street* and its young English cousins the *Teletubbies* now help young children all over the world get ready for school (Arnove 1976, project Headstart web site, *www.nhsa.org*).

The key idea here is that of improving school effectiveness, and this could be the best way forward for younger children. It may be timely to consider exploring further the informal and low-cost approaches of multichannel learning, at primary level in and around schools, incorporating where possible uses of new information and communication technologies. A good way to approach this is through supporting teachers, either in the classroom, or through offering in-service training at a distance to upgrade their skills and learn new teaching techniques.

Convergence

The principal function of most open schools is to transmit the formal curriculum to those out of school. Open and distance learning methods are quite good for delivering traditional knowledge-based curricula. Such curricula are frequently criticised. But open schools cannot reasonably be criticised for conservative curriculum content when the specification of curriculum is a matter for the national authority.

But in the not-too-distant future there are new issues to tackle. First, consensus is growing globally that human values lie at the heart of good education. This principle is enshrined in the curriculum framework of four pillars of education proposed by UNESCO's Commission for Education in the Twenty-first Century:

- Learning to know
- Learning to do
- Learning to live together
- Learning to be   (UNESCO 1996)

Second, competence in the use of computers and new information and communications technologies is now widely acknowledged as a basic skill for employability; young people from marginal communities who complete school without such skills are in danger of further marginalisation. Further, information and communications technologies are beginning to have a broad and profound impact on education, on content, resources and methods of learning.

As mainstream education develops in line with these new demands, the ideal of equity underpinning open schools could be eroded and disadvantage compounded, as long as they depend on old-fashioned curricula and old-fashioned technology.

But there is an alternative. Until recently, open schooling meant taking learning out of the classroom to learners elsewhere. Now new information and communication technologies are turning it into two-way traffic. There is increasing convergence between traditional classroom methods of teaching and learning and those of distance education. On-line learning is spreading fast, as a component of classroom activity. The idea of the open classroom is the result, where teachers and pupils in school are connected to learning outside.

The impact on teachers is very similar to that familiar from the open schools – their role broadens and changes, as they become more facilitators and counsellors, less purveyors of knowledge.

Of course the reality is that, even in rich countries, the use of information and communications technologies in schools is still patchy. We know little about the effects on quality, we know little about the costs. But there is no doubt that on-line learning is here to stay.

Is it too soon to consider the impact on the disadvantaged – poor children, and poor countries? Can we see a future where, instead of making those at the margins even more marginal, the new technological possibilities make the quality of learning in any open classroom, at any level, as good as learning in any other environment? Perhaps the base schools of Indonesia, the *telesalas* of Brazil and the learning centres of BOCODOL will all become connected classrooms at the same time as traditional schools.

Such outcomes depend partly on the vision of policy makers, partly on the resolution of issues and dilemmas such as those we have raised in this chapter. But one point has been clear throughout our analysis – the importance of the teacher in an open school (and the sad results when teachers are insufficiently valued and rewarded). The most crucial activity for improving open schooling is almost certainly through using the powerful tools of open and distance learning to help their teachers and facilitators to discover new ways to deliver the best education to all. One way forward is to use the communications technologies of the information age, to support teachers and create networks which connect them. Organisations such as UNICEF are already doing so, through their on-line resources for school teachers all over the world. The best hope for the future of open schooling lies in enabling its teachers to shape and control its future (Jenkins 1999, Jenkins *et al.* 1998).

Notes

1 As elsewhere in this book, basic education is taken to cover the equivalent of the first nine years of schooling. However some examples considered extend to higher levels, for example secondary-level open schools which cover complete 5–7-year secondary cycles.
2 The European Distance Education Network (EDEN) adopted the name for its school-level activities and held three Pan-European conferences under this banner between 1995 and 1999.
3 Data taken from entry in the International Centre for Distance Learning (ICDL) on-line database.
4 'Multiple media' is now widely used in place of the term 'multimedia', formerly used to describe combinations of media, e.g. print + radio, but now used for computer applications.
5 Now closed (Fraser and Restrepo-Estrada 1998).
6 1992 study.
7 Data from NOS annual reports, NOS Profile 1997–8, and personal communications from former Chairman Professor Mohan B. Menon.
8 Personal communication, Dr David Warr, DFID Technical Adviser.

References

Anzalone, S. (ed.) (1995) Multichannel Learning: Connecting All to Education, Washington, DC: Education Development Center.

Arnove, R. (1976) Educational Television: A Policy Critique and Guide for Developing Countries, New York: Praeger.

Barnadib, I. et al. (1985) Evalluasi DMP Terbuka, Jakarta: Pustekkom.

Bernal Alarcón, H. (ed.) (1978) Educación Fundamental Integral: Teoría y Aplicación en el Caso de ACPO, Bogota: Editorial Andes.

Calderoni, J. (1998) Telesecundaria: Using TV to Bring Education to Rural Mexico, Education and Technology Technical Notes Series, Washington, DC : World Bank.

Calvano, M. and Sadiman, A.S. (1983) Case Study of the Open Junior Secondary School, Jakarta: Pustekkom.

Curran, C. and Murphy, P. (1989) Distance Education at Second Level in Six Countries in Africa, Dublin: Higher Education for Development Co-operation.

de Moura Castro, C. (1999) 'Brazil's Telecurso 2000', in the on-line journal TechKnowLogia November/December. Available HTTP: http://www.TechKnowLogia.org

de Moura Castro, C., Wolff, L. and Garcia, N. (1999) 'Mexico's Telesecundaria', in the on-line journal TechKnowLogia September/October. Available HTTP: http://www.TechKnowLogia.org

Dock, A. and Helwig, J. (eds) (1999) Interactive Radio Instruction: Impact, Sustainability and Future Directions, Washington, DC: World Bank and USAID.

Ehrmann, S. (1996) Adult Learning in a New Technological Era, Paris: OECD.

Fraser, C. and Restrepo-Estrada, S. (1998) Communicating for Development: Human Change for Survival, London: Tauris.

Gamlin, M. (1996) Keynote presentation at Open Classroom Conference, Oslo.

Jenkins, J. (1989) 'Some trends in distance education in Africa: An examination of the past and future role of distance education as a tool for national development', in Distance Education, 10, 1, 41–63.

Jenkins, J. (1999) 'Teaching for tomorrow: The changing role of teachers in the connected classroom', in A. Scucs and A. Wagner (eds), Shifting Perspectives: The Changing Role and Position of Open and Distance Learning in School Level Education, Budapest: EDEN.

Jenkins, J., Lieberg, S. and Stieng, I. (1998) The Connected Teacher, Oslo: National Centre for Educational Resources.

Kartasurya, K. *et al.* (1993) *Baseline Study for Open Junior High School*, Jakarta: UNESCO/ UNDP, INS/88/028.

Laymaman, C. (1999) 'Malawi College of Distance Education to move to resource-based open learning', Paper presented to COL tenth-anniversary conference, Brunei.

Mayo, J. (1999) 'Radio's role in education and development: Introduction and overview', in A. Dock and J. Helwig (eds) *Interactive Radio Instruction: Impact, Sustainability and Future Directions*, Washington, DC: World Bank and USAID.

McTigue Zirker, J. (1990) *Interactive Radio Instruction*, AID Science and Technology in Development Series, Washington, DC: USAID.

Naidoo, G. (1999) 'To the grassroots by air: The South African radio learning programme', in *Open Praxis*, 2, 21–26.

Ortiz, V. (1999) 'Open and distance education in Latin America', in G. Farrell (ed.) *Virtual Learning*, Vancouver: Commonwealth of Learning.

Perraton, H. (ed.) (1982) *Alternative Routes to Formal Education: Distance Education for School Equivalency*, Baltimore: Johns Hopkins University Press.

Rowntree, D. (1992) *Exploring Open and Distance Learning*, London: Kogan Page.

Rumble, G. (1992) *The Management of Distance Learning Systems*, Paris: UNESCO Institute for Educational Planning.

Sadiman. A.S. and Rahardjo, R. (1997) 'Contribution of SMP Terbuka towards lifelong learning in Indonesia' in M. Hatton (ed.) *Lifelong Learning: Policies, Practices and Programs*, Toronto: APEC Publication.

Sadiman, A.S., Rahardjo, R., Siswosumarto, S. and Almunawar, M. (1999) *Open Junior Secondary School: Contribution for Successful Universal Nine-Year Basic Education in Indonesia*, Jakarta: Country Report.

Sadiman, A.S., Seligman, D. and Rahardjo, R. (1995) *The Open Junior Secondary School: An Indonesian Case Study*, Jakarta: UNESCO/UNDP, INS/88/028.

Schramm, W. (ed.) (1967) *New Educational Media in Action: Case Studies for Planners*, Paris: UNESCO/IIEP.

Siaciwena, R. (1994) 'Zambian open secondary classes', in M. Mukhopadhyay and S. Phillips (eds) *Open Schooling: Selected Experiences*, Vancouver: Commonwealth of Learning.

Sutaria, M.C. (1995) 'Multichannel Learning: The Philippines experience', in S. Anzalone (ed.) *Multichannel Learning: Connecting All to Education*, Washington, DC: Education Development Center.

Tiffin, J. and Rajasingham, L. (1995) *In Search of the Virtual Class*, London: Routledge.

UNESCO (1996) *Learning: The Treasure Within*, (Delors report) Paris: UNESCO.

Visser, J. (1994) *Distance Education for the Nine High Population Countries: A Concept Paper*, Paris: UNESCO.

World Bank (1998) *Education in Sub-Saharan Africa*, Washington, DC: World Bank.

Young, M., Perraton, H., Jenkins, J. and Dodds, T. (1980) *Distance Teaching for the Third World*, London: Routledge.

Part 4

Conclusion

Chapter 13

Outcomes: what have we learned?

Chris Yates

> We can interpret the growth of open and distance learning as something which has provided education to thousands, even millions, for whom it would not otherwise have been available. Many have been disappointed by what has been on offer. But others have benefited and we can interpret this widening of education as a move towards equity. The alternative view is harsher. Open and distance learning is regarded by students and ministries of education as a second-rate system used to offer a shadow of education while withholding its substance. It is an inefficient but cheap way of containing educational demand without meeting it. Through its existence it helps insulate the elite system from pressures that might otherwise threaten its status or ways of working. The evidence will fit either interpretation.
>
> (Perraton 2000: 199–200)

This concluding chapter summarises some of the evidence on the outcomes of basic education delivered through open and distance education (ODE), particularly as it relates to policy dimensions and challenges. It considers evidence on questions of access and reach, cost efficiency, equity, quality and effectiveness, innovation and sustainability, relevance and redress. Out of this discussion, and from the body of experience presented in earlier chapters, it draws some preliminary conclusions concerning the contribution of ODE to Education for All (EFA).

Access and reach

Distance education models have a proven record of being able to reach large numbers of students, wherever they live. This is no less true for the basic level of education than for higher education. Projects using print and broadcast combinations, in particular, have reached very large numbers, and in some cases have done so for decades. Two ETV projects, the Mexican Telesecundaria and Brazil's Telecurso 2000, whose forerunners were established in the 1960s, now provide access to basic education for hundreds of thousands of people. In Asia we have seen the emergence of the large-scale 'open schools' model. The Indian, Indonesian

Table 13.1 Enrolment in key ODE institutions operating at the basic level

Institution or project	Year of most recent data	Enrolment ('000)
ETV/Teleschools		
Mexico Telesecundaria[1]	1999	817
Portugal Telescola[2]	1997	200
Brazilian Telecurso 2000[3]	1999	200 out-of-school, 200 in-school
Asian open schools		
Indonesian Open Junior School[4]	1999	376
Indian National Open School[4]	1998	130
Bangladesh Open School[5]	1997	45
South Korean Air Correspondence High Schools[6]	1992	35
Study-centres model		
Malawi College of Distance Education		
– study centres[6]	1999	150
Zambia – study centres[14]	1990	11
Zimbabwe – study centres[14]	1992	23
Papua New Guinea College of Distance		
Education[6]	1992	27.7
New African open schools		
Namibia NAMCOL[7]	1998	5.9
Botswana BOCODOL[17]	1999	0.894 Junior Certificate 1.4 General Certificate of Education
Schools of the Air		
Victoria Australia MoE[8]	1993	0.301 (basic), 2.3 (secondary)
Canada British Columbia MoE[8]	1993	2.8 (grades 1–7), 38 (grades 8–12)
Radio-based models		
Radio ECCA Canary Islands, Spain[9]	1999	64.3 (includes students from mainland Spain)
Colombia ACPO[10]	1987	160–220 p.a.
Venezuela – IRI, Maths is Fun[11]	1999	600
South Africa – IRI, English in Action[11]	1999	100
Tanzania – Man is Health radio campaign[12]	1973	2,000 (estimate)
Multichannel learning		
Pakistan FEPRA/BFEP project[6]	1997	9.0
Mexican Teleprimaria[2]	–	2,500+
Basic education training programmes		
West and central Africa INADES-formation[6]	1996/7	11.8
AMREF[4]	1995	4.0
Brazil Logos II[13]	1993	24.4
Tanzania primary teacher upgrading		
programme 1979–84[13]	1993	45.5
Uganda primary teacher education 1992–7[15]	1997	2.7
South Africa UNISA adult basic education project[16]	1999	4.8

Sources:
1 Farrell (1999); 2 Yates (1998); 3 *TechKnowLogia* (1999); 4 This volume, chapters 11 and 12; 5 Ali, Enamul Haque and Rumble (1997); 6 Perraton (2000); 7 NAMCOL (1998); 8 Mukopadhyay and Phillips (1994); 9 Radio ECCA website. Available on HTTP: http://www.radio-ecca.org; 10 Fraser and Restrepo-Estrada (1998); 11 Dock and Helwig (1999); 12 young *et al.* (1991); 13 Perraton (1993); 14 Perraton and Creed (forthcoming); 15 Wrightson T. (1998) ; 16 McKay, personal communication (2000); 17 Warr, personal communication (2000)

and Korean open schools, in particular, now attract hundreds of thousands of students to their programmes. And basic education, through teacher education and other forms of adult training programme, still receives significant attention from ministries and aid agencies alike (Perraton 1993, 2000, Wrightson 1998, McKay 1995). Other smaller scale, basic level adult training models, like those operated by AMREF for health and INADES-formation for farmers, continue, if somewhat precariously. It is only in Africa that the study centres model and the radio campaign seem to have been rejected. Table 13.1 gives an indication of the scale of activity.

Costs and efficiency

The Jomtien WCEFA forum called for the judicious use of instructional technologies, efficient use of resources and adequate training of staff in efforts to provide basic education for all. However, it is difficult to draw strong conclusions on the cost-efficiency of providing basic education through open and distance education models, not least because of scarcity of information. Despite the longevity of some projects, few have undertaken detailed cost, or more importantly cost-efficiency or cost-effectiveness, studies. Nevertheless, we do have some evidence. Some of it is presented in table 13.2.

The evidence on costs suggests three main conclusions. First, where open and distance learning models have been used as alternatives to residential and face-to-face basic education programmes, they can generally be designed and operated more cheaply than their school equivalents. Out-of-school models like the new Asian open schools, and even the older African study centres model, tend to deliver cost-efficiency even when they are providing an equivalent school curriculum. This is partly because staff salary and capital costs for buildings are lower. Secondly, and in contrast with the first point, in-school models like IRI, ETV and computer-based learning approaches, which are frequently designed to complement and improve the quality of existing provision, rather than substitute for it, all tend to increase unit costs. As Orivel demonstrates in this volume for computer-based education (chapter 8), it is only when countries reach a per-capita GNP of $7,300 that computer-based learning may reach a break-even point where costs match those of conventional education. In countries which have per-capita GNPs below this figure, the costs of employing a primary teacher are so low that teachers are still by far the cheapest way of delivering basic education. Third, both adult formal (for example, primary teacher or health worker education programmes) and non-formal training programmes (for farmers or village dwellers) have demonstrated their cost-efficiency over several decades in comparison with residential or face-to-face equivalent approaches. Nevertheless non-formal and adult basic education through ODE remains a light which, so far, has never shone (Perraton 1993, 2000).

Orivel's conclusion on distance education and cost-effectiveness, reached in the mid-1990s (Orivel 1996), also holds for basic education through ODE today:

Unless massive misallocation of resources occurs as a result of poor management decisions, distance education projects are most of the time cost-effective, even though the advantage of economies of scale is offset by the higher cost of developing multimedia, self instructional materials. But this conclusion is insufficient as a basis for policy making. Not only are more case studies needed that compare actual costs and results, but studies should also investigate, in different contexts, the optimal mix of media that leads to the highest possible cost-effectiveness ratio. Otherwise educational technology choices will be mostly determined by hardware and software producers, telecommunication firms, and innovative entrepreneurs, whose objectives and interests do not necessarily coincide with those who finance education or with the learners themselves.

(Orivel 1996: 847–8)

Questions of equity

The argument for ODE, even at the basic level, is often based on economic considerations. The assumption is that ODE should first demonstrate the ability to provide education more cheaply than alternative means. This is clearly feasible, particularly with mass standardised systems of delivery, constructed to reach out to large settled, stable and sedentary populations which enjoy a high degree of cultural stability and uniformity. But we have also seen that ODE models can further equity goals. The El Salvador ETV experiment, for example, was the first school resource to offer grades 7–9 education equally throughout the country. In the mid-1990s the Indian NOS was attracting 23 per cent of its enrolment from scheduled tribes and castes or disabled people. And even relatively small-scale ODE projects, like INADES-formation, have shown that it is feasible to serve a wide variety of cultural groups by translating their materials into over fifty languages.

The research and experience reported in this book also illustrate how ODE can play an important role in reaching out to small mobile populations like nomads and migrant groups. In refugee crises, and in other situations where cultural maintenance is an issue, ODE can be used to help stimulate education among learners on their own terms, rather than expecting learners to change their lifestyles in order to adapt to existing inflexible structures. We have seen how 'bottom-up community dialogue' has become increasingly central to the successful integration of ODE programmes and to the wider development of civil society. In an age of increasing globalisation, the cultures of the marginalised, who sometimes constitute majorities, can be seriously threatened by forces of homogenisation. Where ODE can be used to support indigenous and locally controlled cultural development, as in the case of the Fulani in Nigeria or the Gobi Women's Project, it at least offers the potential, in theory, to help maintain cultural diversity and thereby improve equity. After all, decentralised project operation has been shown to work even in contexts like Mongolia, where centralised systems of planning and control

Table 13.2 Costs of basic education at a distance

Model/project	Scale and duration	Cost per learner	Currency 1998 US$ Cost comparison
Educational television			
Mexican Telesecundaria [1&7]	Running for more than 30 years in 1998–9, 817,200 students in over 13,000 schools supported by more than 38,000 teachers	In the range $441– 589 per student	Cost per learner has remained relatively stable over a long period. Costs understood to be of a similar order of magnitude to costs in conventional schools. A recent study has reported a 16% increase over the costs of conventional secondary schooling
Brazilian Telecurso 2000[2]	Running since early 1990s, though first generation began in 1978. Now serving 40,000 students both in schools and through study groups – *telesalas*	n/a	Costs of out-of-school provision reported at a similar level to conventional schools
Côte d'Ivoire Educational Television Project[3]	Ran from 1968 to 1981 before being abandoned by government and donors	Cost per pupil per year for primary education with television estimated at $143 compared with $104 for primary education without TV – giving a yearly add-on cost of $39 (1977 figures)	ETV input increased the cost per learner by US $104.90 (at 1998 equivalency)
Radio learning groups			
Zambia radio education campaign on co-operative movement[4]	4,730 participants, ten weekly meetings	$22 per student	Cost per learner lower than cost of training at farmers' centre, higher than primary school costs
Schools broadcasting			
Interactive Radio Instruction (IRI) projects[4]	Over 20 projects ran over 25 years reaching audiences in the range 10– 250,000	In the range $0.97– 16.97 per learner across a wide range of curricula, contexts and developing country settings	Costs are usually add-on in primary schools – but costs for training adults often lower than by other means

continued...

Table 13.2 Costs of basic education at a distance (continued)

Model/project	Scale and duration	Cost per learner	Currency 1998 US $ Cost comparison
Bolivia IRI – Radio Math[5]	Ran 1986–97 reaching 185,000 students in 1996	n/a	
Radio schools Radio schools in Latin America e.g. Acción Cultural Popular, Colombia (ACPO)[1&6]	Ran 1947–87 before being closed down; 160–220,000 participants reached at any one time in over 20,000 radio schools; 2.25 million peasants participated in first 20 years	In the range $50–88 per student per annum	Cost at ACPO less than at primary schools
Radio Santa Maria (RSM), Dominican Republic[1]	20,000 students, one-year course offering primary equivalency		Comparable with primary, lower than evening classes
Open schools National Open School, India[1&4]	Running from 1989 to present, annual enrolment 130,000 (1998–9); 400,000 in full roll; weekly tutorials one hour per subject	Cost per learner $10 (1997–8); cost per graduate $92 (1997–8); graduation rate 43%	Comparative cost per learner in formal school is $27, about 63% of cost of government school
Indonesian Open Junior Secondary School (OJSS)[4&7]	Ran on a pilot basis from 1979, recently scaled up, reaching 376,620 students in 3,773 locations in 1998/9; by 2004 plans to serve 2.25 million students	Cost per student currently reported at $21.8	Expenditure is limited to 60% of the cost of regular schools – costs kept lower by government policy; currently reported at 39% of JSS conventional schooling
South Korean Air Correspondence High School[4]	Has run from 1976 to present – currently serving circa 20,000 students	$171 per student per annum	Cost per student 24% of alternative; cost per successful student 29%
Malawi College of Distance Education (MCDE)[4]	Has been running since 1965; recently government has moved to transformthe institutional outreach system; enrolment 150,000 in 1998	Using 1988 enrolment figures $107 per student; $378 per pass	Cost per pass reduced to 34% of the day-school rate

continued ...

Table 13.2 Costs of basic education at a distance (continued)

Model/project	Scale and duration	Cost per learner	Currency 1998 US $ Cost comparison
Multichannel learning			
Functional Education Project for Rural Areas (FEPRA)[1]	Ran as an experimental research project 1982–5 – small-scale, eight weekly meetings reaching 1,500 participants per cycle, now institutionalised as part of AIOU's programming	About $46 per student	Low in comparison with other alternatives – but more expensive than primary schools
Basic education training programmes			
INADES-formation courses in business and agriculture for farmers and agricultural extension workers[4,7]	Training programme began in 1970s – still continuing – serving 11,853–15,737 students per year 1993–7; enrolment recently declining	Cost per graduate estimated $982 in 1977; estimated $235 in 1996/7	Though quite high, costs compare favourably with equivalent costs for residential farmer training; 80% of costs currently met externally
AMREF health worker programme[4,7]	Programme began in 1980 and reached over 6,000 paramedical staff by mid 1990s; in 1995 4,090 learners were reported active	$155 per successful student in 1996	Costs about one-sixth of conventional face-to-face training combined with potential for multiplier effects in field situations
Primary teacher education, Uganda (NITEP)[8]	Project ran 1993–7, enrolling 2,750 teachers	$2,000 per successful student	Lower than the equivalent college-based programme
UNISA adult educators literacy training programme[9]	Programme commenced in 1995 enrolling 2,200 learners and a further 4,000 in 1996, 5,500 1998 and 4,800 in 1999	n/a	Assumed lower than residential model of training

Sources:
1 Perraton and Creed (forthcoming); 2 de Moura Castro et al (1999); 3 Ba and Potashnik (in press); 4 Perraton (2000); 5 Dock and Helwig (1999); 6 Fraser and Restrepo-Estrada (1998); 7 See this volume; 8 Wrightson (1998); 9 McKay personal communication (2000)

Note:
n/a = not available

have long held sway. ODE initiatives based on this bottom-up 'difference approach' can do much to further goals of social equity, particularly when they serve to challenge deficit notions of citizenship.

But it is not all good news. Paradoxically, basic education ODE systems set up to provide extended educational opportunity to underprivileged groups also often exploit those who work for them. Many of the literacy campaigns, including for example JAMAL, depended to a large extent on unpaid labour for delivery in the field. The Gobi Women's Project depended on people who worked without pay to provide support services in the field (Robinson 1999). Similarly, payments for marking student assignments in the MCDE system were kept so low for so long, and tutors had such high workloads, that the quality and reliability of the education available were seriously undermined. While in some ways the use of voluntary labour can be viewed as admirable, such practices can also be regarded as inequitable, as states seek to exploit the good will and social conscience of those involved. States may, in the case of ABET through ODE, be too ready to rely on the argument that the scale of the problem, and the cost of meeting it, are so great, that initiatives cannot be funded from regular taxation. Thus they avoid making politically difficult choices affecting policies on taxation and social welfare.

Further, we can find many policy contradictions at the institutional level. The case of the Indian open school offers an example. Given that the stated mission of the Indian National Open School is 'to provide education for all and to achieve equity and social justice' (Mukhopadhyay 1995: 94), it appears paradoxical that NOS should also be required to achieve this by drawing most of its funding from the sale of books and materials and from student fees (Perraton 2000: 38). It will be recalled that the Indian government requires NOS to recover around 75 per cent of its operating budget from such sources. The case of the Brazilian primary teacher education project, Logos II, provides another example. In one assessment of this project Oliveira and Orivel concluded: 'from a structural point of view the project can be seen as reinforcing inequality: regular schools for the teachers in the best cities and distance education for the rural areas' (Oliveira and Orivel 1993: 92).

So there are situations where distance learners are required to pay a disproportionate part of the cost of their education, compared with those who attend more conventional institutions. This represents a kind of double inequity for those who cannot access conventional provision. While the state taxes citizens in order to provide funding for conventional schools, to which many do not have access (or where they do not stay long enough to complete the basic cycle), it at the same time requires them, through various forms of cost recovery, to pay yet again for the distance education system which they can use. Further, many of the children attending open schools come from families with below average incomes (Gaba 1997: 44, Jenkins and Sadiman in chapter 12 of this volume). Where states make open school provision available on the same terms as schools, as in the case of the Indonesian Open Junior Secondary School, such inequities can be seen as being mitigated.

Thus we can find evidence to support the view that ODE is being used to provide for the marginal, predominantly rural 'majority' at cost, while conventional schooling is available for more privileged, often urban, learners, through subsidy. By a strange inequitable quirk of policy, ODE learners may be said in some instances to be subsidising the inefficiencies of conventional education. In such a case, ODE is masking, rather than addressing, issues of social equity and democracy.

Quality and effectiveness

Reaching audiences is not the same as teaching them, and teaching a student is not the same as supporting individualised learning and autonomous personal development, as Anderson and Spronk make clear in chapter 3 of this volume. For direct teaching of large illiterate or newly literate audiences, the evidence suggests that current models of ODE have little to offer. To be economic they need to operate on a mass scale, and recent ideas on literacy and post literacy suggest that the complexity and diversity of local context and individual need preclude this.

There are two possible exceptions to this rule. The first would appear to be where refugee populations are involved. In this case, the numbers are often large and the people are frequently required to live in restricted and controlled areas. In these circumstances, education through ODE, as in the case of the SOLO experience, would appear justifiable, not least because it has offered a lifeline of hope (see chapter 3 in this volume and Thomas 1996 for a wider discussion). The other exception is in the case of 'big-small situations'. This is where policy makers are faced with delivering education to relatively small, scattered and in some cases highly mobile populations, which may range over very large physical areas, as in the case of Mongolia or northern Nigeria. In such circumstances, where few other options are available, ODE models for post-literacy groups, based on the 'old format' of simple print, regular radio broadcasts and supported study groups, have been shown to work relatively effectively (Robinson 1999, Pennells and Ezeomah in chapter 10 of this volume). But such schemes have often been dependent on external aid and hence are difficult to sustain.

Where ODE methods do appear to hold significant promise for helping illiterate people is in the task of training the thousands of basic education teachers, literacy workers and support cadres needed to deliver EFA. The UNISA basic education programme for adult literacy is one example which operates on a mass scale for this purpose, and, despite problems and criticisms (Geidt 1996), seems to offer considerable promise (McKay 1995, McKay et al. 1996). UNISA has an extensive infrastructure, and the professional capacity to help further the goal of redress. Nevertheless, programmes such as these do need to continually engage with the professional research debates and contribute to them. UNISA is tainted with the legacy of a discredited educational philosophy, that of 'fundamental pedagogics' (SAIDE 1995: 66–7). Designing and developing mass training programmes based on a celebration of individual difference, notions of multiple literacy, constructivist learning principles and the use of authentic materials, presents considerable challenges which are yet to be well understood or addressed.

As regards in-school models for children, the ETV systems and IRI initiatives have demonstrated their potential for teaching effectively. The body of evidence we have from ETV projects in Niger and El Salvador, from recent initiatives in the US and India (*Sesame Street* and the BEST project), and from over two decades of experimentation with IRI, offers strong evidence that the mass media can work effectively to complement existing education systems and raise quality outcomes.

The emerging Asian open schools, however, are yet to be tested, while the African study centres model sadly appears to have been too starved of resources to deliver quality education to its students (Perraton 2000).

Innovation, politics and sustainability

The introduction of new ways of teaching and learning, in whatever context, is essentially as much about politics as about pedagogy. In chapter 2 of this volume, Unterhalter, Odora Hoppers and Hoppers suggest that ODE is being presented in policy texts as more democratic than may be justified. Despite considerable success in reaching large audiences, and in some cases promoting effective behaviour change, distance learning models have often been poorly supported financially. Governments have used them primarily to save money.

The Mexican Telesecundaria, one of the largest and longest-running basic education projects in the world, was established in 1968. Early in its history Mayo had this to say about its origins:

> The vast majority of Mexico's rural communities (those with less than 2000 inhabitants) produce fewer than thirty 6th grade graduates per year, and under such circumstances the government has not felt it *economically feasible* to provide the same kind of secondary schools found in the larger Mexican towns and cities.
>
> (Mayo 1973: 1–2, our emphasis)

The Malawi College of Distance Education (MCDE), for example, has provided basic education for more than thirty-five years to those who could not get into secondary school. Even in 1994 the country had a gross enrolment rate at the secondary school level of only 4 per cent. The chances for a child of getting a place in a secondary school in Malawi are slim indeed. In this situation it is MCDE or nothing. But MCDE has never been well funded. In the late 1980s over 80 per cent of the education budget available for secondary education was allocated to schools, leaving less than 20 per cent for MCDE, despite the fact that it enrolled more students than all the secondary schools put together. As a result the quality of the education on offer often left much to be desired. One might argue that MCDE was used by the Malawi state to contain demand for secondary education throughout the whole of the Banda era. Similarly, in Papua

New Guinea the College of Distance Education enrolled 27,780 students in 1990, about half the total figure for all the secondary schools. However, it received only 3 per cent of the education budget, while the secondary schools were allocated 56 per cent (Perraton 2000: 44).

Today the long-serving study centres model, found in countries like Malawi, Zambia and Zimbabwe, looks set for either transformation or terminal decline. After a long period of operation, this model, in its older form of cheap print and correspondence, combined with radio and regular face-to-face meetings, may well have lost what little appeal it once had. It has either failed to go to scale or, for a variety of reasons, including regular underfunding and government neglect, failed to deliver consistently high-quality education. However, recently, after more than four decades of low rates of examination passes (often below 30 per cent), MCDE in the mid-1990s reported much improved pass rates at the junior certificate level of 88 per cent in 1996 and 84 per cent in 1997. Nevertheless, pass rates at senior certificate level remain low, at 11 per cent and 9 per cent respectively. The Malawi government is now encouraging the MCDE study centres to convert to regular community schools (Perraton 2000: 41–5).

Interestingly, and in contrast, other more stable or recently democratised states of southern Africa are now encouraging new approaches to open schooling. Institutions like the Botswana College of Distance and Open Learning (BOCODOL) and the Namibian College of Open Learning (NAMCOL) have been established to provide basic education opportunities for adults and adolescents who cannot, or do not want to, go to the conventional secondary schools. These innovations may yet help to engineer a future for alternative basic education delivery for youth and adults in sub-Saharan Africa. At this point, however, it is too early to pass judgement.

The first charge then is one of financial inequity and neglect. Many distance education colleges offering basic education have not received a just share of the resources available to enable them to produce education of equivalent quality to their school counterparts. The education on offer has often been poor. As a result they have been unpopular with many of the parents and students forced by circumstances to use them, and ironically with the politicians who have made use of them.

The story of ACPO, the Colombian radiophonic school, told so generously by Fraser and Restrepo-Estrada (1998), illustrates a further political point. The ACPO radio-school model provided basic education to peasant farmers and their families for almost forty years (1947–87). It was intimately linked with the church, state and big business. At one point it even attracted a visit from Pope Paul VI. The model was also successfully internationalised, being exported to over twenty countries in Latin America. During its life it attracted considerable external funding and technical help from both multilateral and bilateral aid agencies. Its achievements are remarkable:

> By the end of its life, ACPO had broadcast more than 1.5 million hours of radio programmes from its various stations; it had printed 76 million copies

of its newspaper; it had distributed about 6.5 million textbooks and 4.5 million copies of other books; and it had trained almost 25,000 peasant leaders and community development workers.

(Fraser and Restrepo-Estrada 1998: 160)

But ACPO became too successful. It challenged powerful interests directly and as a result its activities were opposed. Fraser and Restrepo-Estrada argue that, having lost some of its most powerful supporters in church and government (including both the Archbishop of Bogota and the president of Colombia), its challenge to Colombian forces of reaction was just too strong for the time and it was effectively suppressed. They conclude that it was an innovation ahead of its day, born of a philosophy of democracy and liberation too weak to survive in the climate of the time.

The second charge, then, is that mass adult and basic education projects using ODE are subject to political patronage and interference. In such circumstances their laudable goals can easily be undermined and distorted. Even when a programme has enough funding, from a variety of sources, it can be almost impossible to remain above the infighting.

Thirdly, we have seen, from the radio study group campaign experience in Africa and elsewhere, that once the primarily political objectives were achieved, the model quickly disappeared, despite its obvious success as an educational and developmental tool. Some governments control the media very tightly and even withhold important information, which might influence the health and well-being of their citizens (Pridmore and Nduba in chapter 11 of this volume). It is not unknown for governments to use, and in some cases abuse, their citizens through their distance education systems.

But it has not all been doom and gloom. In favourable democratic contexts, radio and ETV programming particularly, if it has remained sensitive to stakeholder and audience needs and succeeded in capturing indigenous resources (whether public or private), has been sustained. The world's longest-running radio serial, the BBC's *The Archers*, continues to engage millions after almost fifty years. Mexico's Telesecundaria has reached millions and Brazil's Telecurso 2000 may yet do so. Where ETV can be indigenously funded and can strike the right balance between entertainment, information and education, it too has significant potential and appears sustainable. ETV may yet get a second wind.

Both radio and ETV can effectively reach massive audiences. But the circumstances needed to do this have often been unavailable. The African radio study campaigns were expatriate-led and often reliant on external funding. Balancing the right blend of entertainment, information and education requires considerable professional skill and cultural awareness. Mass media can promote effective basic education and reach mass adult audiences. But the programming blend has to be culturally sensitive, which requires regular monitoring and audience research. The political, economic and professional resources needed to develop and deliver the programming must also be sustained over long periods. In such circumstances a stable democracy appears both a prerequisite and a beneficiary.

In terms of schooling for children, the only model to show any real promise has been IRI. This model has been thoroughly researched, evaluated and exported on a large scale to over twenty-five countries over the last twenty years. The findings we have, which are extensive, suggest that IRI can deliver consistent and improved learning gains to both children and adults, including teachers, in a wide variety of in-school and out-of-school settings (Klees 1995, Bosch 1997, Leigh and Cash 1999). Learning gains have been demonstrated across the range of basic education subject areas, including health education and child development. But some hard questions remain. First, IRI has in all cases achieved these results at an increased cost. These costs, though modest (averaging US $1–6 per student for audiences ranging from 25,000 to 250,000 per year, see Adkins 1999), have still often been too great for governments of poor countries to bear, particularly during an era of structural adjustment. The great majority of IRI projects have been externally funded, often in the initial stages by USAID. Second, IRI, like the ETV model before it, has in some cases been perceived negatively by teachers. It has the potential to disempower or deskill teachers through the promotion of inflexible, overly-centralised or outdated pedagogy, and ultimately to give the state or big business the opportunity to replace them with less well-qualified monitors. Thirdly, IRI's research findings have been largely generated internally by those in the employ of the aid agencies. This suggests an argument for more host-government and independent external validation. For all these reasons, IRI has a mixed record of being sustained.

As long as IRI remains an add-on cost to basic education it is unlikely to be successfully institutionalised in poor developing countries. Essentially this means that effective learning technologies like IRI will need to substitute for other educational inputs. This is, once again, more a matter of politics than of pedagogy.

Relevance, redress and NICT

The application of new information technologies and software tools is often claimed to improve the efficiency of education, its reach and its quality, and hence to have the potential to redress existing educational inequalities borne by underserved marginal groups (World Bank 1995: 84). This book has found little firm evidence that this is so. Unterhalter, Odora Hoppers and Hoppers (chapter 2) have highlighted the yawning gap between the rhetoric and reality at the policy level. Orivel's suggestion, that states need to reach a GNP per-capita level of at least $7,300 before it will be even theoretically cost-efficient to substitute computers for teachers, is a sobering one (chapter 8). There is a danger that the claimed universality of technology may be being used to promote a new metonomic shift, to the detriment of the EFA goal. Technology should be viewed critically and seen almost as much as a problem as it is a solution. Technology must not be regarded as having all the answers embedded in its form. The solutions for EFA are at least as much political, organisational and pedagogic as they are technological. Research needs to be undertaken to investigate the implications of patterns of ownership and control of NICT, and in particular the implications of its deployment for professional practice as this relates to EFA.

Conclusion: in search of a third way

One of the central messages repeated throughout this book is that the old existing models and methods are not up to the task of providing EFA. New methods have to be found, funded, tested and applied on a large scale if EFA is to become a reality by 2015. However, much of open and distance education practice remains problematic. Some ODE experience is certainly promising, but it does not have all the answers. Perhaps what we are looking for is a third way: systems of education provision which better integrate and use the strengths of the different modalities available. But to find this we will need to think more holistically and systemically about how education systems might be re-engineered and reconfigured.

If education systems are to be reconfigured to combine the strengths of face-to-face provision with those of self study and new forms of digital learning, teachers working in the education systems of tomorrow will need considerable support and improved professional development to ensure it can all work effectively. The diversification of education and the closer integration of its structures will call for a more flexible, responsive and highly skilled teacher force. Teachers are likely to need the capacity and capability to work with a wider range of audiences, located in multiple settings and using more, and more complex, media combinations and learning modalities. This will need investment in better systems of initial and ongoing teacher education and professional development. Education planners and policy makers will need to look at how they can up-skill their teacher forces considerably in the years to come. This point does not apply only to school or college teachers. Professional development will be needed for the whole range of people working to provide training and basic education, including extension workers, community health workers and NGO personnel.

Integration or parallelism?

Just as there is no substitute for the teacher, clearly we cannot do without our schools. The evidence presented in this book in no way suggests that we can replace schooling systems. However, schools do need to become more flexible and diversified if they are to respond to changing social expectations, deliver EFA for 2015, and help to provide learning opportunities throughout life. ODE and conventional education structures can either do this by working towards closer integration, or continue to develop along relatively separate lines. Large-scale systems, like ETV and the Asian open schools, may continue to provide alternative cost-efficient routes which remain only weakly linked to conventional schooling. In some contexts it may make sense to continue with a parallel strategy. However, in relatively homogeneous settings, and particularly in small states, there is evidence that moves toward deeper and more fundamental integration are afoot. For example, we have seen how in New Zealand, the open school and the district education authorities and local schools have been working together to make use of the Internet and flexible learning resources to improve reach and delivery (chapter 12, p. 220). Similar moves are apparent in Botswana, through the newly established BOCODOL and the country's schools.

But it is not just about re-engineering existing structures. ODE has often been dominated by Western notions of learning and has been sometimes slow to adopt new research findings. ODE has tended to champion independent and individualistic learning approaches. But children and adults without basic education need to feel supported and worthwhile in a social sense. While they need education which is both culturally and vocationally relevant, they also need a well-organised and supportive social context in which to meet the new educational challenges and to take risks with their learning. Learning needs to be individualised but not made individualistic. And its social content needs to be recognised and celebrated, not undermined. Standardised prescriptions, based on notions of deficit and transmissionist pedagogy, will not serve our future citizens well. ODE needs to learn from the best practice in conventional education and move away from the dominant individualistic and objective notions of knowledge. A lot of new curricular thinking and research needs to be undertaken to make use of recent advances in areas like educational psychology, information technology and organisation theory. In this respect the early ideas of the multichannel advocates would seem to offer a particularly fruitful route for future research and enquiry.

A series of better integrated models may yet evolve, with schools changing from within to take on board some of what ODE has been pioneering over the last forty years or so, and ODE structures moving to emulate the best practice developed in school and university settings. The systems need to evolve together and to learn more effectively from each other. It will be important in the future to plan for better integration and linkage within and across the emergent structures and their modalities of operation. Such arguments are being made now in higher education (Peters 2000; Inglis, Ling and Joosten 1999). They are likely to have relevance at other levels too.

Teacher education

If more diverse and integrated systems are to evolve, teacher training programmes will also need to broaden. Teachers need to be helped to work with a much wider range of media and materials, including independent learning materials and technologies like IRI, ETV and the Internet. This shift in the philosophy and form of teacher education will necessarily be part of a wider shift in the role, function and organisational configuration of the school and teacher training college. During this century we will need our teachers to become more highly skilled than before. They will need to become knowledge facilitators, information managers and, above all, to know how to celebrate, build on and extend individual difference. Perhaps there is some truth in the dictum that 'The teacher who can be replaced by a machine should be', but such a policy would in many ways run counter to the global call to deepen democracy. We should not aim to replace our teachers, but seek to enhance their quality through effective and available continuing education – some of which should be delivered through ODE. Teachers are as much guardians of democracy, as they are gatekeepers of culture.

Radio: the forgotten medium

We have seen throughout this book that there is much support for the use of the little media, particularly radio, for supporting EFA. AMREF has used 'Dr AMREF' successfully for over a decade; new variants of the radio soap opera continue to be popular, as in the case of the BBC-produced *New Home New Life* series in Afghanistan. And some open schools, like the Indonesian OJSS, make substantial use of radio through weekly broadcasts. But in an age of fast-moving commercialism and a plethora of information tools, it is easy to forget or disparage the familiar and longstanding. The modernisation paradigm still dominates much education development thinking, particularly when it involves the use of media. This is well illustrated by the general neglect of educational radio for EFA. Radio, once a medium thought to have so much potential for education, is in serious danger of being overtaken by enthusiasm for the more sophisticated, more visible and expensive technologies. Radio is becoming 'invisible' as an educational tool, a medium of last resort, as resources are increasingly channelled into the new information technologies. If this happens, it will be a betrayal of the people who have been excluded from EFA. Radio is a proven resource. NICT is not. It is time to give radio a new revival.

Research and evaluation

If we are to develop truly responsive systems of lifelong learning provision, ODE needs to be much more heavily researched. Detailed investigation, particularly at pre-tertiary levels, needs to be carried out. ODE may yet play a central role – but at the moment its quality and sustainability remain in question. Currently we know next to nothing about how teachers, learners, policy makers, parents, employers and other educational stakeholders view ODE at the basic level. And we have no confirmed body of opinion or research which unequivocally claims ODE to be an equaliser or opener of educational opportunity, particularly for marginal groups.

Further, if synergies are to be discovered and obtained, the implications of closer system integration need to be researched much more fully. The education and training systems of the future may provide all learners with access to some of their education though face-to-face and some through ODE modalities. Such provision will go far beyond the requirement for regular homework or the guided personal project work common in the better schools and colleges of the last century.

The need to combine and integrate more effectively the systems which we have is an important area for research.

In particular, there is a need to carry out large-scale cross-cultural studies to examine the cost-effectiveness of the different models of experience, particularly in relation to media-based and computer-based education. It is important that ODE should be configured to serve local community needs, and not to further alienate or impoverish the already marginalised. For this to happen, it needs to work ever more closely with the teachers and structures of the mainstream – and they with it. Without a more critical and reflexive practice, which embraces change and uncertainty much more readily, the structures we have will continue to fall well short of society's expectations. We noted in chapter 1 that education is just one of many 'shell institutions' currently undergoing transformation. Shell institutions have rigid but weak exteriors, particularly when their content is being emptied. Let us hope that they will not crack under the pressure of intensifying policy challenges.

Finally, to return to Perraton's conclusion cited at the opening of this chapter, perhaps it is not so much that ODE is either threatening or insulating the way existing systems of education work. Rather, what is happening is that agencies are becoming more transparent and accountable, as a consequence of our increasing realisation that for the first time in history we are all closely interconnected and interdependent. For us to achieve a socially just world, EFA is a requirement. It is not enough just to postpone the target date for achieving it. We have to develop new strategies for doing so.

References

Adkins, D. (1999) 'Cost and finance', in A. Dock and J. Helwig (eds) *Interactive Radio Instruction: Impact, Sustainability, and Future Directions*, Education and Technology Notes Series, 4, 1, Washington, DC: USAID/World Bank.

Ali, M., Enamul Haque, A. and Rumble, G. (1997) 'The Bangladesh Open University: Mission and promise', in *Open Learning*, June, 12–28.

Ba, H. and Potashnik, M. (in press) *The Côte d'Ivoire Educational Television Project: Revisited 20 Years Later*, Draft report, World Bank.

Bosch, A. (1997) *Interactive Radio Instruction: Twenty-Three Years of Improving Educational Quality*, Education and Technology Technical Notes Series 1, 1, Washington, DC: World Bank.

de Moura Castro, C., Wolff, L. and Garcia, N. (1999) 'Mexico's Telesecundaria', in *TechKnowLogia*, September/October, Knowledge Enterprise Inc. Available HTTP: *http://www.techKnowLogia.org*

Dock, A. and Helwig, J. (eds) (1999) *Interactive Radio Instruction: Impact, Sustainability, and Future Directions*, Education and Technology Notes Series 4, 1, Washington, DC: USAID/World Bank.

Farrell, G. (1999) *The Development of Virtual Education: A Global Perspective*, Vancouver: Commonwealth of Learning.

Fraser, C. and Restrepo-Estrada, S. (1998) *Communicating for Development: Human Change for Survival*, London: I.B. Tauris.

Gaba, A. (1997) 'Open Learning in India: development and effectiveness', in *Open Learning*, 12, 3: 43–9.

Geidt, J. (1996) 'Distance education into group areas won't go', in *Open Learning*, 11, 1, February, 12–21.

Inglis, A., Ling P. and Joosten, V. (1999) *Delivering Digitally: Managing the Transition to the Knowledge Media*, London: Kogan Page.

Klees, S. (1995) 'Economics of educational technology', in M. Carnoy (ed.) *International Encyclopedia of the Economics of Education*, Oxford: Pergamon.

Leigh, S. and Cash, F. (1999) 'Effectiveness and methodology of IRI', in A. Dock and J. Helwig (eds) *Interactive Radio Instruction*, Educational Technology Technical Notes Series, 4, 1, Washington, DC: World Bank.

McKay, V. (1995) 'Training adult basic educators for post-apartheid South Africa using the methods of distance education', in D. Sewart (ed.) *One World Many Voices: Quality in Open and Distance Learning*, Milton Keynes: Open University.

McKay, V., Sarakinsky, M. and Sekgobela, E. (1996) 'Distance education into group areas wont go: A response', in *Open learning*, 11, 2, June, 52–56.

Mayo, J. (1973) *The Mexican Telesecundaria: A Cost Effectiveness Approach*, AID Studies in Educational Technology, Washington, DC: Agency for International Development.

Mukhopadhyay, M. (1995) 'Multichannel learning: The case of the National Open School, India', in S. Anzalone (ed.) *Multichannel Learning: Connecting All to Education*, Washington, DC: Education Development Center.

Mukhopadhyay, M. and Phillips, S. (eds) (1994) *Open Schooling: Selected Experiences*, Vancouver: Commonwealth of Learning.

NAMCOL (1998) *Annual Report*, Windhoek: Namibian College of Open Learning.

Oliveira, J. and Orivel, F. (1993) 'Logos II in Brazil', in H. Perraton (ed.) *Distance Education for Teacher Training*, London: Routledge.

Orivel, F. (1996) 'Evaluation of distance education: Cost effectiveness', in A. Tuijnman (ed.) *International Encyclopaedia of Adult Education and Training*, Oxford: Pergamon.

Perraton, H. (ed.) (1993) *Distance Education for Teacher Training*, London: Routledge.

Perraton, H. (2000) *Open and Distance Learning in the Developing World*, London: Routledge.

Perraton, H. and Creed, C. (forthcoming) *Applying New Technologies and Cost Effective Delivery Systems in Basic Education*, Cambridge: International Foundation for Research in Open Learning.

Peters, O. (2000) 'The transformation of the university into an institution of independent learning', in T. Evans and D. Nation (eds) *Changing University Teaching: Reflections on Creating Educational Technologies*, London: Kogan Page.

Robinson, B. (1999) 'Open and distance learning in the Gobi desert: Non-formal education for nomadic women' in *Distance Education*, 20, 2, 181–204.

SAIDE (1995) *Open Learning and Distance Education in South Africa: Report of an International Commission, January–April 1994*, Manzini: Macmillan.

TechKnowLogia (1999), November/December, Knowledge Enterprise Inc. Available HTTP: *http://www.techKnowLogia.org*

Thomas, J. (1996) *Distance Education for Refugees: The Experience of Using Distance and Open Learning with Refugees in Africa 1980–1995, With Guidelines for Action and a Directory of Information*, Cambridge: International Extension College.

World Bank (1995) *Priorities and Strategies for Education: A World Bank Review*, Washington, DC: World Bank.

Wrightson, T. (1998) *Distance Education in Action: The Northern Integrated Teacher Education Project*, Cambridge: International Extension College.

Yates, C. (1998) *Review of Open and Distance Learning Research in Primary and Adult Basic Education*, Cambridge: International Research Foundation for Open Learning.

Young, M., Perraton, H., Jenkins, J. and Dodds, T. (1991) *Distance Teaching for the Third World*, Cambridge: International Extension College (second edition).

Index

aboriginal education 78, 125–6
ACACIA, International Development
    Research Council 160
access to education 30, 31, 34, 35, 41–2,
    43, 67, 91, 133, 147, 157, 175, 179,
    193, 215, 220, 229–31, 236; to
    primary education 3, 6, 126
Accion Cultural Popular (ACPO),
    Colombia 11, 15, 22, 73, 97, 104, 209,
    230, 234, 239–40
ACPH, Honduras 11
action research 99, 100, 117
ACTIONS model of technology
    selection 124
adult basic education; literature 157–8;
    training of trainers 19, 159
Adult Basic Education and Training
    (ABET) Project, South Africa 19
adult education 105; in-school ODL
    programmes 8, 10; learning principles
    and strategies 161–2; open schools
    17–18; out-of-school ODL program-
    mes 9, 97–100; remedial programmes
    57–8; through ODL 155–70
adult literacy 87, 102, 162, 183; estimates
    of illiteracy 4, 27; leader training 11,
    programmes 157, 237
Afghanistan 160, 168, 179; see also
    individual projects
Africa 4, 14, 21, 29, 31, 55, 65, 66, 69,
    75, 80, 88, 103, 140, 161, 173, 181,
    184, 193, 195, 199, 220, 221, 231,
    238, 240; see also Central Africa, East
    Africa, Southern Africa, Sub-Saharan
    Africa, West Africa
African Medical and Research
    Foundation (AMREF) 11, 98, 192,
    193, 197–9, 230, 231, 235, 244

African Virtual University 125
AfriSat satellite 21
agricultural programmes 99, 102, 157,
    183, 184
aid; to basic education 5
AIDS see HIV/AIDS
Alberta Distance Learning Centre,
    Canada 128
All India Radio 14, 131, 132–3
Allama Iqbal Open University, Pakistan
    79–80, 98, 117–8, 162, 235; see also
    FEPRA
Alpharoute Project, Canada 77–8, 102
American Samoa 8, 10, 11
Amman; 1995 Education for All mid-
    decade review 27, 30, 33–4
Arab States see Middle East
Argentina 150
Asia 4, 21, 55, 65, 69, 75, 80, 91, 129,
    140, 193, 195, 229, 231, 238, 242; see
    also East Asia, South Asia, South East
    Asia
assessment, examination and testing 103,
    114, 115, 116
audiences for basic education at a
    distance 51–64, 79, 87, 88, 95, 96–7,
    101–2, 181; characteristics 52–5
audio 125; via streaming technology 20
audio cassettes 79, 98, 99, 102, 123, 127,
    130, 131, 160, 179, 180, 187, 211, 214
audio-vision 99
audioconferencing 71–2
Australasia see Oceania
Australia 8, 11, 16, 73, 78, 89–90, 91,
    117, 125–6, 127–8, 135, 178, 181,
    193, 206–7, 230; see also individual
    institutions, schools of the air

Bangemann, EU Commissioner 220
Bangladesh 9, 91, 160–1; see also
    individual institutions
Bangladesh Open University Open
    School 9, 11, 17–18, 22, 205, 230
basic education; audiences 88; curricula
    65–84, 87, 88–9; in-school for
    children 107; models of provision
    9–20; non-formal curricula 74–81;
    rationale 65–6; relationship between
    content and methods 67–8; social and
    political dimensions 80–1; use of
    media 69
basic education training schemes 10, 11,
    19–20, 230; costs 235; training of
    basic education teachers 237; see also
    primary teacher education, adult
    literacy; leader training, worker
    training, farmer training, health
    worker training
Basic Education Support Television
    (BEST), India 130, 238
Basic Functional Education Programme,
    Allama Iqbal Open University,
    Pakistan see FEPRA
Bates, A.W. 123, 124
Beijing; 1995 women's conference 30
Benin 11
Bolivia 11, 14, 54–5, 196; see also
    individual projects
Botswana 9, 14, 15; see also individual
    institutions
Botswana College of Distance and Open
    Learning (BOCODOL) 221–2, 224,
    230, 239, 243
Brazil 17, 205, 224; see also individual
    institutions and programmes
Brisbane School of Distance Education,
    Australia 185
Britain see United Kingdom
British Broadcasting Corporation (BBC),
    United Kingdom 131, 160, 168, 240,
    244
broadcasting 102, 125, 206–10, 229;
    access to infrastructure 106; see also
    radio, satellite, television
Brunei; 1999 Pan-Commonwealth
    Forum 102
business and entrepreneurship
    programmes 99, 181

cable television 122, 123
Cairo; 1994 conference on population
    and development 30

California Distant Learning Program,
    United States 128–9
Canada 8, 11, 14, 15, 29, 71–2, 73, 76–8,
    89–90, 91, 126, 127–8, 135, 206–7,
    230; see also individual institutions
    and programmes
Canary Islands see Spain
Caribbean 142, 143, 145, 146, 193; see
    also individual countries
Central Africa 11, 91, 94, 230; see also
    individual countries
Central Institute for Educational
    Technology (CIET), India 131, 132
Central Institute of English and Foreign
    Languages, India 131
Central Institute of Indian Languages,
    Mysore, India 131
Centre National d'Enseignement à
    Distance (CNED), France 222
chat services 20
Child Media Lab, National Centre for
    Educational Research and Training,
    India 132
Children Enrichment Experiment Radio,
    India 131
Chile 148, 149, 150
China 141, 142, 143, 145, 146, 193
CIPP (Context-Input-Process-Product)
    approach to evaluation 113–15
'classical' approach to evaluation 115–17
clockwork radio 135
collaboration 101, 107, 220
Colombia 8, 10, 11, 92–3, 196, 240; see
    also individual institutions
Commonwealth 12, 98; see also
    individual countries
Commonwealth of Learning (COL) 36,
    73, 97, 128, 160–1, 199
community education programmes 8, 99,
    101–2, 159, 160, 181
community learning centres 160
Community Skills Centres, British
    Columbia, Canada 73
completion rates 131
computer-based audiographics 123
computer-based learning 123, 231, 245
computer conferencing 123
Computer Literacy and Studies in
    Schools (CLASS) Project, India 131
computer-mediated communication 39
computer software 127, 133
computers 102, 129, 131, 148, 149, 210,
    218, 224

CONFINTEA V (Fifth International Conference on Adult Education) 30–1
convergence 36, 223–4
Co-operative College, Tanzania 124–5
Co-operative Education Centre, Moshi, Tanzania 126
Copenhagen; 1995 social summit 30
Correspondence School, New Zealand 126, 207
correspondence schools 127, 206–7, 214, 221
cost-effectiveness 20, 84, 159, 245; compared with conventional education 96; of distance education 231–2; of open schooling 215; of radio and television 147
cost efficiency 229, 231–2
Costa Rica 11, 148, 149
costs 96, 111, 118, 138–50, 202; compared with conventional education 102–3, 105, 107, 213, 232; in relation to nomadic education 187; of basic education training programmes 235; of digital radio 21; of education 5; of educational television 10, 127, 194, 233; of interactive radio instruction 90; of multichannel learning 235; of new technologies 39, 40, 147–8, 163, 165, 166–7; of non-formal education programmes 104–5; of open schools 18, 215–17, 234; of radio learning groups 233; of radiophonic schools 234; of schools broadcasting 233; of technologies 133
Côte d'Ivoire see Ivory Coast
counselling 95, 214
Countrywide Classroom, India 163
course materials; design 186; development 63, 79, 198, 214; instructional design 159; production and distribution 113–14, 162
courses; delivery 87–107, 182, 198
Croatia 150
Cuba 193
curricula in basic education 65–84, 87, 88–9, 94, 95, 101–2, 103, 106, 168–9, 177, 181, 182, 186–7, 205, 211, 213, 214, 217, 222, 223; learner-centred curricula 81–3
Czech Republic 150

Dakar; 2000 Education for All Forum 27
Deccan Development Society, India 169
definitions; adult education 155–7; assumed synergy between distance learning and open learning 33; basic education 7; basic learning needs 7; distance education 7; distance learning in relation to open learning 40–1, 43, 46; literacy 155–7; medium 122; nomads 174; open learning 7; pastoralism 174; refugees 173–4; technology 122
Denmark 113, 129
DFID (Department for International Development, UK) 35, 36, 40
digital radio 21, 135
disadvantaged groups and individuals 91, 97, 99, 107, 112–15, 125–6, 158, 193, 224, 232, 236
distance education see open and distance learning (ODL)
Distance Education Programme – District Primary Education Programme, Indira Gandhi National Open University, India 132
distance learning centres 127
District Primary Education Programme, India 34
Dominican Republic 9, 11, 16, 209; see also individual institutions and projects
dropouts see completion rates
Durban, South Africa; Seventh Conference of African Ministers of Education 34

earnings-related education 101–2
East Africa 11, 197; see also individual countries
East Asia 94, 142, 143, 145, 146; see also individual countries
East Timor 29
Eastern Europe 142; see also individual countries
Ecuador 196
Education Development Center, United States 72
Education for All 4, 5, 27, 31, 45, 158, 206, 211, 229, 241, 242, 244, 245
Education for Development 63
educational television 8, 10–12, 70–1, 103, 104, 127, 193, 194, 229, 230, 232, 233, 238, 240, 242, 243

Egypt 160
El Salvador 8, 10, 11, 208, 232, 238
electronic library 125
electronic mail 20, 102, 123, 126
empowerment approach 14
English in Action, South Africa 13, 230
Enrichment School Telecasts, India 131
equity in education 5–6, 10, 41–2, 105,
    220, 229, 232–7
Eritrea 98, 180
Ethiopia 56, 98, 139, 147, 159, 180, 198
Europe 29, 140, 174; see also Eastern
    Europe, Western Europe, and
    individual countries
European Commission 126, 130
European Distance Education Network
    (EDEN) 225
European Information Technology
    Summit 1995 220
European Union 185
evaluation of programmes 102–3, 103–7,
    100–21, 170, 194, 202; see also CIPP
    approach, 'classical' approach
Experimental World Literacy Programme,
    UNESCO 4

face-to-face support 95, 99, 102, 129,
    158, 163, 180
farm forums 11, 14
Farm School Programme, India 14, 133
farmer training programmes 11, 56–7, 99,
    118, 132, 157, 185, 231; see also
    agricultural programmes
fax 126, 218
FEPRA, Pakistan 11, 19, 55, 57, 79, 230,
    235
formal education programmes; in-school
    70–2, 88; out of school 73–4, 205–24
France 29, 140, 148–9, 151, 222
Fulbe (Fulani) people, Nigeria 178, 183,
    232
functional courses 57, 79
funding 101, 104, 105, 129, 134, 167,
    201–2, 208, 238
funding agencies 100; see also individual
    agencies

The Gambia 196
gender equity 6, 13, 53, 133
Ghana 9, 11, 14, 98; see also individual
    projects
Ghana, Ministry of Education Non-
    formal Education Division 98

Ghana Community Broadcasting
    Services 81
globalisation 29, 232
Gobi Women's Project, Mongolia 98,
    102, 112–15, 129, 160, 168, 181, 186,
    222, 232, 236
government ministries 105
graduation rates 97
GTZ-BEFARe Project, Afghanistan 179
Guatemala 55
Guyana 53; see also individual
    institutions

Hadzabe people, Tanzania 174
Hamburg; 1997 conference on Adult
    Education 4, 34, 44
Hawthorne effect 119
health and environment programmes 98,
    99, 102, 129, 157, 180, 184, 192–202,
    222, 231, 241
health worker training 11, 242
Healthcom Project, Philippines 194
HIV/AIDS 53, 54, 75–6, 83, 193, 196
Honduras 11; see also individual
    institutions
Hungary 150

INADES-formation 11, 55, 56–7, 118,
    230, 231, 232, 235
income-generating programmes 129, 181,
    184, 222
India 5, 9, 11, 15, 17, 91, 115, 130–3,
    141, 142, 143, 146, 159, 160–1, 163,
    180, 181; see also individual institu-
    tions, organisations and programmes
India, Department of Women and Child
    Development 131
India, Directorate of Education, Delhi,
    Television Branch, India 132
Indian National Satellite (INSAT) 131,
    132
Indira Gandhi National Open University,
    India 132
Indonesia 9, 11, 17, 91, 92–3, 94, 95, 97,
    104, 205, 211–13, 218, 221, 224,
    229–31; see also individual institutions
information and communication
    technologies (ICT) see new
    information and communication
    technologies (NICT)
Information Village Project, India 168
Institute of In-service Teacher Training
    (IITT), Somalia 179–80

integrated services digital network (ISDN) 125
interactive radio instruction (IRI) 8, 9, 11, 12–14, 16–17, 32, 39, 72, 90–1, 103, 104, 105, 129, 135, 192–3, 195–6, 197, 201, 209–10, 230, 238, 241, 243
interactivity 162; via the Internet 20
International Development Research Council (IDRC), Canada 32, 36, 160
International Extension College (IEC) 55, 58, 97, 100
International Research Foundation for Open Learning (IRFOL) 158
Internet 20–1, 39, 102, 123, 125, 126, 128–9, 133, 149, 160, 187, 218, 220, 243
Internet Radio Project, Sri Lanka 167
Ivory Coast, Programme for Educational Television 8, 9, 10, 11, 70, 127, 194, 208, 233

Jamaican Movement for the Advancement of Literacy (JAMAL) 116, 236
Japan 21
Jhabua Development Communication Project, India 162, 163
job training programmes 73–4
Jomtien; 1990 World Conference on Education for All 3, 5, 6, 7, 27, 28, 30, 31, 32, 33, 34, 35, 36, 37, 41, 42, 43, 44, 45, 46, 66, 139, 231
Jordan 27

Kagiso Trust, South Africa 130
Kenya 5, 11, 104, 180, 181, 197, 209; see also individual institutions, organisations and programmes
Kenya Institute of Education 198
Kheda Communication Project, India 163, 169
Kidd, J.Roby 84
Korea 17, 229–31
Laiwo Karen Multichannel Learning Project, Thailand 11, 19
Latin America 9, 15, 16, 21, 65, 66, 69, 75, 80, 91, 92–3, 94, 95, 97, 127, 140, 142, 143, 145, 146, 148, 150, 193, 195, 209, 234, 239; see also individual countries
learner support 17–18, 71, 78, 107, 113–14, 122, 129, 135–6, 212, 218; see also counselling, face-to-face support, tutorials

learners and their needs 51–64, 70–1, 79–83, 87, 88, 95, 96–7, 106, 112–3, 117, 130, 161, 164, 169–70, 176, 177, 197; 'deficit' and 'difference' conceptualisations 59–62
learning centres 212
Learning for Life Project, Mongolia 129
learning groups 95, 130
Learning Without Frontiers, UNESCO 36, 222
LearnTech, United States 90, 129
Lesotho 8, 11, 185
literacy 102, 127, 222; campaigns 14–15, 236; eradication of illiteracy 3, 138; estimates of illiteracy 4; functional literacy 97, 98, 120, 129, 132; levels 124; 'new literacy' approach 8–9; out-of-school programmes 11, 73; programmes for illiterate and neo-literate audiences 79–80, 98, 99, 147, 159, 160, 181, 184–5, 207; tests 116; through ODL 155–70; web-based literacy training 77–8
Literacy Mission, India 132
Logos II, Brazil 20, 230, 236

M.S.Swaminathan Research Foundation, India 168
Makerere University, Uganda 125
Malawi 9, 17, 91, 92–3, 94, 96, 239; see also individual institutions
Malawi College of Distance Education 221, 230, 234, 236, 238, 239
Malawi Correspondence College 92–3
Man is Health, Tanzania 11, 15, 126, 230
Mandela, Nelson 29
mass media campaigns 8, 9, 194, 197
Math Readiness Programme, Saskatchewan, Canada 78
Maths is Fun, Venezuela 230
media use in basic education 69, 102, 111, 113–14, 117, 122–36, 162, 167–8, 245; training 168
Mexico 55, 193, 205, 217; see also individual programmes
Middle East 21, 142, 143, 144, 145, 146; see also individual countries
Minerva, Brazil 11
mobile schools 182, 187
Mongolia 112–5, 232, 235, 237; see also individual projects
monitors 95
Monrovia; 1979 declaration 4

Montreal; 1960 World Conference on Adult Education 156
Mozambique 53
multichannel learning 8, 9, 18–19, 210, 218, 223, 230; costs 235
multimedia 123, 124
multiple literacies approach 157, 237–8
Mumbai Doordarshan Kendra, India 132

Namibia 9; *see also* individual institutions
Namibian College of Open Learning 230, 239
National Centre for Educational Research and Training (NCERT), India 131, 132
National Correspondence College, Zambia 92–3
National Extension College, United Kingdom 69, 73–4
National Open School, India 11, 17, 91, 92–3, 94, 95, 96–7, 104, 105, 106, 194, 195, 205, 214–15, 216, 217, 225, 229–31, 232, 234, 236
National Teachers' Institute, Nigeria 184
National Technological University, United States 125
Nepal 5, 11, 196
Netherlands Development Assistance 35
new information and communication technologies (NICT) 20–1, 35, 37–8, 39–40, 102, 120, 125, 126, 129, 135, 136, 138, 147–50, 155, 157, 160, 163, 220, 223, 224, 241–2, 244; linked with aspirations for equality and democracy 28, 31, 42; use for literacy and adult education 164–70
New Life, Afghanistan 160, 168, 244
New York; children's summit 30
New Zealand 89–90, 91, 126, 127–8, 135, 206–7, 220, 243; *see also* individual institutions
Nicaragua 11, 12, 72, 194, 209
Niger 8, 10, 11, 14, 70–1, 238
Nigeria 173, 174, 178, 180–1, 182–4, 193, 196, 232, 237
nomadic and itinerant groups 8–9, 173–88, 232; *see also* individual projects
Nomadic Fulani Educational Radio Programme, Nigeria 184
non-formal education programmes 74–81, 89, 100, 101, 103, 104, 105–6, 107, 112–15, 127, 158, 161–2, 163, 166; integration into educational system 104

North America 128, 139, 149; *see also* individual countries
Northern Integrated Teacher Education Project (NITEP), Uganda 20, 235
numeracy programmes 73, 98, 102, 159, 160, 184–5, 222

Oceania 142, 143, 145, 146, 221; *see also* individual countries
on-line courses 110, 128–9, 224
On The Move, United Kingdom 11
open and distance learning (ODL); at primary level 31–2, 197; changing the relationship between content, learner and context 68; contribution to Jomtien challenge 6; equalising potential 43–4; for health and the environment 192–202; for literacy 159, 237; for nomads 184–6; generations of distance education 124; implications of 'deficit' and 'difference' notions 62–4; in agency policies 34–7; in international policy discourses 31–4; in-school programmes 8, 10–12; out-of-school programmes 8–9; potential and requirements list 158–9; problematic nature in the context of basic education 32–3; provision and models at basic education level 7–22; 'synergistic effect' 37–8, 44, 45
Open Junior High School, Indonesia 194–5, 230
Open Junior Secondary School, Indonesia 11, 211–13, 215–16, 218, 219, 230, 234, 236, 244
open learning 34, 35; and the Jomtien Declaration 33; *see also* open and distance learning (ODL)
Open Learning Systems Educational Trust (OLSET), South Africa 90–1, 129, 209–10
open schooling 205–24, 239
open schools 8, 9, 11, 17–18, 22, 31, 91, 92–3, 94, 95, 193, 194–5, 197, 205, 207, 210–15, 218–20, 222, 223, 224, 229–30, 231, 236, 242, 243; costs 234; curricula 17, 205; use of media 17
open universities 19, 22, 157, 206
Operation Black Board, India 132
Organisation for Economic Co-operation and Development (OECD) 5, 150–1
Organisation of African Unity 4

organisational structures 87–107
Outback Digital Network, Australia 125–6
Oxfam 6, 35

Pakistan 11; see also individual institutions
Papua New Guinea 14; see also individual institutions
Papua New Guinea College of Distance Education 230, 238–9
PETROBRAS, Brazil 11, 19–20
Philippines 193, 194; see also individual projects
political support 104, 105, 200, 240
policy issues and formulation 6, 27–46, 80–1, 111, 165, 201–2, 236
Portugal; see individual programmes
post-literacy programmes 98, 237
Preventive Health Programme (PARI), Bolivia 195–6
primary education 88, 105, 116, 129, 132, 182; completion rates 3–4; expenditure 4–5; in-school ODL programmes 8, 10–12, 16, 70–2, 89–91, 130; out-of-school ODL programmes 8–9, 91–97; teacher education 11, 20
printed materials 14–15, 16, 20, 69, 71–2, 79, 95, 98, 99, 102, 113–14, 117, 122, 124, 126, 127, 130, 136, 147, 158, 159, 160, 180, 185, 186, 187, 206–7, 210, 211, 214, 218, 229, 237, 239; delivered via Internet 20
Project ACESSO, Brazil 19–20
Project Alphabetizar Constructir, Brazil 11
Project Headstart, United States 223
Project No Drops, Philippines 11, 19, 210
Project on Radio Education for Adult Literacy, India 132, 159
project planning and management 164–6
Pustekkom, Indonesia 212

quality of education 5, 17, 18, 22, 89, 90, 104, 107, 110–21, 130, 131, 179, 193, 194, 200, 207, 217–20, 237–8, 239, 241, 244

radio 12–17, 39, 69, 81, 90, 95, 98, 99, 101, 102, 106, 113–14, 116, 124, 125, 126, 127, 129, 131, 132, 133, 135, 147, 158, 159, 160, 168, 183, 184, 186, 187, 193, 196, 198, 206–7, 211, 218, 219, 230, 237, 240, 244; schools radio 8; see also clockwork radio, digital radio, interactive radio instruction (IRI)
Radio Ada, Ghana 81
Radio-Assisted Community Basic Education Project (RADECO), Dominican Republic 195–6
radio campaigns 9, 11, 14–15, 126, 193, 194, 231
radio clubs 9, 14–15
Radio ECCA, Spain 11, 15–16, 126–7, 230
radio forums 9, 11, 14–15, 115, 116
radio learning groups 9, 11, 233
Radio Math, Bolivia 234
Radio Plateau, Nigeria 184
Radio Santa Maria, Dominican Republic 11, 234
radio schools see radiophonic schools
radiophonic schools 9, 11, 15–17, 91, 92–3, 94, 95, 97, 104, 127, 193–4, 209, 230, 234, 239–40; problems in supplementing primary provision in-school 16
Radioprimaria, Mexico 9, 11, 193
RealAudio 123
RealVideo 123
Refugee Adult Education (RAE) Programme, Somalia 179
refugees and displaced persons 55–6, 98, 99, 159, 173–88, 232, 237
Rio; 1992 conference on the environment and development 29
Roberto Marinho Foundation, Brazil 10
Romany gypsies 174
Rwanda 29, 178

satellite television 8, 21, 122, 123, 125, 130, 131, 163
Satellite Instructional Television (SITE), India 130, 132
Scandinavia 88; see also individual countries
School Broadcasting Unit, Malawi 92–3
School Television, India 163
schools broadcasting 9, 11, 233; see also interactive radio instruction (IRI)
schools of the air 11, 16, 126, 128, 206–7, 230
Science, Technology and Mathematics Programme, Southern Africa 73

secondary education 17, 20
Secundo Grau, Brazil 11
Senegal 11, 14, 27
Sesame Street, United States 223, 238
Siaciwena, R. 103
Slovenia 150
social and personal development
    programmes 74–8, 196
social marketing 192–3, 196–7, 201
Somalia 29; see also individual projects
South Africa 9, 11, 14, 54, 72, 80, 84, 90,
    104, 124, 125, 129, 159, 178, 180,
    196; see also individual institutions
    and projects
South Africa Radio Learning Project 11
South African Extension Unit (SAEU),
    Tanzania 180
South African Institute for Distance
    Education (SAIDE) 40, 80–1, 124,
    125
South Asia 3, 22, 29, 142, 143, 145, 146,
    157; see also individual countries
South East Asia 9, 193; see also individual
    countries
South Korean Air Correspondence High
    School 230, 234
Southern Africa 9, 73, 91; see also
    individual countries
Soviet Union 112, 141, 142
Spain; see also individual institutions
Special Orientation Programme for
    Primary Teachers, India 132
Sri Lanka; see individual projects
Stanford University, United States 72, 90
Star Schools Project, United States 128
streaming technology 20
Strengthening Primary Education
    Programme, Kenya 34
study centres 91, 94, 95, 96, 220, 230,
    231, 239
study groups 8, 9, 14–16, 69, 79, 98, 99,
    101, 102, 159, 179, 180, 187, 218,
    221, 237, 240
Sub-Saharan Africa 3, 22, 54, 142, 143,
    144–5, 146, 160, 209, 239; see also
    individual countries
Sudan; see also individual institutions and
    projects
Sudan Open Learning Organisation
    (SOLO) 55–6, 98–9, 159, 180
Sudan Open Learning Unit (SOLU) see
    Sudan Open Learning Organisation
    (SOLO)

sustainability of programmes 103–7, 111,
    114, 133, 159, 229, 244
Sweden 117
Swedish International Development
    Authority (SIDA) 35

Taleem Research Foundation, India 130
Tanami Network, Australia 125–6
Tanzania 9, 11, 14, 15, 22, 56, 88,
    116–17, 124–5, 126, 174, 180, 181,
    193, 198, 230; see also individual
    programmes and institutions
Tarahumara Indian Project 193–4
teacher education 11, 20, 21, 39, 130,
    132, 179, 223, 230, 231, 243–4
technologies; ACTIONS selection model
    124; choice 217–8 implications of use
    in ODL 122–3; problems in use
    133–5, 241; use in basic education
    122–36, 163
telecentres 102, 160, 161
Telecurso 2000, Brazil 9, 10–12, 159–60,
    210, 216–17, 219, 222, 229, 230, 233,
    240
telemedicine 126
telephone 102, 123, 127, 128, 218
Teleprimaria, Brazil 222
Teleprimaria, Mexico 230
Telescola, Portugal 10–12, 230
Telesecundaria, Mexico 10–12, 91, 92–3,
    94, 95, 96, 104, 205, 208, 216, 217,
    219, 221, 229, 230, 233, 238, 240
teletext 123
Teletubbies, United Kingdom 223
television 83, 90, 95, 102, 116, 122, 128,
    130, 131, 132, 133, 147, 159, 162,
    168, 193, 196, 207–8, 209, 214, 218,
    219, 222; see also cable television,
    educational television, satellite
    television, and names of individual
    projects
television schools 9
Thailand 3, 209; see also individual
    projects
Thailand, Department of Non-Formal
    Education 91, 92–3, 94, 95, 96, 97,
    104, 105, 106
TOPILOT Project, United Kingdom 178
Tuggeranong Flexible Learning Centre,
    Australia 73
tutorials 95, 102, 124, 127, 158, 159, 180,
    214; on-line 218

Udaipur; 1983 conference on literacy 4
Uganda 198, 230; see also individual
　organisations and projects
UNESCO 3, 4, 14, 22, 27, 35, 36, 39, 43,
　61, 65, 112, 113, 129, 139, 142, 143,
　145, 146, 223; see also individual
　programmes
UNHCR 54, 98, 174, 179
UNICEF 53, 132, 224
UNICEF Nomadic Education Project,
　Sudan 185
United Kingdom 11, 15, 17, 29, 73, 88,
　117, 181, 185, 193; see also individual
　institutions and programmes
United Nations Declaration of Human
　Rights 4, 29
United Nations Development Programme
　(UNDP) 29, 52, 54
United Nations International Literacy
　Year 1990 30
United States 5, 29, 55, 115, 119, 128–9,
　148, 149, 223; see also individual
　institutions
Universal Service Fund, United States
　128–9
universities 101; see also names of
　individual universities
University College of Dar-es-Salaam,
　Tanzania 126
University of Fort Hare Adult Basic
　Education Project, South Africa 130,
　160
University of Guyana 55, 57–8
University of London, United Kingdom
　100, 198
University of Nairobi, Kenya 20, 198
University of Namibia, Centre for
　External Studies 99–100
University of South Africa (UNISA) 11,
　19, 159, 230, 235, 237–8
Uruguay 150
USAID 12, 72, 90, 104, 129, 194, 241

Venezuela 14; see also individual
　programmes

video 83, 102, 122, 123, 125, 127, 131,
　211, 214; via streaming technology 20
videoconferencing 71–2, 123, 125
viewdata 123
virtual education 128, 129, 206
virtual reality 123
vocational programmes 8, 19, 20, 99, 214

web-based programmes; literacy training
　77–8, mathematics education for
　aboriginal learners 78
West Africa 56–57, 230; see also
　individual countries
Western Australia Ministry of Education
　Schools of Isolated and Distance
　Education 128, 207
Western Europe 139; see also individual
　countries
world wide web 123, 185
Wolsey Hall, United Kingdom 180
women's education 30, 81, 97, 98, 99,
　103, 112–15, 129, 132, 157, 160, 161,
　163, 185, 192; see also Gobi Women's
　Project
worker basic education training 11, 19
World Bank 34, 35–36, 37–40, 41–2, 43,
　141, 150, 209
World Conference on Education for All,
　1990, Jomtien, Thailand see Jomtien;
　1990 World Conference on Education
　for All
WorldSpace Corporation 21

Yashwantrao Chavan Maharashtra Open
　University, India 99
Yugoslavia (former) 29

Zaire 178
Zambia 5, 9, 11, 15, 91, 92–3, 94, 96,
　160–1, 195, 198, 221, 230, 233, 239
Zanzibar 185
Zimbabwe 22, 90, 96, 196, 221, 230, 239